Identifying *the* Enemy

CHARLOTTE LAUVER

Copyright © 2024 Charlotte Lauver
All rights reserved
First Edition

PAGE PUBLISHING
Conneaut Lake, PA

First originally published by Page Publishing 2024

ISBN 979-8-89315-053-7 (pbk)
ISBN 979-8-89315-072-8 (digital)

Printed in the United States of America

This book is dedicated to the memory of my brother Lance Corporal Barton "Bart" E. Haynes. He was born July 19, 1948, and was killed in action in Trang Quai, Vietnam, on October 22, 1967. Bart and Bruce Springsteen were teenage friends and up-and-coming musicians. Their band was called the Castiles, and Bart was the drummer.

Gone too soon were his quick wit, humor, and warm smile, which will always be etched in my memory. He lost his life because he joined the Marines to escape the horrors of his homelife.

Contents

Preface vii
Chapter 1: Promising Beginnings 1
Chapter 2: Constant Terror 15
Chapter 3: Two Steps Forward, Three Steps Backward 33
Chapter 4: Unexpected Help 49
Chapter 5: False Hope 60
Chapter 6: A Geographical Cure 68
Chapter 7: Rebellion and Courage 85
Chapter 8: A Trap, Not a Way Out 108
Chapter 9: False Promises 129
Chapter 10: From Bad to Worse 160
Chapter 11: Spousal Abuse Continues and a New Baby 182
Chapter 12: Abuse and Reward 220
Chapter 13: Fighting Back 240
Chapter 14: Brief Reprieve before the Divorce 260
Chapter 15: Effects from Years of Abuse Surface 284
Chapter 16: Healing Takes Place 303

Preface

In my attempt to write short stories, I soon realized that I needed to tell the whole story in its entirety for it to make any sense. So here is my early life as it happened. It was simply too painfully complicated to try to explain it any other way than to put it down on paper. This is my gift of the truth to my children, grandchildren, and whomever else it may benefit. I will write about the environment I grew up in and how I survived the unending trauma that continued into my adulthood. I will include memories of my earliest childhood as far back as I can remember and how my childhood slowly turned into days of terror, fear, and violence. Finally, I will describe a marriage that recreated much of the same and how I was trapped in a fearful and treacherous situation with no money, no place to go, and three very young children. Today, women who find themselves in similar situations can get help and support by calling the National Domestic Violence Hotline at 1-800-799-SAFE (7233), which was not available at the time I needed it.

My family of origin and their thinking, beliefs, and addictions were a great source of stress and confusion most of my life. As a child, I had no way to cope with it. As I approached adulthood, I became desperate for an escape route. The fear of talking about my family was too overwhelming; I had no idea how to put my thoughts and emotions together to make any sense out of it. Who would ever be able to understand? Who would even believe it? I knew of no one I could trust who would have the inclination to listen. My mother's alcoholism and her unpredictable behavior were an embarrassment to me. My dad's strong conviction that I should never tell and it should all just be forgotten made it impossible for me to have a clear understanding of who I was. He insisted that telling was a shameful thing to do, and I feared that he would reject me if I did not honor his beliefs. Because I was never able to discuss and understand the events of my childhood, I made, in my turn, many wrong and regrettable decisions that resulted in devastating consequences.

The news of my mother's sudden death in 1968 brought me back to vivid memories of her life. It was a life of great possibilities that never happened because her life was overtaken by alcoholism, a form of mental illness that in her case took the disease's most severe possible form. The sudden shock of learning of her death brought me extreme sadness but, more than sadness, relief. I knew that putting the past in its proper perspective was going to prove to be a real challenge because I was haunted with memories that I did not know what to do with. Without a place to unload, I only recreated the trauma from which I so desperately sought to escape.

Today has brought me to a place of safety, sanity, and contentment. For a long time, I have felt not only the need but the obligation to share the events of my past, and I finally started to write these memoirs in 2005. How grateful I am for today because of what I have escaped. I feel lucky, blessed, and grateful that I have grown emotionally strong enough to tell about it. My scars cannot be seen, only felt. This memoir is about my life, my family, and the horrors we endured. Finally, my story is about God's grace that called me out of the darkness, a divine miracle for which there is no other logical explanation.

Chapter 1

Promising Beginnings

My dad's name was Alva; everyone called him Al. He grew up in Grand Isle, Vermont, the third son of Charles Moses Haynes and Charlotte Barton Haynes. There were five boys in his family, a second family for Charles, who was called Mose. Mose was thirty years older than Charlotte, and he had already raised one family through a previous union. Mose was sixty years old when my dad was born. These boys lived a hard childhood with few advantages. When Mose died, Daddy was only in the eighth grade, and he had to quit school to help support the family. They were very poor, and winters on Lake Champlain were brutal. In addition, the boys were poorly supervised, and their medical care was inadequate. One of the brothers, Eb, was only three years old when he was hit by a train and lost his leg. He was fitted with a peg and had to walk with crutches. The oldest brother, Ferd, had a dislocated hip that was never properly set, leaving one leg shorter than the other. Daddy was luckier by far; his worst injury occurred when his nose was broken by a kick from a horse. He was left with a crooked nose, but that paled in comparison to what his brothers had to deal with. In the end, Daddy outlived all his brothers.

In his early teens, Daddy's first job was a milk route, driving horses across frozen Lake Champlain in winter. This was no easy task for a boy his age. Daddy never talked much about his childhood; I can only assume that it was filled with pain, struggle, and worry. Although he was highly gifted with exceptional people skills and personality, his lack of education was always an embarrassment to him. Despite not having a formal education, he excelled in math. He and his brothers were a great bunch of horse traders; they were funny, witty, and good at buying and selling things to make a profit. Daddy and Eb shared a close bond. Eb always put excessive strain on his body trying to keep up with the others, and Daddy admired Eb's unrelenting determination. As the boys grew up and left home, Eb was left behind, living at home with his mother until she died. I remember reading a telegram that he sent notifying his brothers about their mother's death. Eb wrote, "I not only lost my mother but my home also." Shortly after she died, Eb dropped dead of a heart attack; he was thirty years old.

My mother grew up in East Clifton, Quebec, the youngest daughter of Henry and Agnes Thompson. She had ten brothers and sisters. Henry was a lumberman whose family was originally from Scotland. The family owned many acres of picture-perfect land and rolling hills with blue sky and green grass as far as the eye could see. It was a simpler life than what we know today, and it was by no means easy. Henry built a large two-story house for his family on their property, with no indoor plumbing and no refrigeration. Henry had a beautiful singing voice. He sang at church on Sundays, and when my mother was three, she would sing with him, standing on a stool next to him. People would come from neighboring towns just to hear them sing hymns together. As the story goes, Henry was cleaning a gun one day, and it accidentally fired and killed him. He was only forty-two years old. He left Agnes with a house full of children to raise, the youngest less than a year old. Two years later, their oldest son, George, was killed in action in World War I. The family worked to keep the farm going; the boys did the farming, and the girls helped with the meals and younger siblings. Agnes was an exceptional woman. Not only did she raise her children, but she made sure they were educated. My mother attended Mary Fletcher School of Nursing in Burlington, Vermont, graduating second highest in the state of Vermont with an RN degree.

My parents met through friends who socialized in the same circles. After a relatively short courtship, they were married in

Burlington, Vermont, on January 28, 1938. The ceremony took place in the manse of the First Church. I have been told that many of Daddy's well-meaning relatives tried their best to convince him not to marry my mother, which makes me think that she already had a poor reputation, which was known by many. The wedding was an event which took some planning, and I was surprised when I read the details in the newspaper because it all looked so perfect, so polished and proper. Who could have predicted how it would all play out?

Because drinking was socially acceptable in both my parents' families, all the warning signs were ignored. My dad prided himself on being able to handle his liquor, and drinking together was clearly the tie that bound them. Dad worked on an estate in Sag Harbor, New York, when my parents were first married. It was a beautiful area, and Daddy loved working the land. An apartment was provided for them to live in. My mother had no trouble getting a nursing job. However, with the war on and the Depression, Daddy lost his job on the estate. Jobs were scarce, and finding another one proved to be a challenge. He was finally offered a job at a company called Irvington Varnish, which required my parents to relocate to New Jersey. This was a factory job running a slitting machine. His job would be filling orders of different cuts and types of tape for large companies. The slitting machine cut the tape to specific sizes once it was set up at the right measurements. The job required excellent math skills, which Daddy had. My parents moved to Springfield, New Jersey, and my mother landed a job at Ohrbach's, a large department store. She was hired as a nurse to sell baby needs and layettes for mothers having their first babies. She was a hit; she had the personality and credentials to succeed. My parents were doing well and purchased their first house, a nice two-story with a large backyard, the perfect place to start a family. Looking from the outside, they were indeed the perfect couple, bound for a life of prosperity and success.

My older sister, Constance Agnes ("Connie"), was born in July of 1942, and I was born fourteen months later. They named me Charlotte Marie after my grandmother. However, not long after they brought me home, my mother decided that instead of taking the risk that I would end up with the nickname Lottie as my grandmother did, I would be called Charlene. This decision has caused me many difficulties throughout my life, forcing me to explain why I have two different names. In the workplace, I was called Charlotte, and outside the workplace, I was Charlene. In fact, I didn't find out my real name was Charlotte until I applied for my first job and needed my birth certificate to get a social security card.

My mother didn't adapt well to staying home with two babies, and her mother came to stay with her for a while to help out. Motherhood was a demanding and less-than-glamorous existence, compared to what she was used to. Connie was full of mischief and always running away. There was a brook that ran along the back of the property, and my mother was terrified that Connie would find her way to the water. Even though they fenced in the backyard, Connie would escape by pulling a garbage can up to the fence, rolling over the can, and away she would go. Through the trials and tribulations of raising two babies, life was good to my mother. She had a good family and strong family ties; she visited her sisters and brothers often, and sometimes the whole family went. I remember train trips to Canada at no more than three years old, sleeping in what was called a berth. My mother's family also came to New Jersey to visit us on occasion. In June of 1944, my mother became an American citizen.

Daddy was always planning and scheming new ways to make money. After a few drinks, his focus always went to how he could make money without working for someone else. He believed that rental property was the best option, and in many ways, he was right. My parents found the opportunity they were looking for in an apartment building located on Franklin Terrace in Irvington, New Jersey. Franklin Terrace was the first house that I remember. It was a large square brick building that sat on a corner. The yard was to the right of the house, with a driveway and a two-car garage on the far side of the yard. The building had a front entrance, and two apartments were rented on the first floor. The second floor had two apartments also; one was rented to Arnie and Mary, friends of my parents. We occupied the larger apartment on the second floor, which also had a private entrance. An outside stairway led up from the yard directly into the bedroom that Connie and I shared. All the rooms were large and bright with lots of windows. The kitchen had no counters, and the double sinks were not enclosed but had the plumbing underneath exposed. The dining and living rooms were open, almost as if they were one room. We had nice furniture, including a large mahogany dining room suite that my parents had bought shortly after they were married. A pretty set of china filled the china cabinet. The living room contained a sofa and Daddy's easy chair; a large wooden floor radio sat in the corner where Daddy would listen to the news in the evening. Sometimes he and my mother would listen together to a radio program called *Amos 'n' Andy*.

My family did not yet have a car, but my father was saving for one. Since Arnie had a car and he and Daddy both worked the day shift at Irvington Varnish, they rode back and forth to work together. We lived within walking distance of Stuyvesant Avenue, which was a busy main street with lots of businesses, one of which was the Welcome Tavern. My dad liked living within walking distance of the local bar, and this was where he hung out. He and my mother both loved the bar atmosphere. Although Daddy was a drinker, he never appeared to be drunk, and if he was, it was not obvious. I remember their friends Slim and Josie, a couple they met at the tavern. They had two girls our ages, and we would visit each other's homes. I remember overhearing my mom and dad talking about Josie being sick and in the hospital. I remember my mother calling the hospital and asking about Josie's condition. As she hung up the phone, she said, "Josie's gone." We never saw the girls or Slim again, but I remember Daddy telling my mother that Slim had died. I asked lots of questions about Slim and the girls, but they didn't want me to know what really happened to Slim. I knew he hung out at the Welcome Tavern. The girls must have gone to live with other relatives after Josie died. I always listened closely to my parents' conversations about Slim. I remember Daddy telling my mother that Slim had hanged himself in the room he rented, across the street from the Welcome Tavern. I didn't understand what the word *hanged* meant, but I was sure it was something very bad.

My parents were not a churchgoing couple. My dad's family was for the most part what you would call humanists or agnostics. My dad believed as they did, in human reason, in thinking for yourself instead of relying on a God that he believed did not exist. He thought going to church or having a spiritual life was nothing more than a bunch of nonsense. He believed in human rights. He had a kindness about him and a compassion for others. I never knew what my mother believed. My understanding was that they were Christian. If church or religion were part of her life as a child, it did not stick with her into adulthood. Priorities were never church-based. They had many friends who came to visit, and we were also invited to visit with them. All their friends were drinking people, most of whom they had met at the Welcome Tavern.

I was three when my mother decided to go back to work, and she had no trouble getting a nursing job at a local hospital. She was working the midnight to 8:00 a.m. shift, so she hired a lady named Roxie to come and stay with Connie and me while she slept in the daytime. We loved Roxie. She was good to us; she played games with us and was always a loving, kind lady. My earliest memories of my mother were her coming home early in the morning as I was just waking up. I could hear the sound of her footsteps coming up the outside stairs as she opened our bedroom door. She always had a habit of stepping harder on her last step into our bedroom, and she seemed to enter with a sigh of relief. I noticed her white stockings and how pretty she was in her nurse's uniform. I remember her smiling at me as she took off her white hat with the black stripe along the top that distinguished her as an RN. Sometimes she would bring home gifts that patients had given her as a gesture of gratitude for being their nurse. I loved her, and I felt her love for me also. I was glad that she was my mother. The words "I love you" were never spoken, but her kindness and the patient way she spoke to me were how I felt her love. She wore pretty clothes, smelled good, and always dressed up when we went somewhere. When she died, I thought back to this memory, how much we all loved her, and how highly we all valued and trusted her.

The first time I noticed the conflicts between my parents was one night when I was around four years old. I awoke to their loud arguing, and as I wandered into the living room, my mother said that she was going for a walk. It was late at night, and I was crying to go with her. She told me to get her shoes, put them on her, and she and I would go. I did as she asked but had a hard time getting her shoes on; they were high heels with lots of straps. I worked at it and finally managed to get them on. I reached for her hand and the railing as we walked down the long steps off the bedroom. When she stepped onto the sidewalk, she was all over the place, almost falling off the curb. I asked her what was wrong with her, and she said, "You put my shoes on wrong." That was my very first memory of what was to come. There was surely an enemy now among us.

However, there were still some good times during my childhood. On Halloween, we all, even my parents, dressed up in costumes and went trick-or-treating as a family. We wore simple homemade costumes, and my sister and I carried white pillowcases to stash our goodies. We walked down to Stuyvesant Avenue, stopping at all the businesses for a treat. We had other fun family times at Olympic Park, an amusement park not far from where we lived. Sometimes we would all go together and spend the day. Connie and I would be all excited when we knew we were going. Daddy would take us to the kiddie rides while my mother found a picnic table and bought a pitcher of beer. My sister and I rode all the rides, played games of chance, and had lots of fun. I remember how I loved the sound of the music that played on the merry-go-round. One particularly wonderful day was July 26, 1947, Connie's fifth birthday. Aunt Bea, one of my mother's sisters, came to visit, and we all went to Asbury Park for the weekend. Aunt Bea even let Connie and me ride in the rumble seat of her car.

My mother quit work when she found out she was pregnant again. We sadly told Roxie goodbye, but I was happy that my mom was going to be home with me all day now. Connie had started school, and it was just Mom and me at home. Some days I knew there was something not right about her, but I wasn't old enough to figure it out. Sometimes she would be crying when my dad got home from work, and he had to cook supper. I would ask why she was crying, but she would never answer me.

On July 19, 1948, our brother Bart was born. Connie and I went to stay with Arnie's and Mary's family in Morristown. They were like substitute grandparents to us. They lived out in the country, and we had a wonderful time with them, going on picnics and nature walks in the woods. We stayed for a few weeks so that my mother could have some time to rest and get used to the new baby. I could tell that Daddy was very excited when he told us we had a baby brother. I remember the day Daddy came to take us home. Arnie drove him to pick us up, and on the way home, we stopped at a shopping plaza. Daddy told us we could pick out something that we wanted, and we left with shiny new patent leather pocketbooks. Mine had a shoulder strap with a pattern of blue-and-pink swirls all over it, and I loved it. I could hardly wait to get home and see Mommy again. We walked through the front door with our new pocketbooks slung over our shoulders, and Mommy sat at the dining room table, waiting for us. She looked pretty and well rested, and her hair was pulled back with a bow. Connie and I wanted to know the first thing about our new baby brother. She led us into her bedroom, and there was this very tiny new baby sleeping in a small crib. We all whispered as we asked questions about when he would wake up. We were all eyes and ears the first time we heard him cry to be fed. Sometimes my mother would let me sit on the sofa and hold him. Connie wasn't as interested as I was and didn't get to help as much as I did. When Bart was a few months old, Mommy got out the big carriage that had been stored in the basement. She dressed Bart in some warm clothes and let me push him around the block in the carriage, all by myself. I wanted all the neighbors to see me; I felt so very special and much older than my five years.

About the time Bart was born, television was the latest and greatest invention. Everyone was in awe of this new discovery that seemed just too phenomenal to believe. Very few people owned a television since they were very expensive. We didn't have one yet, but the family next door to us did. Connie and I would quietly walk up on their front porch and try to look in through the window to see if we could get a glimpse of it. I always hoped they would invite us in to see it, but they never did. I wasn't even sure what it was, but from overhearing the grown-ups, I knew it was something big, too big for me to even imagine.

IDENTIFYING THE ENEMY

The Christmas season always increased my parents' efforts to make us look like a normal happy family. Every year, we had a Christmas tree and lots of gifts. For Christmas of 1948, my parents had Christmas cards made up with our picture on them. Connie and I were sitting in Daddy's big easy chair, holding Bart between us. My parents were especially proud of Bart since he was the first boy, and they wanted all their friends and family to see him. My mother signed the card "Al, Et, and All." That sounds strange to me now since my mother never referred to herself as Et. In fact, not many people even called her Ethel. My dad always called her by the nickname Tommy, a name she had acquired before her marriage because of her maiden name Thompson.

Before Bart was two years old, my parents decided it was time to move again. The new plan was to give up the rental idea and buy a single-family house. My parents found a house they liked just a mile away, still within walking distance of both our school and the Welcome Tavern. The house was a nice two-story with three bedrooms and a bath upstairs and a living room, dining room, kitchen, and sunroom downstairs. Even though money did not seem to be a problem, they were never satisfied and were always looking for changes that did not involve addressing their larger issues. With my mother's escalating drinking, any plans they made or houses they bought were never going to work to either their advantage or ours.

I was six years old now and in the first grade. I liked our new neighborhood, and many of my school friends were our neighbors. My dad bought his first new car, a 1949 green Dodge. I loved the new car and was always ready to go for a ride. My mother never had a driver's license. We also bought our first television that year. It was a big box with a tiny picture. There were only two stations, and the picture was black-and-white and very snowy. It was pretty amazing though; people in New York were singing and dancing live on the little screen in our living room. Connie and I loved to watch the Farmer Gray cartoons, which were the only cartoons they showed. Variety didn't matter; we watched intently no matter how many times they showed the same cartoon. To us, television was really something!

My parents wanted Connie and me to take piano lessons, so they purchased a new Steinway. Connie started first. She hated taking lessons, and she didn't want to practice. I remember Connie standing in the driveway with a suitcase in her hand and an angry look on her face. When I asked where she was going, my mother would say, "She's leaving home because she doesn't want to practice her piano lesson." Since Connie disliked lessons so much and refused to practice, my parents ended her piano instruction. After that, they never mentioned my taking lessons either, and I was glad because I didn't want to take them. However, since my mother could read music and play a little, we kept the piano. When I was asked to sing in the Christmas program at school, my mother helped me practice. She played the song, and I was to sing it until I remembered all the words and could follow the music. On the night of the Christmas pageant, my parents were as excited as I was when I sang a solo on the big stage in front of a huge audience. My song was one of the popular Christmas songs of the day, "All I Want for Christmas Is My Two Front Teeth," and it was the perfect song for me since my two front teeth were really missing. I remembered all the words, and I knew my parents were proud of me.

Although our new house was in a very nice neighborhood, it was predominately German, and my mother was not happy with that. She kept a low profile and did not make many friends. She probably didn't want the neighbors to find out about her drinking problem, but it was likely that most of them already knew. One day, she got into a shouting match with the lady across the street and called her a Nazi. This woman took her to court. It was a family court, and we all had to go. The lady told the judge that Mrs. Haynes had called her a Nazi. When it was my mother's turn to speak, she came up with a cock-and-bull story about how she had a little dog, and the dog's name was Snazi, and she was merely calling her dog. I knew that my mother was lying because our dog's name was Zipper. However, the judge believed my mother and threw the complaint out of court. Daddy bragged on and on about how clever my mother was and how she got off so easy because she had them all fooled. As young as I was, I felt sad because I knew she had lied, and I also knew it was wrong.

The Welcome Tavern was still my parents' favorite hangout. If they didn't have a babysitter on Saturday nights, they would take us with them. They would dress Bart in his cowboy outfit and let him take his guitar. When we got to the tavern, Bart would be hoisted up on the shuffleboard table. He was barely two years old, just strumming the guitar and making sounds no one could understand, but he was a hit as he entertained the half-crocked bar crowd. Did either of my parents ever think this was not the place to take children? I hated the smell of the tavern, but they liked it, and that was where their friends were. If I went to the store on a Saturday with Daddy, we always ended up at the Welcome Tavern. I went there so many times that I made friends with the kids who lived in an apartment over the bar. They invited me up to their house to play. What a mess! I knew I was lucky that I didn't live there. Their parents were always at the bar. One of our nights out at the Welcome Tavern, two men got into a fistfight, just like you would see in a movie. It was scary, with fists flying and blood everywhere. An ambulance was called, and I remember crying that I wanted to go home.

We walked home from school every day for lunch. Some days, my mother would be asleep on the sofa when I got home, and I could smell the liquor on her. I would try to wake her up, but she was out cold, and nothing I did to wake her up worked. I didn't know what to do. I didn't tell anyone; I just went back to school without lunch. When Connie was in the first grade, my mother invited her teacher over for lunch, and the pattern continued with my first-grade teacher as well. My mother made such a big deal out of it, so I couldn't tell her I didn't want my teacher in our house. I knew the visit would happen whether I liked it or not, and I knew my mother was planning to put on an act to cover up what was really going on. She fixed a very nice lunch, and I remember the strange softness in her voice as she tried to impress her company. We had a pretty dining room that was reserved for company only. Lunch for the teacher was one of the few times we ate at the dining room table because other than the teacher visits, we never had any company. The day my teacher was supposed to come for lunch, I was on edge all morning, worried that my mother had forgotten. All morning at school, I imagined myself walking in the front door with my teacher, only to find my mother passed out on the sofa. Worry had become my constant companion.

Larry and Linda Barrs, who were friends my parents met at the bar, had children our age. One weekend, Daddy took us over to their house to spend the night. When Daddy came to get us, I overheard him telling Linda about my mother going to the hospital. I started crying and demanding to know what happened to her. They kept saying that it was nothing and she was fine, but we had to stay another night. Because of my endless pleading for the truth, Linda finally told me that my mother had fallen down the stairs and hurt her arm, but it was all taken care of now, and she was fine. When we got home, my mother's arm was in a cast. I asked her what had happened, and she said she slipped on the stairs. I knew she fell because she was drunk; I was wiser to what was going on than either of my parents thought. I was seven now, and I was very much aware of the difference between drunk and sober.

Daddy liked to play poker. One Saturday night, a group of his friends got together at our house for a game, and the game was still going strong when I went to bed. In fact, when I came downstairs the next morning, the game was just ending, and dollar bills were stacked all over the table. Daddy had offered to give one of the guys a ride home, and I wanted to ride with them. I climbed into the back seat, leaning toward the front so I could hear their conversation. As soon as we rolled out of the driveway, the guy said to my dad, "Your wife swiped a twenty-dollar bill from Joe."

"She did?" Daddy replied, with a tone of surprise in his voice. I thought he was more embarrassed than surprised.

"Yeah, I saw her." He went on, "She swiped it right off the table when Joe wasn't looking."

"Well, I'll make sure Joe gets it back," Daddy answered. I didn't know what was ever said to my mother about it or if Joe ever got his money, but I knew my mother had stolen a twenty-dollar bill.

One summer evening when my parents were embroiled in a heated argument, my mother stormed out the door and took Connie with her. Into the late hours of the night, she had still not returned. Daddy told me to come to bed with him. Bart was asleep in his crib in the same room. I knew Daddy was not sleeping but just trying to let me think he was. At some point in the night, I woke up, and

Daddy was gone. I was scared and couldn't go back to sleep. I started slowly walking around the house in the dark, trying to find him. I was scared Bart would wake up, so I quietly climbed back into bed. Just as I did, I heard Daddy come in the back door. I ran downstairs, asking him where Mommy and Connie were. He said he didn't know and had gone out to see if he could find them. He put me back into bed. I must have drifted off to sleep because when I awoke again, it was morning, and Mommy and Connie were back home. I knew something bad had happened, but I never really knew what. I do remember that after that, detectives began coming to our door to ask my mother questions. I also knew that she was terrified of one particular detective, whom she referred to as "the man with the white hair." She told me that if I saw him coming to run in and let her know. I remember also that she stayed sober more often. I tried to listen to the conversations about that night, but I could never make any sense of them. I asked Connie where she went with Mommy, and she said that they went to the Welcome Tavern. She added that she and my mother left with a man from the tavern; they went to his house, and that was all she remembered.

I enjoyed school and had lots of girlfriends. We would walk to and from school together, playing games as we walked. One game was Ts and Hs. The sidewalk was divided onto blocks; some had Ts, and some had Hs. We did "eeny meeny miny moe" to determine who got the *T* and who got the *H*. The winner was the one who stepped on her letter the most. On the weekends, we played hopscotch, or we went to the school ground and played on the swings. If we played inside, I always went to one of my friends' houses instead of them coming to mine. My best girlfriend was Dorothy, who lived five or six houses down from mine. Her family had a TV, and sometimes we would watch the Farmer Gray cartoons together. I especially loved it when it showed raining cats and dogs. The cats and dogs would all fall down from the sky and run away as soon as they hit the ground.

One morning, as Dorothy and I walked to school together, she told me the most exciting story I had ever heard. She said that while watching a Farmer Gray cartoon on her TV the night before, Farmer Gray had popped right out of the TV. She said he was running around her living room as she tried to catch him. I listened intently, believing every word she said. "Did you ever catch him?" I asked.

"Oh, yes, I finally caught him in a fishing net," she answered.

"What did you do with him?" I asked, in awe of the fun she must have had catching this little animated guy who looked a lot like today's Pillsbury Dough Boy. I also asked, "What did your mother say about it?"

"She doesn't know. I hid him in my closet. When I get home from school, I am going to get him out and play with him." I begged and pleaded with her to let me come to her house after school to play with Farmer Gray. I promised with all my heart never to let her mother or anyone else know. Of course, I never was invited to play with the Farmer Gray cartoon that she kept hidden in her closet. I used to imagine him jumping out of my TV and me catching him and hiding him in my closet. I wanted more than anything else to have my own secret Farmer Gray. I was going to tell him all the things I knew, things my parents tried to hide from me, but I knew anyhow.

I loved my dolls. All my dolls were girls, and they were all named Linda. I wished my name were Linda instead of Charlene. I hated my name. No one else in school was named Charlene. How could I be like everyone else with a name like Charlene? I loved to dress and undress my dolls, pretending that I was their real mother. Trying to get Connie to play dolls with me was wasted energy. She was never interested. Most of the time, I would just play by myself in my world of pretend. I pretended a lot. I pretended that I wasn't scared when my mother was drunk—that she wasn't like she was, that she really loved me, that I didn't notice when she was drunk when I knew she was, and that I didn't have to worry about whether she would be sober or not when I came home for lunch.

When I heard my mother complaining about the neighbors and the neighborhood, I knew it was time to move again. Now it was back to another apartment house, with big plans for extra income. A common word they used was *gold mine*. My mother's out-of-control drinking had escalated, and it was so much bigger than any house they could find. They both looked the other way at the huge pitfalls on the road ahead.

Chapter 2

Constant Terror

It was the summer of 1951 when Daddy announced the news that we were moving to Wyoming Avenue in Elizabeth, New Jersey, a suburb of Newark. I didn't want to leave my friends and start third grade at a new school, but that was the plan. Daddy took me with him one Saturday to see our new one-hundred-year-old house. The first time I saw this house, I was amazed at the size of it. It was huge, three stories high, big rooms, high ceilings, and old, very old. It had a funny smell to it that Daddy said I would get used to. We occupied the first floor and rented rooms and a small apartment on the second floor and a large apartment on the third floor. One of my schoolmates told me that our house was once a hospital. She said that her mother was born in our house.

The front of our new house was Victorian, with a large wrap-around porch and bay windows laced with gingerbread eaves. The heavy double front doors led into the foyer, which contained a winding staircase that led up to the second floor. The foyer ceiling must have gone up twenty feet. To the right was the door to our section of the house. The two large front rooms, which were separated by a pocket door, each had a fireplace, and one room had two bay windows. At the beginning, one room was our living room, and the other our dining room. Later on, my mother combined the dining room and living room so that the front room became my parents' bedroom. Things were always changing. There were two other bedrooms and a bathroom on the first floor. A long wide hall led to the kitchen at the back of the house, a utility room, a screened porch, and the stairs to the basement. Our property went from the front on Wyoming Avenue straight through to the street at the back, so you could come into the house from the front or back streets. There was a walkway that came up the back, which made it easy to go either into the house or through the hatchway into the basement. A back stairway zigzagged from the third floor down. This allowed all the apartment renters to have front and back entrances and exits. This rare find was in the Elmora section of Elizabeth, New Jersey, which was known to be one of the best areas in Elizabeth. The neighborhood was littered with doctors, dentists, and many other professional people.

The rooms and apartments were all rented furnished. That way, there was no moving of furniture in and out by the tenants. Daddy went to estate sales and picked up used furniture and kitchen supplies. Because the neighborhood was desirable, the rooms and apartments rented quickly. Daddy kept his job with Irvington Varnish, but my mother's job was to rent the rooms and clean and change the sheets for room renters once a week. Her laundry duties gave her a cover story when she went down to the basement to drink, and the basement hatchway gave her a secret entrance she could use to take her newest bottle directly from the store to her hiding place. The garbage cans in the basement were filled with empty liquor bottles underneath an old blanket and some towels.

After our move to Wyoming Avenue, I never went to the Welcome Tavern again. I knew that Daddy still stopped by there every once in a while because I heard him talk about it. If my parents ever went out together, it was to hang out at other bars and have drinks. That was their pastime, their thrills; that was what their lives were about.

The grammar school was just one block over on the next street. Connie and I could walk to school and come home for lunch. Anyone observing our family coming and going from our large house would mistakenly get the idea that we were the perfect family with all the bells and whistles necessary to prosper.

"East side, west side all around the town, boys and girls together, London Bridge's falling down." This was the song the kids sang on the only Saturday morning kids' show on TV. The show was televised live from New York. The kids would sing or dance, and the show would air film clips of *Our Gang* in between musical numbers. Of course, the commercial for the Castro Convertible played every ten minutes or so. I loved to wrap up with a blanket in Daddy's easy chair and watch TV on Saturday mornings before anyone else was up. On school days, most of the kids' shows were on around 4:00 p.m. I loved *Howdy Doody and Buffalo Bob*. The characters were puppets, and Buffalo Bob was a live person who interacted with them. Nothing was taped back then; all the shows on TV were live. All the kids on *Howdy Doody* sat in a special section called the Peanut Gallery. In spite of the poor reception, once you had a TV, life would never be the same without one. Televisions were still expensive but much improved from just a few years before. The screen was bigger now, and in the evening, they had shows for the whole family, but there were only two or three channels to choose from. Sitcoms were starting, and on the *Ed Sullivan Show*, anyone could see entertainment that was previously available only in New York City. Television was an amazing contraption that was always improving and which allowed for much better communication. Instead of listening to the news on the radio, you could watch it on TV and actually see the person explaining it.

As that year passed and summer came, my mother's drinking got worse. One glance at my mother's face was all I needed to tell if she had had her first swallow. A small sip and her whole demeanor changed; her eyes became glassy and focused differently. She wouldn't look directly at me when she spoke to me, and her manner of speech was different. She slurred her words; her voice was much louder and full of anger and hate. The loving smiles of yesteryear had turned into viciousness. I was getting older and wiser to the schemes of the devil, and I learned how to avoid her when I knew she was drinking. I was much smarter about her goings-on than she ever knew. By the time I was ten, I had already acquired a wealth of information that no one knew I was carrying around in my head. I had the scoop but no one to tell, at least no one that I felt safe enough to trust.

Connie and I did not have a lot to do in the summer. We had no rules and were pretty much free to come and go as we pleased.

Most of our girlfriends came from more affluent families and spent summers at the shore, but we never went anywhere. Connie and I set up a lemonade stand on the driveway across the street from the back of our house. We made the lemonade, bought a pack of paper cups, dragged a card table across the street, and put up a sign. We used an empty cigar box for the profits and started with four quarters. We were in business. Our plan was to make enough money to go to Linden Pool. It took two buses to get to Linden Pool, and of course, Connie, being older and smarter than I was, knew how to get there. Our lemonade stand was a success, and after one day of selling lemonade, we had enough money to fund an entire day at Linden Pool. We even had enough to buy a hot dog at the concession stand. We were up early the next day and ready to go. We rolled our bathing suits in a towel, left a note for Daddy to pick us up when he got home from work, and off we went. Some days when my mother was very drunk, we would take Bart with us. After a few days at the pool, Connie and I both learned to swim. There was a grassy area near the highway where we would wait for Daddy. Sometimes he was very late, but he would always show up. Linden Pool was such great fun!

That same summer, my mother rented the large front room to an older lady. This kind of spoiled a lot of our fun or maybe enhanced it, depending on how you looked at it. The large windows in the front room came down almost to the bottom of the front porch. The new tenant put a small sliding screen in the window at the bottom that easily moved in and out. We were told not to play on the front porch so she would not be bothered by our noise. She was always complaining about how hot it was. Every day, she would—as she called it, "wash out her drawers"—walk around to the back of the house and hang them on our clothesline. We laughed and made jokes about how big her drawers were. We named her Ms. Drawers. She would tell us she was going to the movies in the afternoon to get some relief from the heat. One day, as we sat quietly on the front steps, Ms. Drawers came out the front door with her basket of wash on her way to the backyard. Once she was out of sight, Connie said, "Let's go in her room and get something."

"Okay," I replied.

Connie said, "You watch for her coming back, and I'll go in and get us something."

"Okay," I agreed. Connie carefully pushed the screen apart and quietly stepped in through the window. I walked over to the walkway at the end of the house to watch for the tenant. Just as Connie got into the room, I saw Ms. Drawers coming along the walkway around the side of the house. I ran up on the porch to alert Connie, loudly whispering through the window, "She's coming. Hurry up." Connie quickly opened her refrigerator, grabbed two plums, and climbed back through the window as I helped her put the screen in place. We just had the screen in place when Ms. Drawers came into clear view of us. We ran to the other end of the porch, climbed over the banister, ran around to the side of the house, and ate our plums as we giggled our butts off.

Although Connie was only fourteen months older than I was, she looked much older and more mature. Some days she would be gone all day, hanging out with her friends or whatever else she did. I would stick around the house. Sometimes I would visit with the family who rented the third floor or go over to the school playground. But sometimes I would hang around the house just because I knew that my presence was an annoyance to my mother. I was always aware of the times when she was trying to get rid of me, and I knew why. I would make it a point to hang around her because I knew she didn't want me to and because I knew it was more difficult for her to drink if I was right under her nose.

When our front door bell rang, it was loud and echoed throughout the house. One summer day, around late morning, the doorbell rang. I ran to the door, my mother running as fast behind me. It was a delivery man from the liquor store. When I saw who it was, I quickly stepped out of the way and let her open the door. I watched as she pulled some bills out of her pocket. As she handed the man the bills, he handed her a bottle wrapped in a brown paper bag. I knew what it was. There was a barrel down in the basement filled with empty bottles with the same shape and size as this one; some of them still had the brown paper bag wrapped around them. I sensed her sober embarrassment as I stood and watched the transaction take place.

"Well, now you know. Come on in the kitchen, and I will fix a 'cocktail' for us," she blurted out nervously as if I were one of her lady friends and we were going to have cocktails together. I sat down at the kitchen table as she mixed the drinks. I carefully watched her every move as she poured from the paper bag-wrapped bottle and then from the soda bottle. She placed my drink on the table in front of me. She then sat down across the table from me with her drink. The smell of the liquor was strong. I knew the smell very well, and I hated it because I knew what it did to her. I tried to act as if I were going along with her game so she wouldn't get mad at me. I put my glass up to my lips as if to take a drink, my lips barely getting wet, then I swallowed to let her think I had really taken a drink. The taste and smell reminded me of something like rotten vinegar mixed with Coca-Cola. I wanted no part of her evil potion because I feared that I would become like her if I drank even a sip. My face would become twisted, my eyes glassy, and my words slurred, then ranting and raving. Oh, no! I wasn't going for it. I looked her straight in the eye and said, "I don't like it! I think I will go to the playground." I knew that was exactly the reaction she wanted from me. I ran through the house and out the front door as if there were an evil monster after me. I knew when I came back home she would be drunk, either passed out or in a rage.

I became very streetwise for my age. The business district was only a few blocks from where we lived. It was a busy corner with buses going to downtown Elizabeth, Linden, Newark, and New York City. On the corner, there was a grassy area with park benches, a drugstore, restaurant, five and ten, and a bank. This was a very high transient area with its share of crime and loitering. Farther down Elmora Avenue were the grocery store and the movie theater where I hung out with my girlfriends on Saturdays.

I loved the beginning of the school year. I loved the coolness in the air and the leaves changing color. At the beginning of each school year, Daddy would give me money for school clothes and school supplies, and I would catch a bus to downtown Elizabeth to do my shopping. I was always alone on these bus trips; my girlfriends were never allowed to go where I went and do the things I was allowed to do. In many ways, I felt much older than I really was.

The phone was always ringing when an ad was in the paper for a room or apartment for rent. I took the calls more often now. I knew how to give directions to our house, and I could answer any questions about the rooms. Sometimes I would get some flak from a potential renter, who would say, "Could I speak with an adult?"

Since my mother was usually not in any shape to take the calls, I would just say, "Are you calling about the ad in the newspaper to rent a room?"

"Yes," they would reply.

"I can help you with that," I would say.

"And how old are you?" would be the next question.

"Almost ten, but I do this all the time," I would answer as I tried to convince them of my competency. If they still gave me flak, I would just say, "Either you can call back later, or I can help you now." This usually changed the conversation to questions about the room for rent. I would give exact directions and wait for the loud bell on the front door to ring. My small stature made me look even younger than I really was. The potential tenants were always surprised when they first saw me that I could really do this, but if they wanted to rent the room, they were stuck with me. The ring of keys was stored on the mantle in the dining room with the receipt book. There was a master key that opened all the doors to every room and apartment. When people came, I would show the room, answer their questions, take their money, count it in front of them, and write out a receipt. The carbon copy was always left in the receipt book. I knew that I was good at this job, and this knowledge gave me an adult sense of confidence. I rented more rooms than anyone else. Daddy told me I was never to give the rent money to my mother; I was to give it to him. If he wasn't home, I was to hold on to the money until he got home. I understood why, and I always did what he told me because I trusted him.

Daddy worked the swing shift, days one week and nights the next. I hated when he was on the four-to-midnight shift. This was the worst time for me because my mother would start drinking as soon as Daddy's car pulled away from the curb. I knew there would be no dinner; it was fend-for-yourself night, and the ranting and raving would start. My mother's tirades always took the form of four-letter words that no child should be exposed to. These episodes sometimes lasted for hours on end as my mother kept repeating the same story over and over until she would finally give up or pass out. Her theme was always the same—her hatred for my dad. She asserted that when he said he was at work, he was really with other women, that he set these women up in apartments and bought them luxuries, while she sat at home taking care of his children.

She never talked like this when she was sober, but there was no reasoning with her when she was drinking. In fact, her hatred extended to me if I tried to defend my father. She called me "Daddy's little girl—go tell Daddy everything, you little bitch." Her hatred also extended to my father's family, which was why we never got to see them. She said Daddy's father died of venereal disease, and he was going to die the same way. She called Daddy's brothers "low-life s——t slingers." She made sure that Daddy's family never felt welcome in our house, while priding herself on letting them think that it was Daddy who was the problem. She tried to make them think that Daddy couldn't support us and that we barely had enough money to eat. Our infrequent visits to Daddy's brother Virgil ended for good when my mother stole money from Virgil's family, bought some booze, got drunk, and started a scene. Virgil's family seemed relieved when Daddy finally got her in the car and we left.

Both parents were smokers. My mother began to get careless with her smoking, and one night, she fell asleep in Daddy's easy chair with a lit cigarette in her hand, and the chair caught on fire. I poured some water on the chair, trying to put the fire out without waking her, but it kept smoking. I ran upstairs and knocked hard on the door of a group of guys who were renting the third-floor apartment. One of them quickly opened the door. "Please come and help me! There is a fire downstairs!" I cried in a panic. He ran down the stairs with me, pulled my mother out of the chair, and dragged the chair out to the front porch, where it burst into flames and burned up to nothing.

Nights were terrifying because I could feel my mother's hostility toward me. She knew I told Daddy things that went on when he wasn't home. One day, I heard her on the phone telling a neighbor what a troublemaker I was. I had lost all trust in her and feared what she might do to me when Daddy wasn't home. Some days when Daddy was on the day shift, I would wait for him on the street across from the school, where I knew he would be driving by. As soon as he saw me, he would stop to let me jump in. I usually did this when there was some news I felt he should know about. It was a way for me to talk to him in private.

Sometimes on the weekends, Daddy would get all dressed up. He would deck out in his good suit and tie, and I knew he would be gone all day. "Where are you going, Daddy?" I would ask.

"Oh, I have some business to take care of," he would say.

"Can I come?" I knew his answer would be no, but I always asked anyhow.

"No. It is not a place for children."

I suspected that he was on his way to the Welcome Tavern, but I didn't really know where he went. That annoyed me. I usually took off for the movies or found another place to go, but some Saturdays, I would hunt him down. I knew all the bars that he hung out in, so it was pretty easy to find him; I just had to look for his parked car. I would hang around outside until he came out; sometimes it would be hours, and sometimes it would be dark. When he finally came out, he would act surprised to see me and would say, "What are you doing here?"

"I was waiting for you to give me a ride home."

"Okay, let's go," he would say, without any hint of annoyance in his voice. I loved Daddy; I tried to help him by giving him as much information as I could. I always asked him not to let my mother know what I told him. He never did because he knew how vicious she was when she was drinking. He also knew she didn't like me watching her and telling Daddy what she did.

Some Fridays, my mother would give me a list and send me to the grocery store on Elmora Avenue. I was supposed to get everything on the list. When I had everything in the cart, I was supposed to wait for Daddy to come to pay for the groceries and take me home. Sometimes it would be hours before he came. Sometimes it would be dark. I trusted that he wouldn't forget, and he always showed up.

The other women would see me there doing the shopping, and one day, one of the women asked, "Are you doing the shopping all by yourself?"

"Yes," I replied in a prideful sort of way.

"How old are you?" she asked.

"I'm almost ten," I told her.

"Where is your mother?" she asked in a nosy tone.

"At home," I answered and pushed my cart away so I didn't have to answer any more of her questions. The women seemed to think it was quite amazing that I was doing the grocery shopping, but I didn't think too much of it. It wasn't hard; I knew how to read and could follow the list. The part I hated was waiting for Daddy because I never knew how long it would be before he got there. I lived in a world of great confusion, and I even had trouble with my identity. Sometimes I wondered if I was really an adult masquerading as a nine-year-old child. I felt different from other kids who had real parents. My world was chaotic, and I was always fearful, always on guard.

On nights when my mother's drunken ranting and raving episodes got really bad, I would run down to the corner drugstore, call my dad, and plead with him to come home. I knew he hated those phone calls. I would explain that she was drunk, and I was afraid to go in the house. I would let him know that I would be waiting for him on the front steps. Sometimes he would come, and other times he wouldn't. Even if he didn't come when I called him, I knew that he would get off work at midnight and would be home before 1:00 a.m. It was a great relief when his car finally turned the corner and pulled up to the curb in front of our house. I never went back in the house until Daddy was home. It only felt safe when he was there; he was my only protection. Sitting on the front steps some nights, I thought I would freeze to death before he arrived. My mother tried to hide her hostility toward me from Daddy. That was one reason that I needed to tell him what was really going on, so Daddy would know why I was waiting for him. Very little was ever said about what was going on unless I brought it up, and I knew better than do that if my mother was anywhere around. I took advantage of every opportunity to have time alone with Daddy to speak my piece, even though nothing I said ever changed anything. I would sometimes hear Daddy berating my mother for her hateful attitude toward me. He knew because I told him everything. He also knew the stress I was under when he left for work. Some nights I would beg him not to go, but my begging never worked.

One summer Saturday afternoon, Daddy asked me, "What would you like to do today if you could do anything you wanted to?"

I quickly answered, "Olympic Park."

To my disbelief, Daddy said, "Okay, let's go!"

"Just us?" I asked.

"Yeah, just us," he repeated.

I had not been to Olympic Park since we lived in Maplewood. We walked out the front door and climbed into his car. I was still in a state of awe that this was really happening. Daddy was always happy no matter the situation. As we walked into the park, we laughed as we looked at each other in the curved mirrors that distorted our image. We walked up to the "go fish" booth. Daddy gave the man a dollar, and the man gave him ten dimes so I could play. After that, Daddy ordered a pitcher of beer, and we found a picnic table. He gave me money to go ride whatever rides I wanted to. I lapped up cotton candy; rode the merry-go-round, the whip, and the teacups; and had a ball. The music played, and for the few hours we were there, I forgot about the terror at home. I knew this was one of the happiest days of my life.

As my mother gave up any pretense at housekeeping and parenting, the house was always a mess, and we all just fended for ourselves, including Bart, who was only four. There was no such thing as mealtime, especially when Daddy worked the night shift. We would just fix a sandwich or whatever we could find. There was no place to get away from my mother's rants and do homework or just tune her out. I felt very unsafe when Daddy wasn't home.

One night, during a particularly bad episode with my mother, I ran down to the corner store to call Daddy. I knew which stores had a phone booth, and I usually went to a small grocery store that was never very busy. There you could buy things like bread, milk, and other staples that today you would pick up at a 7-Eleven. In that small store, the phone booth stood along the back wall. On the night of the bad episode, as I walked straight to the back of the store, the man behind the counter quickly asked if he could help me. "Just came in to use the phone," I mumbled while wiping off my glasses that were all steamed up after coming in from the cold. I slid into the phone booth, closed the door, and dialed Daddy's number. I felt as though the man was watching me, even though I knew he couldn't hear me. I sensed his eyes glancing my way as I pleaded on the phone with Daddy to come home. When I was finished, I wiped my eyes, embarrassed that the man might have seen me crying, slipped my glasses back on, opened the door of the booth, and headed for the door. I was a small kid, and I weighed no more than fifty pounds. It was pretty late at night, around 9:00 p.m. As I walked toward the door, the man asked if everything was okay. "Yes," I answered flippantly as I strutted past him without looking up. The bell on the front door clanged as it closed behind me. The cold night air felt harsh as I crossed the busy intersection on my way back home. The darkness of the night became blacker as I walked away from the flashing lights and headlights. I took my time walking home, wishing I had another place to go. I hoped that I had convinced Daddy to come home. I was unaware at the time of the danger that could have lain in wait for a child alone in the night, and I now believe that God must have been with me, protecting me. At the time, I was sure I could outrun anyone who tried to get me, and these nighttime trips to the phone booth were how I survived what seemed to be endless drunken rampages.

 I always entered our property from the back street and walked around to the front of the house, sat on the front steps, leaned against the banister, and waited. On this particularly bad night, I held out little hope of Daddy actually coming, but all of a sudden, to my surprise, there he was pulling up in front of the house. It was now around 10:00 p.m. A feeling of relief came over me as I heard the engine stop and the car door open. He walked up to the steps. "I'm so glad you are here," I said with the thrill of surprise in my voice. We walked in together down the long hall to the kitchen. The ranting of my mother's voice could be heard as soon as the door to our part of the house opened. Daddy entered the kitchen first, and I was right behind him. I could see the stunned look on my mother's face when Daddy appeared in the kitchen. I felt that she knew he had come home because of me. I wasn't afraid then, but I knew that somehow she would find a way to pay me back. I wanted to tell Daddy, "This is what we put up with when you're not home," but I didn't. He said something to her, and she left the room. She quieted down, and we thought she had gone to bed. Daddy and I began cleaning up the kitchen, which was a mess. We were standing at the sink; Daddy was washing the dishes, and I was drying. She kept coming back into the kitchen, ranting and raving. Daddy told her to go to bed and sleep it off, but her anger was at full steam. Our backs were to her as she kept coming back into the kitchen, slurring her negative remarks like, "Daddy's little girl couldn't wait to tell." We kept working, ignoring her remarks. Suddenly, she picked up a heavy glass off the table and threw it in our direction. The glass hit Daddy in the temple, and blood spewed everywhere. I was terrified, and I screamed as loud as I could as I ran upstairs and banged on the door to the small apartment. As soon as the tenant opened the door, I shouted as fast as I could get the words out, "Please come and help me. My dad is hurt, bleeding badly. Please take him to the hospital." The tenant promised he would be right down.

    Daddy had a towel wrapped around his head as he and the tenant left for the hospital. Everything quieted down after that. I went to bed crying, worried about whether Daddy would be okay. The next morning, I thought about my hopeless situation and wondered whether life was worth living as it was. Nevertheless, I got dressed and walked downstairs. As I got closer to the kitchen, I could see Daddy at the kitchen table, a white bandage wrapped around his head and almost completely covering his face. I could hear him scolding my mother for the way she treated me. She was stone sober. Daddy smiled at me, and I asked if he was all right. He made jokes about his experience in the emergency room, and soon the room was filled with laughter. This was his way of making light of the situation. I laughed with them, but the humor to me was just another part of the nightmare. Nothing was ever a big deal to Daddy; just sweep it under the rug and forget about it. Maybe he could forget about the previous night, but for me, it was another episode in the unending terror. I felt hate for this woman who injured my father. She was an unloving person and never showed any remorse for what she had done. I knew there would be a next time and feared that, the next time, she might kill one of us. Who would be her next victim if someone didn't intervene and find a solution? My greatest fear was something really bad happening to Daddy and my being stuck with my mother as my only parent. Who would defend me then? Who would be on my side? Who would I call? What would happen to us? This was a brutal environment for children. Some so-called child experts say that all parents should be allowed to raise their own children, with no exceptions, without government interference. However, if these experts had seen and experienced what went on in our house, they might think differently. They have no clue what goes on in homes where no one steps in to rescue children from their wayward, drunk, or mentally deranged parents.

Daddy stayed home from work that day. My mother stayed sober for three full days, and in those three days, she made a skirt for me out of a piece of light-purple cotton cloth she had. I remember her old Singer sewing machine, the kind that was in a cabinet and had a knee pedal. Although the sewing machine was seldom used, my mother had many talents and could do just about anything she set her mind to when she was sober. She carefully threaded the machine, measured me all over, and began her project. There was no pattern to go by, just the measurements. It was a simple skirt with a waistband and pleats. It fit me perfectly, and I loved it! I couldn't wait to wear it to school so my friends could see it. I felt as if the skirt was my mother's way of saying she was sorry without actually saying it. "If only things could stay this way" was a wish I held out little hope of coming true. As I think back to those days, I realize how grateful I was for the tenants who came to my rescue so many times. They were quick to respond, and they asked for nothing in return. I will always remember them with gratitude.

I clearly remember the day my mother told Connie and me that she was going to have another baby. She said, "I told the doctor that I just have to have a baby for my two girls." I was not impressed with this asinine statement. *Oh no!* I thought; it was all I can do to take care of myself, and this would just be another responsibility that would be shoved off on me. She would be too drunk to do it. She couldn't take care of Bart, so how was she going to take care of a new baby? It wasn't hard to guess who was going to get the job.

The drinking didn't stop when my mother became pregnant. One Saturday afternoon came to mind. She had been gone all night, and we didn't know where she was. The phone rang; Daddy answered, and it was the police. They wanted him to come down to the police station and get my mother as soon as possible; she was in the drunk tank, ranting and raving. My father told me about the phone call. I said, "Why can't we get rid of her? Why do we have to put up with her?"

He said, "What can we do?"

"Well, we could move and not tell her where we move to," I said.

"No, we can't do that," he said. I knew this was his problem to figure out, not mine. The real problem was that he did nothing. He just looked the other way and acted as if it wasn't happening. On that Saturday afternoon, as soon as the police called, he left and went down to get her.

September 29, 1953, was my tenth birthday. In our house, birthdays were ignored. There were many years that my birthday came and went without my realizing it until weeks later. With all the problems I had to deal with, a missed birthday was of little significance. I became used to it, and I had no expectations.

One weekend, Daddy spent the morning putting together a small crib and setting it up in the sunroom. My mother had a table that she said would be perfect to use as a changing table, which she claimed was a necessary item for taking care of a new baby. The table was scrubbed, sanded, and painted white. A stack of new diapers, baby lotion, and other baby needs were placed on the table also. In the days ahead, I used to go into the sunroom and look at the small crib sitting there with the sun shining in on it and wonder what this new baby would look like. I also wondered how she would be taken care of. I was excited about it and sad at the same time. I worried about how a new baby could survive at our house. It was a huge worry for me.

A week later, on October 5, 1953, the new baby arrived. When Daddy came home from the hospital and announced that we had a new sister, I was happy. I could hardly wait to see her. My mother named her Marjorie Ellen, and we called her Margie. She was tiny, only five and a half pounds. The day she came through the front door, I wanted to hold her; she was so tiny and fragile. When my mother said I could hold her, I was very careful to do exactly as she instructed. It wasn't long before all fear was gone, and I felt very comfortable picking Margie up and holding her.

I remember my mother staying sober, gently feeding and taking care of this new baby, as capable as any hospital nurse. Margie slept most of the time and only woke up to be fed and changed. While Margie slept, my mother showed me how to make her formula. There were no premixed formulas in those days. There were two or three ingredients that had to be mixed in exact measurements, put in the bottles, and sterilized in a special pot on the stove. The main ingredient was Dextri-Maltose; it was a powder that was mixed with sterile water to make the formula. All the ingredients were stored on the top shelf of one of the kitchen cabinets, and I had to use a stool to reach it all. After I had made the formula a few times, I had it all memorized. My mother showed me how to feed, bathe, and change Margie, and I enjoyed spending the day with my mother as her baby helper. I hoped that maybe since she had a new baby, she would stop drinking. I knew that wasn't going to happen, but I allowed myself to wish it. I also knew why she was so precise in showing me how to take care of this baby. Because I was more of a worrier and was home more than Connie, I knew from the beginning that the responsibility for this child was going to be mine.

When my mother was sober, you could not imagine that such a calm and capable person was ever drunk, raving and slinging obscenities from her foul mouth. But the alcohol had tremendous power to change her, and it proved to be more powerful than any new baby. As for me, I had too little parenting and too many adult responsibilities.

I was never a child but saw myself as an adult. I became attached to this baby and felt the need to protect her since she had no way to protect herself. I would always check to see if my mother was sober before leaving for school. If she was drunk, I would stay home. She was resentful when I stayed home; she threatened to report me to the school and refused to write an excuse note for me. However, I easily solved that problem by writing my own notes, and nothing was ever said to me about them. If I did go to school when I knew my mother was drinking, I had trouble concentrating. My thoughts were consumed with worry about what was happening at home. The minute school was out, I would race home to check out the situation.

Christmas day the year Margie was born was different from any other because my mother was not drunk as she had been every other Christmas. When a small light of hope flickered, I always wanted to have it written in stone for fear that, in my next breath, it would be gone. After we had all opened our gifts and made a huge mess, Connie dressed up in her new clothes and took off to visit her friends. My mother very soberly told me that she and my dad needed to go somewhere, and she wanted me to take care of Margie. She never explained where they were going or when they would be back. Margie was now two months old, and this was the first time my parents were leaving me alone with her. It was late morning when they left, my mother sporting her trusty old winter coat with the large fur collar.

I fed Margie and changed her as I had been shown. She slept for a long time. When she woke up, I fed and changed her again, but this time, she didn't want to go back to sleep. She kept crying, and nothing I did seemed to make her happy. The day was quickly becoming night, and my parents were not home yet. I was getting annoyed and tired of babysitting. I was mad at my parents for leaving me alone with this tiny crying baby for so long. By 9:00 p.m., I was close to tears myself. My parents had been gone too long, and they hadn't left a phone number that I could call in case there was a problem. Well, now there was a problem, and I had to figure out what to do by myself. I thought about the neighbor across the street, Mrs. Lieberman, who had babies of her own. I knew her well, and I knew that if she was home, she would help me. I looked out the window and saw that her lights were on. I put my coat on, carefully wrapped Margie in a blanket, carried her across the street, and rang the doorbell. Just as her door opened, Daddy's car pulled up in front of our house. I explained my predicament to Mrs. Lieberman, thanked her, and told her that my parents had just gotten home. As I walked back across the street, my parents were just getting out of the car. I handed Margie to my mother, explaining what had happened. She was not happy with me and started yelling at me. "I showed you how to take care of her! You didn't need help from a neighbor!" she yelled.

"Why didn't you come home sooner?" I asked.

"That doesn't matter," she yelled back angrily.

She said no more, and neither did I. Daddy didn't say anything. I was glad they were home, and I was no longer responsible for a crying baby. I went to my room and got out my secret Bible, which had been left by one of the tenants. I closed the door, opened the Bible, and started reading it. The beginning was too hard, so I went to the middle, but I still didn't understand much of what it said. That night, I was very angry. I didn't want to be an adult; I wanted to be a kid. The babysitting incident brought home to me how unrealistic my parents' expectations of me were. My parents were wrong, and I knew it, but things always had a way of becoming my fault. What my mother was really mad about was that Mrs. Lieberman now knew that she had left a ten-year-old child alone all day and all evening with her two-month-old baby. My mother had told everyone what a troublemaker I was and how I did nothing to help her, and now Mrs. Lieberman knew that what my mother told the neighbors didn't exactly match the truth. In the midst of my anger, reading my Bible gave me a sense of peacefulness, even though I didn't understand all the words. Daddy always told me that God wasn't real, but I believed he was, and I just kept that belief all to myself. My faith helped me to cope with many injustices over the years.

Chapter 3

Two Steps Forward, Three Steps Backward

I never understood my parents' relationship. It was a strange union. In fact, I often wondered if they were really married. Neither of them wore a wedding ring, and there were no wedding pictures. If I asked them when they were married, they would just brush me off and say it was too long ago to remember. The only thing they seemed to enjoy together was drinking. I remember them sitting together in the dark drinking beer, planning their future together. It was only when they were both drinking that they seemed to like each other; any other time, my mother hated my dad with a vengeance. I thought it strange that they always had the lights off when they drank together. Did they think no one could see them in the dark? If I tried to turn the light on, they would yell at me. Their common thread was the alcohol, and it was in the darkness that they found their harmony. I believed that they somehow needed each other in a way that I couldn't understand. They loved the darkness, but it was that same darkness that was slowly chipping away at their sanity and keeping any light from penetrating our home.

I often wondered if they loved each other. I knew that if I ever brought the subject of love up to either of them, it would make them squirm, so I never pressed the question. I don't believe that true love was ever a part of their lives because they preferred their darkness.

Love was a word never used in our house. I could feel my dad's love for me at times, but I never felt motherly love. There was never a touch, a smile, or a kind word; our home was filled instead with violence, drunkenness, abuse, fear, and the quest for survival.

Before Margie was a year old, my mother announced that another baby was on the way. I was devastated and angry, and I didn't want to believe what I was hearing. I didn't want another baby, sister, brother, or whatever, because there were already enough children without proper care in our house. My mother was now forty-four years old and in no condition to have another baby. She couldn't take care of herself, let alone a baby. Regardless of my opinion, this baby was coming. It was a boy; he was born with an enlarged heart and lived only thirteen hours. The day Daddy came home from the hospital and told us the baby had died, Connie cried. I felt grateful, for us and for him.

During the summer of 1953, a photographer came to take our pictures. My mother told Connie and me to put on dresses and comb our hair. The photographer made many trips out to his car and carried suitcases filled with a large camera, a tripod, special lights, screens, and a table for us to sit on. He set all this equipment up in our living room. My mother had been drinking that morning. The photographer told us how to sit, what to look at, and when to smile. I remember the look of approval on my mother's face as the flash went off. I also remember her glassy eyes, her head tilted cockeyed, and her drunken smile. I hated her silly, unnatural grin; she looked like a clown without makeup, and I hoped the photographer didn't notice. I felt embarrassed, disgusted that she was the way she was, and I remember wishing she wasn't my mother. My friends had real mothers, and I was stuck with her. My loving feelings of years ago were long gone, lying dead somewhere in one of her empty bottles of booze. Many times, I wished she had died along with the love between us. I wanted the photographer to get finished and leave before she got any worse. I didn't know whether Connie knew or not because we seldom discussed what we knew. I just acted as if I didn't notice and kept it to myself.

That fall, I started sixth grade, my last year in grammar school. Connie was now a seventh grader in junior high school. I was pretty much on my own now because Connie was hanging out with the big dogs. She got to eat lunch in the school cafeteria, and she enjoyed telling me how much better she had it—how the food was so good, and I still had to come home and eat the inferior food at home. Sixth grade was my worst year in grammar school; everything went wrong for me. The events of that year provided several good examples of why today's advice to abused children—to "tell an adult"—was not going to work for me. For various reasons, I felt I could not trust the school nurse, the principal, the tenants, or my aunts. I often wished I had someone to tell, but my greatest fear was that I would tell someone, and they wouldn't believe me. Also, if I told, my mother would find ways to punish me. I was never going to win this battle because I was just a kid, and she was the adult. In my world, adults were always right, and the truth didn't matter.

One day, the school nurse called me in to her office and complained to me that Bart was coming to school dirty. She said that I should see to it that he had a bath at night and was dressed and clean to come to school every day. She went on to tell me how the school called and told my mother about it. "Your mother has a small baby at home, and she says that you do nothing to help her." As the nurse repeated my mother's words, she looked at me with disgust. As the words came out of her mouth, I seethed with anger. I knew why Bart came to school dirty, and it wasn't because my mother had a new baby at home. It was because she was too drunk to take care of him. She didn't take care of the baby either; I did. The nurse told me to go to the store and buy a bar of soap and give Bart a bath. Later that day, the principal called me in to her office and wanted to know why I didn't do more to help my mother. I knew better than to tell the true story to either the nurse or the principal. They would have insisted I was a liar and would have told my mother what I had said. I knew I would have been punished, so it was not worth it to me. I just kept my mouth shut. I knew my mother had bad-mouthed me to the neighbors, and now she was doing the same at school, all to cover for herself. After that, I became more afraid of my mother. I tiptoed around her, fearing what she might do next. I couldn't trust her, even when she was sober.

I was also terrified of the principal, who was a large rigid woman who never smiled. I knew that she didn't like me, mostly because of the lies my mother had told her about me. When this woman passed me in the hall, I was terrified that she might call me into her office for some reason or other because she always looked at me with an expression of disapproval on her face.

There was a program in the sixth grade called Young Nurses of America, and all the girls were required to belong. We had white smocks with red embroidery over the pocket that read "Young Nurses of America." Once a month, a nurse would come to the school and talk to us about different things that nurses did. One day, she told us that nurses never wear jewelry, so I took off the ring I had just received for Christmas and put it in the pocket of my smock. When we turned our smocks in at the end of the class, I forgot about the ring. The next day when I remembered where I had left my ring, I asked my teacher if there was some way I could get it back. She called the principal, and I was told to go up to the principal's office, and she would "help" me. I was terrified but did as I was told. I walked into the principal's office almost in tears but keeping my composure. The principal grilled me with questions about the ring, where I got it, how long I had it, why I put it in the pocket, etc. She implied that I was causing her trouble. She finally pushed away from her desk, stood up with a large ring of keys in her hand, told me to come with her, and we walked downstairs to the closet where the smocks were stored. She never spoke to me as we walked. She fumbled with the key ring, finally finding the right key. I stood waiting as she reached in and pulled out one smock at a time, checking each pocket with an annoyed look on her face. She finally found the ring. She pulled it out, flashed it in front of me, and said "Is this your ring?"

"Yes" I said. She proceeded to put on her glasses that hung around her neck on a cord, pulled the ring up to her nose, and examined it. She turned it this way and that way, looking for some clue that maybe it wasn't mine. She finally handed it to me as she shook her head back and forth. Her disapproval of me was a feeling I was getting used to. I never took the ring off again.

June finally arrived, and I was about to graduate from the sixth grade. Daddy gave me his credit card and told me to go shopping and buy whatever dress I wanted for graduation. I took the bus to downtown Elizabeth and went shopping. Not quite twelve years old, I was not sure what to buy for a graduation. I knew only that it had to be a white dress. The first dress I tried on was all white and looked like a ballerina dress. This dress would have been more appropriate for a dance recital, but I didn't know it. I had no one to help me, so I bought what I liked. The top of the dress was white satin, and the skirt was layers of a mesh fabric, almost see-through. It would have even been an okay choice if I had worn a slip, but I didn't know about slips. I liked how I looked in it, so I bought it.

The graduation was in the evening. My mother was drinking that day, so only Daddy went with me. My girlfriends and I all had autograph books that we passed around to our friends and teachers. No negative comments were made about my dress, and I had a fun time. When it was over, Daddy took me to the White Castle for coffee and a doughnut. Because he talked to me and was interested in what I was doing, I always loved the time he spent with me. My mother knew very little about me because she was too preoccupied with herself. How would I ever know how to mother my own children when I had never been mothered myself? My father stood out as the hero without whom I could not have survived. It really worked both ways when I think back because I took care of him as much as he took care of me. The difference was that only my dad had the power to change our lives; I didn't.

We still had Zipper, our beloved little dog, and we also had a cat. My mother loved Zipper, but the cat was not as lucky. She wanted to get rid of the cat and asked my dad to drop him off at a dairy that he drove by each day on his way to work. I asked all kinds of questions about how the cat could survive at the dairy, and as Daddy left that morning with the cat, he assured me the cat would be happier at a dairy than with us. He said that he would have other cats to play with and plenty of fresh milk to lap up.

The next winter, my mother bought "Connie and me" a parakeet. Yeah, right! Actually, she bought it for herself. It looked as if it was ours since the best place to put the cage was in our bedroom. The cage sat on our dresser so the bird could see itself in the mirror. Some days, my mother would open the door of the cage, and the parakeet would come out, sit on the dresser, and look in the mirror. He would also sit on my finger and let me put him back in the cage. I found it strange how my mother seemed to have such a warm attachment to this bird.

One day as I walked in the house from school, my mother said, "Well, guess who's back."

"Who?"

"Our old cat that Daddy dropped off at the dairy eighteen months ago. I guess there is no way to get rid of him," she stammered, annoyed that he was back.

The cat wandered into our bedroom, and there was the parakeet, out of its cage, sitting on the dresser and looking in the mirror. As soon as the cat noticed the bird, all peace and calm ended, and it was now a cat-and-bird scrimmage. The bird was trying to escape, flying around the room and crashing into the walls. I finally caught the bird while my mother caught the cat, but it was too late for the bird. I put him in his cage and closed the door. He seemed okay, but the next morning, the bird lay dead in his cage. All my mother talked about for weeks was "that poor little bird and how that rotten cat killed her." It was, of course, my fault since I was responsible for letting the cat in my room.

One day soon after the bird incident, I heard some commotion down the basement and went down to see what was going on. As I came down the stairs, my mother was sitting on a garbage can she had filled with water; the cat was inside the can, and she was sitting on the lid. She said in her half-loaded voice, "I'll get rid of this cat once and for all." I could hear the cat inside the can hit the top of the lid, squeal, and hit the top again. My mother calmly sat there. I knew she hated the cat, but to kill him so brutally? What she was doing made me sick. I needed to get away, and I started back up the stairs. The cat suddenly stopped hitting the lid. "He's dead," my mother yelled to me as I disappeared from her view. I backed down a step and saw my mother slowly rise up off the can. The cat leaped out of the can, squealing loudly as he raced out the cellar door. I was glad that the cat had outsmarted her. My mother only remarked, "You can't kill a cat. They have nine lives." My mother's vicious plan to kill the cat didn't work, but it made me more aware of her potential for violence. After that incident, I worried that she might try the same thing on me if I made her mad enough. Memories of her cruel behavior haunted me for a long time after.

My mother's drinking led to increasing problems between her and the tenants. She would go into their rooms when they were not home and steal from them, then they would complain about a missing bottle of liquor or some other item she had stolen. Screaming matches between her and a tenant were a regular occurrence. Since Connie and I shared a room on the second floor, we regularly ran into the tenants who rented the small apartment at the end of the hall. One tenant who comes to mind was Eleanor, a young woman in her twenties, who lived with her husband and their two-year-old son. Eleanor's husband was gone most of the time, and Eleanor had a lot of free time on her hands. Sometimes she would knock on our bedroom door to visit, and then she would talk to us about her life and her marriage. After she left, Connie and I would laugh at some of the stupid things she told us. Some days we would see her downtown, walking with her short shorts and high heels, with the little boy in tow. She wore bright-red lipstick that she drew up above her lip line, which only added to her whorish look. We suspected that she had a drinking problem. One night after midnight, Eleanor came down the side stairs into our part of the house after Daddy had just come in from work. I had waited on the front steps for Daddy since my mother had been on one of her drunken rampages. Eleanor was obviously drunk. She kept falling all over Daddy, trying to put her arms around him and asking him to come upstairs to her apartment. Daddy kept pushing her away, telling her to go back up to her apartment. I stood there watching, hardly believing my eyes. Daddy finally told her that if she did not go up to her apartment and leave him alone, he would have to call the police. I was scared to death that my mother would walk in and see what was going on, but she didn't, and Eleanor made her way safely back up to her apartment.

One day, Connie and I ran into Eleanor in the hallway, and she mentioned that she was on her way into the bathroom to take a bath. It was not a school day for us, so we had plenty of time to dally around and get into some mischief. Connie suggested, "Let's climb out on the roof, knock on the window, and say hi to Eleanor while she takes a bath."

"What?" I asked as if I hadn't heard her the first time.

Connie egged me on. "Look, we can just open our bedroom window and climb out on the roof." We giggled and laughed as we opened the window. Connie went first. We were pretty high up on the second floor, and the roof had a slight slant to it, so we had to be careful and find something to hold on to. When Connie got to the bathroom window, she motioned to me to come also, and I carefully inched over to where she was. Connie knocked on the window.

With big smiley faces, we both yelled, "Hi, Eleanor, how's the water?" I could clearly see her nude body as she sat in the bathtub. She was making faces at us and shaking her fist, trying to shoo us away. When the fun was over, I edged over to our window and climbed back in, with Connie soon following. I was afraid my mother might wander up to our room and see what was going on, and I knew that I would have been in more trouble than Connie if we had been caught. I began to worry that if we made Eleanor mad enough, she would tell on us.

"What if she tells Mommy?" I asked fearfully.

"Oh, you worry about everything! Just say Eleanor made it all up to get us in trouble. She can't prove it. No one saw us," Connie insisted. There was a sort of thrill to doing what I knew wasn't right, but I was always worried about getting caught. That time, we were not found out, and it wasn't too long before Eleanor and her husband moved out.

By the time Margie was two and a half, Daddy became concerned about her. He knew Margie was neglected, and he was worried that something could happen to her. Therefore, my dad called my mother's sister Alice and asked if she would be willing to take Margie. This was a clear message to me that Daddy was aware of how serious our home situation was, not only for Margie but for all of us. But did he really think that sending Margie away was a solution? How did he expect the rest of us to cope? Bart was only seven; did my dad not realize how neglected Bart was? The problem was that my father would never stand up and admit what the real problem was, especially if it meant any changes for him. My father wanted us all to believe that there was no problem, that there was nothing wrong with drinking, hanging out at bars, or exposing your children to this lifestyle.

Word of my dad's phone call to Alice spread quickly among my mother's family members, and my mother's two sisters, Bea and Ellen, came to check out the situation. This was their first visit to us since we had moved to Elizabeth; our last visit with them at their place happened when my mother was pregnant with Margie. Of course, my mother was always on her best behavior when she was around her family. For those few days of her sisters' visit, my mother stayed sober, was on her best behavior, and presented a picture of what should be rather than what was. According to her, everything was wonderful, and if there was some kind of a problem, she was not the cause. Except for my dad's failings, we were all perfectly happy. They questioned me when my mother wasn't around, but they got nowhere with that. I knew better than to open my mouth; my mother's drinking was not something that I was free to talk about. I also wondered what their plan was if they did find out. Did they have some sort of solution, or were they just being nosy? I certainly didn't want to go live with them. I was living in a dangerous and abusive environment, but I was used to it. I didn't know my aunts very well, and I didn't particularly like them; I saw them as two nosy old biddies. I also doubted that they would have believed me if I did tell them. I would never have trusted them not to tell my mother, and I wasn't going to risk being the object of my mother's wrath after my aunts were gone. I didn't trust adults in general because they only stuck up for one another. Maybe my aunts wanted to take Bart and Margie, but they never did. I really wasn't sure what their visit was supposed to achieve.

Sixth grade and the summer that followed turned out to be a particularly hard year for me. It became clear to me that if anyone was going to find out what went on in our house, it was never going to be because I told them. I still had my Bible, and I read it more and began to pray and ask God to help me. I didn't understand prayer, but what or who else did I have? Prayer seemed to be a safe method through which to express what went on in my world of fear.

Summers for me were too long, and I was always glad when it was time to go back to school. I loved the coolness of the air, the falling leaves, and seeing my old friends, some of whom I hadn't seen since June. I was in the seventh grade now, and I was sure that this year was going to be different. This school wasn't a block away; it was a mile away. I was going to eat lunch in the cafeteria that Connie had prized so highly. I would also have a homeroom, and the classrooms would change for each subject. Running home to see about Margie was not going to be an option for me now. I would just have to figure out a different way to cope, especially when Daddy was working the four-to-twelve shift.

In some ways, I feared what was ahead for me, but I also looked forward to the changes. I was quiet and kept to myself, never made any trouble, and was never the loudmouth that Connie was. I was unsure of what was appropriate and what was not, so I never wanted to draw attention to myself. Connie was never fazed by consequences; she never compromised her fun. She had the brass and guts that I never possessed. She also didn't care who she hurt or embarrassed. I was shy and uncomfortable around those who were loud and aggressive. Many of the kids I went to grammar school with were now attending other schools, but I still had enough friends. I kept a low profile, did not make any waves, and hoped I wouldn't be judged by the teachers who had Connie in their class the year before. I had one teacher who questioned me about being Connie's sister, and when I assured her that I really was Connie's sister, she remarked, "Oh no, not another one." At times like that, I hated being Connie's sister.

Some days I thought I would explode with all my secrets and just blurt it all out to whoever would listen. Suppressing my feelings took energy and work, but I wanted to avoid the embarrassment that the truth would bring. I wanted to be a kid like everyone else, but how can you be a kid when you have no parents and you in fact have to be a parent? My world was very confusing, but I just took one day at a time and went along with the program. I never knew how to express what I really felt or thought. I always chose the safest place I could find to stay out of trouble and hide who I really was.

On days when my mother was particularly wasted and I knew Margie would be spending the day alone, I stayed home. I had gone to school many days when this was the case, but the worry of it was too troublesome. Since writing my own notes in grammar school had worked so well for me, I continued to do the same in junior high.

Some nights, my mother would be up all night on one of her binges, raging until the wee hours of the morning. When that happened, I knew my mother would be sleeping most of the next day. Sometimes she would live in her housecoat for days or weeks at a time and stay drunk. Her naps were of utmost importance to her. Nothing provoked her anger more than her claim that one of us children had ruined her nap. One Friday, I decided to stay home from school and look after Margie since Daddy was on the day shift. My mother was getting wise to what I was doing, and her anger kicked in when she knew I was staying home because she was drunk. Any indication that I noticed her inability to be responsible fueled her anger. I could be punished for "noticing."

The following Monday when I arrived home from school, she met me at the door, drunk and angry. "Where is the rent money that you collected from Mr. Larsen yesterday?" I had it with me but was not going to let her know I had it, nor was I going to give it to her because Daddy told me always to give the rent money to him.

"I left it in my desk at school," I lied. Her eyes were glassy and mean-looking; the stage between being high and totally wasted was when she was most vicious. She started badgering me about why I didn't go to school on Friday, but I ignored her question and focused on talking to Margie.

She kept it up. "You little bitch. I'll see to it that the school knows why you didn't go to school on Friday. It was just because you didn't want to go and no other reason." Then she started in again about the rent money. "In what classroom, what desk did you leave the money?" Her voice was even angrier than before.

"Homeroom," I replied.

"Well, I'm going up to the school to get it," she snapped back, mumbling to herself as she put on her coat and stormed out the door.

I watched my mother walk up the street, smoking a cigarette as fast as she could smoke. I worried that she might actually be on her way up to the school, but she seldom did what she said she was going to do. I tried to reason it out. She probably wouldn't go all the way up the school because it was too cold for her to walk a mile. However, I also knew that nothing would stop her when she wanted a drink, and she probably needed the money that I told her was in my desk at school. I was terrified that my mother would go to the school and learn the truth. Daddy was on the four-to-twelve shift. I wanted to run down to the store, call Daddy, and let him know what was going on. The fear and anticipation were wearing on me; I tried to do my homework, but I couldn't concentrate.

All of a sudden, the back door slammed, harder than usual. I knew it was her. I knew those footsteps as each one hit the floor, coming toward my room. My bedroom door flew open. I was so scared I was shaking, but I kept calm so she wouldn't know how scared I really was. She screamed at me, "You are a liar! I went up to the school. The principal took me into your homeroom, and there was no money in your desk. Where is it? I want it now!" As she moved closer, I feared she was going to hit me.

"I don't know. That is where I left it. Someone must have stolen it out of my desk," I said calmly, trying not to cry or show fear on my face.

She yelled back "You are a liar! I told Mr. Fancher that you didn't go to school on Friday just because you didn't want to. He is going to put you on the truancy list, and you will be punished." As she walked out of the room, I hated her more than ever before. I knew she wanted the money to buy another bottle, and I knew this was the exact reason Daddy told me not to give her the rent money. I always did as Daddy told me, no matter what, and this was no exception.

I worried about what lies my mother might have told Mr. Fancher. The next morning, I went into the front room to see Daddy.

I had to wake him up. I gave him the money and explained what had happened the night before. "You did good! Do you need a note for Friday?" he asked.

"No, I'm okay," I answered as I left quickly, hurrying to get to school on time. I had already written a note for Friday and turned it in yesterday. Daddy didn't know about my note system, and I never told him. It was one of the many secrets I kept to myself. I walked quickly to school, hoping I wouldn't be late and asking God to help me get through the day. I tried not to think about the consequences I might have to face because of yesterday.

As I sat in English class that morning, the attendance report came around. The teacher read it out loud to the class. First, she read all the students' names who were absent for that day. She hesitated, and then, in what seemed like an unusually loud voice, she said, "Truant, Charlene Haynes." Loud "ahs" from every corner of the room were directed straight at me. Everyone was looking at me with mouths open in disbelief. I wanted to die at that very moment! There was no place to hide, and I could feel my face getting redder by the minute. I was close to tears but somehow was able to keep my composure. The start of the class took the focus off me, but I was still terribly self-conscious, embarrassed, and humiliated. I was never in trouble, always quiet, did what I was asked to, and obeyed all the rules. My classmates couldn't believe what they had just heard. If they only knew the truth, I thought to myself. Finally, the bell rang, and I was out of there.

Later that day, I was told that Mr. Fancher wanted to see me in his office. *Oh no!* I thought, worried what my punishment would be for being truant. I had never been in his office before. I had never even spoken to him before. I walked slowly to his office, taking my time, praying as I walked. His door was open.

"Come in. Close the door and have a seat," he said as he pointed to the chair in front of his desk. Mr. Fancher was tall and balding, with a small patch of hair on the front of his head that looked lost in the middle of nowhere. His voice was soft with a soothing tone to it, which made me feel more at ease. "Your mother was up here yesterday after school was out. She was looking for some money in your desk. She said you told her you had left it there." He paused for a moment, then continued, "She also told me that on Friday you stayed home from school for no reason, except that you wanted to stay home that day." He looked at me straight in the eye as he talked. "Is there something you would like to tell me about all this?"

"I stayed home on Friday to take care of my little sister," I nervously replied. There was a long silence. I felt uncomfortable with such a long pause. I worried that maybe he didn't believe me.

He suddenly blurted out, "Does your mother have a drinking problem?" I sat there, stunned by his question but relieved that somehow he knew.

"Yes," I replied, almost in tears.

"When she was up here last evening, I strongly sensed that she had been drinking. I could smell it on her." Tears welled up in my eyes; as much as I wanted to, I couldn't stop them. I was embarrassed to be crying in front of Mr. Fancher, but the relief I felt was far greater than I could explain. This was the first time in my life that I was not being blamed for my mother's wrongdoing. This principal knew the truth and wasn't afraid to let me know it. My mother had managed to tell the tale herself. I felt empowered and validated that day; it was a real victory for me. "I'm taking you off the truancy list. You can go back to your class." I stood up and walked out of his office, hoping that by the time I reached my classroom, no one would be able to tell I had been crying.

My prayers had been answered. I will never forget that day that began in trauma and ended in joy and gratitude. Mr. Fancher would never know how much he helped me that day. I had always believed that no adult would believe me over my mother, but Mr. Fancher taught me that nothing was more powerful than the truth. I also learned that when the darkness is exposed, it loses its power.

During the year I was in seventh grade, I was stunned when out of nowhere, my mother suggested that she wanted me to go to church with her on Easter Sunday, which was just a few weeks away. She even told me she would take me shopping for a new dress and shoes. I had trouble believing that any of this would really happen since we had never been a churchgoing family. I allowed myself to get excited about the possibility, even though I figured that between now and Easter, my mother would get drunk and forget that she ever suggested either the shopping trip or the church service. Then she might blame me for making it all up.

However, much to my surprise, the next weekend, we were on a bus to downtown Elizabeth. We shopped at one of the nicer department stores so she could use Daddy's credit card. He never gave her cash, but she could use the credit card. I loved the plush carpeting, the smell of perfume, and the sound of the chime when the elevator doors opened at each floor. My mother helped me pick out the perfect Easter dress. I tried on several until I found one we both liked. It was a light-cotton-blue dress in a simple style that made me look much older than my twelve years. We then ventured to the shoe department and found a pair of shoes that matched perfectly. Then came my first garter belt and stockings. Against all odds, I had spent a wonderful day with my mother. I didn't feel her love for me as much as I felt her need to have me believe she could do better. I knew this was a special day that was unlikely to be repeated. I wanted to believe that it could, but I wasn't counting on it. I wondered whether my mother was being nice to me out of guilt, or maybe Daddy had scolded her for how she treated me. Nevertheless, I was looking forward to Easter Sunday as I never had before. It was just a week away, and I was afraid that something was going to thwart our plans. I was well aware that at our house, plans could change suddenly, and promises were not something I could depend on.

The big day finally arrived. I quickly jumped out of bed and ran downstairs to the kitchen just to take a look at my mother's face, to see if all was okay. It was a happy day for me. I thought how grateful I was as I dressed up in my new clothes, taking off tags and looking at the pretty dress and shoes. I was elated and thanked God for letting this happen for me.

It was the most perfect Easter Sunday morning. The sun was shining; there was a fresh smell to the warm breeze as we walked to the church just a few blocks away. I felt a little wobbly wearing my new shoes but soon got used to the higher heel. As we walked in the front door of the church, the organ played softly. We quietly slipped into the pew in the back row. The church was very large, open, and airy. I noticed the wide stained glass windows that climbed up the side of the walls. The worn velvet cushions on the pew felt luxuriously soft. The church began to fill up, and the music became louder. The service began, and the music echoed as the first Easter hymn played. We shared a hymn book and sang together. I felt as if it was some miracle of God that I was where I was with my mother.

When the service ended, the pastor stood outside the front door, at the top of the steps, shaking hands with everyone as they were leaving. My mother seemed to be in a great hurry, but she stopped and quickly shook hands with the pastor. I didn't understand the sudden speed, and I was having trouble keeping up with her. When we finally turned the corner onto another street, she pulled out a hymn book from under her arm. "Oh no! You forgot to put the hymn book back!" I said, assuming she would suggest that I take it back.

"Yes, I did, but it's okay. I will return it another time." When I offered to take it back, she never answered me, and we just kept walking. I felt uncomfortable about the book, but she just changed the subject. Despite my worry, I said no more about it.

Returning the hymn book was never mentioned again. Several weeks later, I noticed the hymn book sitting on our piano. Every now and then, I would see my mother sitting at the piano, tapping out a song from the hymn book. I would always smile to myself as I walked past, thinking back to Easter Sunday and how my mother's motivation finally became so clear. In her eyes, my dad paid for my new outfit, and she got free sheet music!

Chapter 4

Unexpected Help

The McCue family lived on the corner a block away. I always thought their house, a two-story pink stucco, was one of the prettiest in the neighborhood. When I was younger, I used to visit them now and then, but now that I was twelve and in seventh grade, I started to visit them more often. I always felt welcome, even when I showed up uninvited. Mrs. McCue was pleasant and always glad to see me. Her husband, Dr. McCue, was a dentist. The McCues had four children, two girls in first and second grade, a four-year-old boy, and a baby boy. When I visited, I would entertain the children and help the girls with their homework. Sometimes, Mrs. McCue would ask me if I would take the baby for a walk in the stroller, and she would always offer me at least a quarter to do it. When I helped the girls with their homework, they would ask if I could come back tomorrow to help them again. This became a regular routine. The McCue house was a place where I felt wanted and useful. If I stayed long enough, I was invited for dinner. Their house was always clean and neat. Mrs. McCue had lots of help, including a regular maid who came to clean and iron four days a week and another lady who came on Wednesdays to do extra cleaning like kitchen cabinets and bathroom floors. The McCues' house was up-to-date with wall-to-wall carpet, nice furniture, and the latest styles of baby gear. I secretly wished I could have been one of their kids.

One day when I was visiting the McCues, we started talking about birthdays. We all told when our birthdays were; mine happened to be that day, and I hadn't realized it. A few minutes later, Mrs. McCue appeared with a birthday gift for me. I was so thrilled. It was a bottle of perfume, the very first birthday gift I ever remember getting.

After a while, I was going to the McCues' house every night and staying for dinner. The food was wonderful. Mrs. McCue usually broiled steaks that she had a local butcher custom-cut for her. It wasn't long before Mrs. McCue asked me if I would like to clean the kitchen for her every night after dinner, and she would pay me thirty-five cents. I loved the thought of this arrangement; I thought of it as my first job. I told my mother about Mrs. McCue's offer, and she didn't object. This family was an answer to prayer for me, although I didn't realize it at the time. I now had a nice place to go after school every day, and I was earning some money of my own. I was no longer running the streets at night trying to call Daddy to come home; I was only home now on the weekends. I detached myself from the constant problems at home and concentrated on my newfound family. I didn't read my Bible anymore or pray since I was no longer in desperate need. It was clear to me now that I really should have kept closer to God because he was providing me with the relief I had asked for.

The McCues were very generous and included me in all that they did as a family.

I felt so lucky to be with them. As far as I knew, the McCues never knew about my situation at home, or maybe they did and didn't let me know. Nevertheless, they provided me a place of refuge from the constant turmoil and abuse. Some nights after I had cleaned up from dinner, Dr. and Mrs. McCue would play games with us, and it was always great fun. Sometimes I wouldn't get home until 9:00 p.m., but the McCues always insisted on watching me as I walked home to be sure I got there safely.

The McCue house had a walk-up attic, and there was a bed in the attic that Mrs. McCue always said was the best bed in the house. Every now and then, she would invite me to spend the night on a Friday night, and I was honored with the bed in the attic. The girls were always excited for me to spend the night at their house and be there on Saturday mornings. We would watch cartoons together and play games. When Dr. and Mrs. McCue got up with the younger children, they would fix breakfast, and we would all eat at the kitchen table. Their breakfast was usually something special that I never had at home, like waffles or pancakes with blueberry syrup.

Since Connie and I still shared a bedroom on the second floor, I could come in the front door and walk up the winding staircase to the second floor without ever going into my family's part of the house. I seldom saw my parents anymore, except on the weekends. I don't believe they cared because I was out of my mother's hair and no longer waiting for Daddy at the bar or calling Daddy at work in desperation. The best part was that I was off the streets and in a safer environment. Connie was busy with her social life, so neither one of us was home much anymore. I was much happier, more at ease, and adjusting better at school. On the weekends, I hung out at the movie theater with my girlfriends.

Mrs. McCue was very pretty, and her family reminded me of a storybook family. Mrs. McCue was a registered nurse like my mother, but there the similarities end. Mrs. McCue had a calm, patient way about her that would make any child glad she was their mother. She knew what was appropriate and what wasn't. Dr. McCue treated her with love and respect, and I could tell that he valued her as his wife and mother of his children. Mrs. McCue was on a ladies bowling league, and every Wednesday morning, she would leave the younger children with the maid and be free to go bowling and shopping for the day. She had pretty clothes and an attic full of shoes. Every now and then, Dr. and Mrs. McCue would get dressed up and go out for the evening. I remember one night when they dressed up to go out, Mrs. McCue walked down the stairs, and I thought she looked just like Donna Reed as she gracefully stepped into view. Dr. Mc Cue would help her on with her coat just like I had seen in the *Donna Reed Show*. I admired and respected both of them for creating such a loving family, and I was grateful that they so easily included me in much of what they did as a family. Sometimes I did wonder whether somehow they knew what went on at my house. Many times, I wanted to tell Mrs. McCue about my mother, but I never got up the courage to do it. It would have been easy if she had asked me about it, but she never pried or asked any questions. I always wished she would because it would have helped me to spit it all out. Even though telling would have been hard for me, I would have trusted Mrs. McCue to believe me. However, that door just never opened.

One evening, their doorbell rang. Mrs. McCue was busy, and she asked me to answer it. I opened the door, and it was their paper boy, who happened to be one of the boys in my homeroom class. Mrs. McCue yelled to me, "There is an envelope on the desk all ready for him." I found the envelope and gave it to him.

When I closed the door, I smiled and thought to myself, *He thinks I live here and this is my family.* My self-esteem was raised a few notches the next day when I saw him at school. I felt as if I had as much value as any of the other girls in the seventh grade. How would he ever know any different?

One day in the fall, Mrs. McCue told me that she was planning a shopping trip to New York City and asked if I would like to go with her. She explained that I would have to take a day off from school. She also told me that I would have to get my parents' permission in advance so she could make our plans. I told her that would be fine. I told my mother about the invitation, but she was drinking that day and didn't really know what I was telling her. I knew she didn't care what I did or where I went, and I knew there would be no objection.

I was excited the day of our shopping trip. It was a beautiful fall day. I dressed in my usual school clothes and put on my coat and walked out the front door just as if I were going to school, so no questions would be asked. I would write my own excuse note for school on Monday as I usually did. I carefully watched my time so that I was at Mrs. McCue's at eight sharp as she had told me. I could hardly believe I was getting to do this; it seemed odd to me that she chose me to go with her instead of one of her lady friends. I felt very special and honored that she liked me enough to want me to go with her and spend the whole day. I slid into the passenger side of her station wagon, and we were on our way. She parked the car at the train station and said that Dr. McCue would come and get the car since his office was not far from there. As we found our seats on the train, Mrs. McCue told me that she had ordered a leather coat which she would pick up while we were in New York. All of a sudden, I was excited to feel the train moving, and before long, we arrived in New York City, within walking distance of a large department store.

Once we were in the store, as we moved up one escalator and down another, it was obvious that Mrs. McCue had done this many times before and knew exactly which way to go. "Would you like a new dress?" she asked. I didn't answer. "We will go look and see if we can find one that you like." We proceeded to the girls' dress department. I tried on several dresses, and she helped me pick out one that fit well. I loved her helping me and telling me what looked good on me, how it fit, etc. The one we chose was a red-and-gold print which Mrs. McCue said would be good for fall. We kept shopping except for stopping for lunch, and before long, we had acquired two shopping bags full of Christmas gifts. "What can I get you for Christmas?" she asked. I didn't know what to say. "If you don't tell me what you want, I will buy you perfume," she teased.

"I would like a pair of long pants," I blurted out. I don't know how I got the courage to say that. So we proceeded back to the girls' department, and I tried on a pair of red velvet toreador pants, which were the latest rage at that time. "Toreador" style meant the pants came down to just above the ankle and had a small slit on the side of each leg. I loved them! Mrs. McCue saw me turn the tag over to see the price.

"Don't look at the tag. If you want them, you can have them."

"Okay, I want them," I said, so elated I could feel my heart pounding.

It was getting late, and we still needed to pick up Mrs. McCue's leather coat. When we left the first store, we were on a busy street with tall buildings all around us. We walked a few blocks to another store to pick up the coat, and Mrs. McCue explained as we walked that even though the second store was a few blocks away, it was on the way to the train station. She tried the coat on, modeling it in the mirror, and I could tell she loved it. I told her how pretty the coat looked on her. Mrs. McCue chatted with the saleslady as I waited on a chair with the other bags. I thought about how stylish Mrs. McCue was and how different from my mother, who still wore nurse's shoes that laced up and had chunky heels, along with her out-of-date cotton dresses. Mrs. McCue decided to wear the new leather coat home, and we were soon on our way to the train station.

We had had a full day, but it was now dusk, and we were both exhausted. The bags were getting heavy, and we were glad to get on the train. It was dark by the time we arrived at the Elizabeth station. Down the ramp and a few rows back, Dr. McCue was there waiting to pick us up. I hopped in the back seat with my bags, and Mrs. McCue slid in the front. She and Dr. McCue gave each other a kiss as I tried to look the other way. "I was looking for you when you got off the train," he said. "I had to look twice before I recognized you. When I realized it was you, I thought, 'What in the world is that thing she is wearing?'"

"This is the leather coat I ordered," she flippantly replied. I knew his remark and the tone of his voice had rubbed her the wrong way. I ignored the rest of their conversation and kept looking out the window, looking forward to getting home so I could try on my new pants again. Dr. McCue dropped us off in front of their house. As we walked up the front walkway, Mrs. McCue said with a great deal of annoyance, "I don't care if he likes my new coat or not. It doesn't matter to me one bit."

"I like it!" I answered. "I think it looks nice on you." I was trying to soothe her obvious irritation with him.

I had had a wonderful day. Mrs. McCue handed me my bags and watched me as I walked home. I thought about how I had seen Dr. and Mrs. McCue as such a perfect couple. It takes a while to realize that nothing is ever as perfect as it may appear at first, and even this perfect couple had their angry moments.

My parents never noticed or made mention of my red velvet pants. Connie noticed and asked me where I got them. I told her that Mrs. McCue bought them for me for Christmas. I knew they looked good, and I wore them everywhere. Every weekend, I had them on, and it wasn't long before the velvet had worn off in patches in places like the butt and the knees. However, I still wore them until they no longer fit me and were falling apart.

There was a savings program at school, and students could open a bank account in homeroom. Every Friday, we could deposit or withdraw money from our account. Since I now had an "income," I signed up and made my deposit each week, and it wasn't long before I had a little stash. My parents never knew I had this account. I especially didn't want my mother to know because she would have been "borrowing" from me and never paying me back.

On the weekends, I would sometimes visit the family, who rented the third-floor apartment, and one day, I told the lady about my savings account. She asked me if she could borrow $30 and promised to pay me back the following Friday when her husband got paid. I withdrew the money from my account and gave it to her. The next Friday when I got home from school, I learned that they had moved out, and I never heard from them again. I learned a great lesson from that loss, and I never again told anyone about my savings account.

Most of the clothes I had up to this point were what Connie had outgrown. I remember one day a thick Montgomery Ward catalog came in the mail, and I scanned through it for hours. I found a yellow-and-gray pleated skirt that I just had to have, so I filled out the order form, following the directions as to how to place an order. I counted out the exact amount of money I needed, put it in a white envelope with the order form, and put a few stamps on it. The change made the envelope heavy, and I could hear it jingle when I dropped it in the mailbox. I was excited about this new skirt and looked each day for it to arrive. It didn't take nearly as long as I had expected. I came in from school one day, and there was my package, sitting on the piano, wrapped in brown paper and addressed to me. I tore it open, ran upstairs to my bedroom, and tried on the skirt. It was a perfect fit. I was very proud of that skirt. I wore it to school the next day and to the McCues' that night, telling them all about how I had ordered it through the catalog and bought it with my own money.

Christmas was never a big deal for me because it was never a family event at our house. We always had a Christmas tree, but I had no clue what it meant or why we did it, except for the fact that everyone else did it. There were always toys for Bart and Margie. When Daddy asked me what I wanted, my answer was always, "New clothes." Starting when I was in seventh grade, my father would hand me his charge card and tell me to go buy what I wanted. I would hop on the bus to downtown, pick out an outfit, bring it home, and wrap it up. When the big ordeal of opening the gifts arrived, I already knew what I had, so it all seemed so silly to me. The only exceptions were the wrapped gifts my mother's sisters, Aunts Bea and Ellen, mailed to us every year. These were the only presents I had to open that I hadn't wrapped myself. In addition, there was no such thing as Christmas dinner at our house. I never really knew how it was to be in a real family, except for my involvement with the McCues. And even though the McCues welcomed me lovingly and treated me like a family member, I knew I was not really part of them. In my family, there were too many unspoken issues which left us each separated in our own compartmentalized worlds. Christmas for me was just nonsense; the idea of Santa coming down the chimney leaving presents was to me nothing more than a fairy tale that no one wanted to admit wasn't true. I saw the holidays as just another excuse the world accepts as a valid reason to get drunk. That was how our family celebrated. I always knew that in my house, Christmas had nothing to do with religion and everything to do with following a routine, trying to fit in and look acceptable.

 Mrs. McCue told me that on Christmas Day, their family went to visit relatives, exchanged gifts, had dinner together, and returned in the early evening. She gave me a key to their house and told me if I wanted to come over, I could wait for them to return. Late that afternoon, I walked to their house. I felt so grown-up, so trustworthy as I turned the key in the lock and opened their front door. How could I be so privileged to have the key to this huge expensive house? I came in, took off my coat, and sat on the sofa. I had never been in this house before when it was empty of the noise and chatter of kids. I was looking forward to seeing the girls so they could show me their new gifts. As I waited, I thought about how different their lives were from mine; this was a whole different world just a block away. Mrs. McCue saw me in a different light than my mother did, and I felt trusted and safe when I was with her and her family. Thanks to the McCues, I was sure that all the negative things my mother had to say about me to the neighbors, to the school, and to my face were not true. To the McCues, I had value. They had fit my very beat-up life into their world of sanity and love. My mother had no clue who I was, what I thought, or how I felt. She didn't know the McCues either, and I was grateful that so far, she had not intruded on my relationship with them. However, the fear that she might intrude was becoming more of a constant worry for me. When it started getting dark and the McCues had not yet arrived, I wrote them a note. It simply said, "Merry Christmas. Love, Charlene. I'll be over tomorrow." I left it on the table with the key and locked the door behind me. I can still remember the smell of the cold air as I walked home that evening.

In 1956, I was becoming aware of the current songs on the radio. I loved to listen to the top 10, including Patti Page, Johnny Mathis, Frankie Valli, and of course, the hottest sensation of the time was Elvis. Everyone loved Elvis, including me. I had received a wallet for Christmas, and I carved all of Elvis's hit songs on the outside of my wallet in ink. One day, when Dr. McCue saw my wallet, he teased me without mercy, and the girls got a kick out of the teasing. The humor was always fun and in good taste.

That spring, the McCues had a wedding to attend in Connecticut, and I was invited to come along. Mrs. McCue bought pretty new dresses from an exclusive children's shop for her girls for this upcoming event. She explained to me that the only reason they were getting new dresses was because they would be seeing relatives that they had not seen in a long time, and she assured me I would look fine in anything that I wore to school. She was always conscious of making sure I was comfortable with any situation and did not feel in any way out of place. The plan was that I would babysit for her and her sister while they attended the service. I was even going to get paid for watching the children.

This trip was like a vacation for me. It was a cold morning when we set out for the long trip to Connecticut. We arrived at a relative's house, and I stayed with the babies, who were all asleep, while the grown-ups went to the service. After less than an hour, the adults arrived back at the house. They gathered up the children, and we all piled into one of the station wagons on our way to the reception. We pulled onto a winding driveway that I thought was just another street, until I saw a large house in the distance. It looked sort of like the mansions I had seen in movies. I was amazed at the size of this house, and once inside, I was in awe of the openness of the large rooms, the high ceilings, the fancy chandeliers, and the winding staircase which was suitable for a movie star. This was a fantasy world to me, and I had never seen anything like it before. I felt too poor to be there, but who would know it? The house was full of people, and a waiter walked around with trays of food and drinks. I would have felt uncomfortably out of place had it not been for Mrs. McCue, who kept me with her and introduced me to some of their relatives. I felt extremely privileged to be there.

A few weeks later, my nagging fear that my mother would interfere with the McCues turned out to be justified. As I entered the McCues' front door, Mrs. McCue said, "Your mother called this morning and told me that you needed to go to the dentist, so I made an appointment for you to see Dr. McCue."

I shuddered in fear at her words, and it wasn't because I was afraid of dentists. Under my breath, I said, "Uh-oh." It was true that I needed to see a dentist because I hadn't been to one in several years, and my teeth needed attention. My fear came from the first part of Mrs. McCue's sentence, "Your mother called." I wondered who was going to pay Dr. McCue because I knew it was not going to be my mother. I could smell a rat and knew that somehow I needed to weasel my way out of this appointment. The appointment was more than a month away, so I had time to find a way out. I wished I could have sat down and explained my feelings and fears to Mrs. McCue and tell her about my mother, but I never could find the right time or place to do it. I knew how my mother operated and how she seemed to think that other people owed her things. I feared that her greed would jeopardize my relationship with the McCues. I wished my mother would stay out of it, but I knew that this was just the beginning. My mother's motives were generally to the tune of how she could get something for nothing. I was also afraid of what lies she would start telling Mrs. McCue about me. I was afraid, very afraid.

Not long after that, I heard my mother on the phone with Mrs. McCue borrowing a pound of coffee. To my mother, borrowing something was the same as taking it because she never repaid anything she borrowed. Her idea that things were free for her was embarrassing to me. It was like all the things she stole and thought it was okay. Her thought system worked on the basis that if an entity, whether a family or a church, had plenty of something, then they wouldn't miss or need the one item she took. She also believed that the stolen article was rightly hers. That afternoon, I went to the McCues as usual. I told Mrs. McCue that I wouldn't be able to come over anymore because I now had much more homework and needed to spend more time studying. She graciously said that it was okay, and I didn't explain further. I should have; I still feel today that she deserved more than that, but at the time, it was all I had to give. I also owed the McCues a debt of gratitude for all they did for me. They would always hold a special place in my heart, and they would never know the magnitude of how my life was lifted because of them.

When my mother asked me why I didn't go to the McCues anymore, I gave her the same excuse about homework.

Chapter 5

False Hope

After four years, we were still living on Wyoming Avenue; this was the longest that we had lived anywhere. The fifth and last year in our big house was our worst. My mother's drinking was now even more out of control. The ranting and raving episodes would go on for hours at a time, all night long, almost every night. She still repeated the same story over and over, about how my dad kept girlfriends in apartments and how they had all the things that she did not, like big TVs, silk nightgowns, etc., while she sat at home with babies. Whether this story was true or not did not matter to any of the children in the house. All we cared about was that we needed parents who were real adults who could function at an adult level. My mother's hatred for my dad became more obvious as her behavior toward him became increasingly mean and brutal. She worked at making life as miserable for him as she could. The children were all deeply affected by this continual battle that we could do nothing about. Some days when I went to school, I just wanted to scream, scream as loud as I could, just scream and keep on screaming until someone insisted I tell them exactly what was wrong. Of course, I never did this, but there were times when I feared that I would not find the strength to hold it in any longer.

Although Daddy sympathized with his children and did what he could to fix what my mother destroyed, he offered no real solution. Ignoring her behavior only ensured that it would get worse over time. He lived in his own world of denial, and instead of addressing the severity of the problem, he continued to make light of it. He pretended he couldn't see any problems as he stayed calm in the midst of the turmoil. He seldom raised his voice, never uttered a four-letter word, and never ever said anything negative about my mother. My mother always used the filthiest language when she was ranting and raving, words I had never heard of, but I was catching on quickly. I never remember seeing Daddy drunk, and if he was, I couldn't tell. Even when my mother's alcohol problem was at its peak, I would still see my parents sitting together in the dark, enjoying their drinks. If they were able to see the damage my mother's behavior was doing to their family, they didn't care enough to face the problem and make changes. It was many years later that Daddy told me that my mother knew she had a drinking problem and wished she could get it under control. He seemed to be implying that she was clever, almost bragging about the fact that she was aware of her problem. I wasn't impressed because if she knew it and he knew it, why didn't they attempt to figure out some kind of solution?

One Sunday, to my surprise, my mother decided that Connie and I would go with her to church. I don't know where she found this church, but that Sunday, we went with her. I knew she had been drinking. The only other church I had been to so far was a Methodist church, and this one was very different. As we stepped in the door, one of the ladies came up to my mother and greeted her as if she already knew her. The inside of the church was simple, a large room with rows of folding chairs. We slid into a seat on the back row. It was a loud place with music playing and people crying, speaking in different languages, and praying out loud, yelling phrases like, "Praise the Lord," and "Hallelujah." I didn't understand what it was all about. It was different from anything I had ever seen before, and I felt out of place. The whole atmosphere was strange enough to be frightening to me. There were separate rooms where you could go in with the pastor and "get saved." Someone came over and spoke to my mother. I saw her go into one of the rooms; I could hear her crying and yelling, "Hallelujah," her voice not quite right. I was afraid she might use one of her four-letter words; I would have been embarrassed if that happened, but it didn't. Connie and I were approached by two girls our age whose parents attended the church. They were friendly and told us about some things that were going on for teens. The next Sunday, we went back, and the girls invited us to a day at Linden Pool and a sleepover at their house afterward. We went and had a great time. The sleepover was fun; we stayed up late, talked, laughed, and took pictures of one another. The next morning, the parents served breakfast for us; they had a huge dining room table where we all ate breakfast together in our pajamas. The food was plentiful, and it was a fun time for Connie and me. These were nice people, but we could never invite those girls to our house because they would have been terrified of my mother.

It was summer, and the church had a teen Bible school for both boys and girls. One of the boys was the pastor's son, and he was cute. I will always remember him praying with us. He seemed so confident, and the words just came out so naturally for him. I thought about how terrified I would have been if they had asked me to lead a prayer.

I believe it was through this church that my mother was put in touch with AA (Alcoholics Anonymous). I was never told about her going to an AA meeting, so I didn't know she was really seeking help. My dad didn't go because as the fantasy went, it was only she who needed help, not him. My memories are somewhat vague about how long she stayed sober, but I do remember her being sober. The whole atmosphere in our house changed. My mother cleaned up the house. She looked and acted different, much calmer and quieter when she spoke. It felt odd to me, almost uncomfortable. I had become so accustomed to being tense that when there was calm, I became nervous. Things seemed to have gone from black to white overnight, without time to adjust.

One day, my mother told us a friend of hers was coming to visit, and one of the ladies from AA came to our house. When this lady came, she suggested that we all take a ride to her house. My mother, Margie, Bart, and I all went with the AA lady. My mother sat in the front passenger seat, and she and the lady talked. I listened carefully as the lady from AA told my mother about her sobriety and how different her life was now. My mother responded positively with statements that validated her own desire to maintain sobriety. The lady talked about how bad her own life had been before she found AA and how different it was now. Her house sat up on a steep hill. It was an old house, much smaller than ours, in a poorer neighborhood. This lady told my mother that she also had teenagers. As we went into her house, she was telling my mother about how when she was drinking, she would sleep all day and ignore her children, but now that she was sober, she was very involved in their lives. My mother talked to this woman about her own drinking, and I listened intently. I was hearing her not only admit she had a drinking problem, but she wanted to get sober. We got back in the car, and as we rode home, I thought about how different our lives could be if my mother were to stay sober. I had a good time that day. I felt that maybe God had heard her prayer at the church that Sunday, and that was what led her to AA.

When we got home, my mother thanked her new friend as we got out of the car. She cooked dinner that night, and we all ate together. However, less than a week later when I came in from school, I knew that my mother had been drinking, and all was as before; nothing had changed. I suppose my mother had decided not to continue to go to the meetings, stay sober, and work the program. She never went back to church either. Maybe if my dad had made it a priority to go with her and stop drinking himself, it would have made a difference, maybe not. My dad would never have participated in any program that suggested that he believe in God; he still thought that all religion was nonsense. I also believe he feared not being able to drink himself. Maybe if my mother had not been drunk when she went to the church, she could have truly repented with all her heart instead of just yelling out some words. God helps the repentant sinner, but true repentance includes giving up one's sin, and my mother could not give up drinking for very long.

Connie and I were so different from each other that many people were surprised to learn that we were sisters. Connie was popular, and her friends were part of the "in" crowd. She had a quick wit and was always busy going here or there with her friends. I was the opposite. I did my homework and did not get involved with the uppity girls whom I knew didn't like me. Connie called me a "fag," and I was known to her friends as "Connie's fag sister."

Connie's best girlfriend, Phyllis Boff, lived just a few blocks from us. Phyllis had six siblings, and her father was a dentist. In the summer, Phyllis's family rented a house at the shore for the whole summer. Dr. Boff would work during the week and go to the shore on the weekends to be with his family. This summer was no different except that Connie was going to figure out a way to spend a week or two at the shore so that she and Phyllis could be together and have fun. The Boffs would have probably invited Connie to join them at their rental if they didn't have so many children, but Mrs. Boff did help Connie find out about rooms for rent near them. Connie asked my dad if she could rent a room for a week or two, arguing that the Boffs would be staying only a few houses away, and she would be fine. Connie was persistent, and Daddy was easy and usually gave in to her pleading. Daddy suggested that I go along so that Connie wouldn't be renting the room by herself. Connie told me about the plan and pumped it all up, making it sound too good to be true. I was going to get to do this and that, and we would have the greatest time at the shore for a whole week, blah, blah, blah. I agreed to go, but I doubted that I was going to fit in as well as she made it sound or that she and Phyllis really planned to include me. Connie was especially nice to me as the time to go was approaching because I was important to her plan. I didn't really care if I went or not because I wondered what I would be doing while she and Phyllis hung out together. Phyllis was her friend, and I certainly didn't know anyone at the shore. Even so, the idea of spending a week at the shore became more exciting to me as the days grew closer.

We packed our suitcase the night before so we could leave early the next morning. This was new, and the excitement was contagious as Connie and I became best of buddies once again. The shore we would be staying at was Belmar. Daddy piled our luggage into our car, and we were on our way. It took a few hours to get there, but it was fun talking and joking with one another as Daddy drove. We crossed over several large bridges, the last one a drawbridge. As soon as we were on the other side of the drawbridge, the air had a salty smell to it, and as we drove closer, I could hear the sound of the ocean. When the ocean finally came into view, I was in love with it.

We arrived at the Boffs' place, visited for a few minutes, then walked down the street to where we would be staying. The landlady answered the door. She was an older lady who had a mellow voice and looked like a grandmother. We were invited in and shown to our room on the second floor. The room had a row of windows across the front, a double bed, and an old musty smell to it. Daddy went downstairs to pay the lady and to be sure she was okay with the arrangement. Connie and Phyllis stood around laughing with each other and talking about what they were going to do the rest of the day, which of course would include me since Daddy was still there. Daddy gave Connie and me some money for our meals and told us to be careful and have a good time. As he left, he reminded us to be all packed and ready to go the following Saturday when he would be back to get us. As soon as he was out of sight, Connie said, "Let's put on our bathing suits and walk down to the beach." We were changed in no time, grabbed a few towels, and we were off to the beach. Connie and Phyllis walked ahead of me. I knew from the start that for this entire week, I was on my own.

The sound of the ocean and the smell of the air intrigued me as we walked up a few concrete steps to the beach. The ocean was so overwhelming, never-ending, constantly moving. I slowly walked closer to it so that the wave would glide over my feet as I stood there. The water gliding back would give me a strange feeling of unsteadiness. I was in awe of the massiveness of it, and I wanted to stay there and watch it. Connie and Phyllis didn't get as much of a charge out of the sea as I did. Connie had been to the shore before, and to Phyllis, this was old hat; she came every summer and had done so for years. They went up to the boardwalk, and I knew they wanted to get rid of me. They made fun of me, mocking everything I said. I really didn't like them and didn't want to be with them any more than they wanted to be with me. I just stayed on the beach. I was having fun, venturing in a little farther, trying not to step on any broken shells. I was getting hungry by now, and I could tell I was sunburned. I walked back to the room, changed my clothes, and headed for the boardwalk.

The boardwalk was pretty neat. The food smelled good, and there was lots to do—places to play games, places to buy souvenirs or beach clothes, and places to just hang out. Connie and Phyllis were gone by now. I climbed up on a stool and ordered a meatball sandwich. I could hear music playing in the background; it was one of the top hits that year, Patti Page's "Old Cape Cod." I felt a part of the scene she created through her softly sung words about sand dunes and salty air. As I sat on the stool looking out toward the ocean, I knew I would always remember that moment. This place took me out of reality and let me drift into another setting where life was easy, relaxed, and worry-free. I loved the atmosphere. I felt quite adult, as if I had never been a child. Being on my own was familiar to me, so familiar that I had no fear of it. Solitude was what I knew. I played a few games of chance, bought a comic book to read, and went back to the room. This was pretty much my routine for the next few days.

By the end of the week, Connie had acquired an ear infection. Daddy came the next day and took Connie to a local doctor, who gave her a prescription for eardrops. Overnight, the ear infection was on the mend. Daddy spent the day with us, suggesting that we go out for hot dogs and a movie. Then he told us that since it was already Friday, we should all get packed and go home together since he wasn't willing to drive all the way home and come back again. Connie was feeling better now, and she asked if she could stay until Sunday and ride home with Dr. Boff. Daddy agreed. I packed my suitcase and left with Daddy. I had really had a great time in spite of the circumstances. The world seemed safer back then; in today's world, it would have been much different for a twelve-year-old to be hanging around a boardwalk without an adult or even a friend. I believed that God loved me and was always with me, or I would not have survived all the situations that life brought my way. I was also too young to know the danger as I do today. Although I enjoyed my trip to the beach, I had missed Bart and Margie, and I was glad to get home to make sure they were okay.

One Sunday afternoon while we were all home, a group of people from the church came to the door. My mother had never gone back to church, but they were coming to visit us. I was surprised that my mother actually invited them in. I stayed in my bedroom, trying to listen to what the adults were saying. I heard the visitors invite both my parents to come to church. I knew my dad wasn't going to go because as long as I had known him, he had never set foot in a church. I was even surprised that he was willing to stand there and talk to representatives from a church. I was scared that the visitors had somehow found out what really went on at our house—about how Bart and Margie were left to fend for themselves in a violent and drunken atmosphere. I feared that the church people were going to take us away; that was always my fear about anyone finding out our secret. I could hear the visitors praying with my parents, and I knelt down beside my bed until they were finished. Connie was in the bedroom with me; she was laughing about the prayers and trying not to let the adults hear her laughing. All of a sudden, the church people were leaving. After they left, I could hear my parents talking to each other, but I couldn't hear them well enough to know what was said.

A week later, Daddy came home from work and announced that Irvington Varnish was being bought out by another company, and he was being transferred to Freehold, New Jersey. My dad never saw God's hand in this sudden change for us, but I did. The situation had become close to unbearable, especially for Bart and Margie. Daddy said that our new home was a long distance from any stores, so it would be harder for my mother to buy liquor. I wonder if he really thought that would make any difference or if he was just trying to convince me that he had found a solution. I don't know, but I do know that for a time, the move created positive change for all of us.

Chapter 6

A Geographical Cure

How my dad managed to sell that big house with all the furnished rooms so quickly I will never know. It happened so suddenly that school was no sooner out than we were packed up and on our way. I did not see our new house until moving day, and I loved it at first sight. It was a four-bedroom Cape Cod in a subdivision of East Brunswick, New Jersey, about twenty-five miles from my father's new job in Freehold. The first thing I noticed about East Brunswick was that it seemed a safer place than Elizabeth, where crime was plentiful and on the rise. In Elizabeth, I had been freely running the streets and riding buses alone. Connie and I had no rules; no one knew where we were most of the time, and I was on the streets alone more than she was. Many times at night, I would see a man standing in front of a large apartment building on Elmora Avenue with his penis out, just standing there. I knew he was dangerous, but I always thought I could outrun him if he came after me. Now that I was an adult, I knew I was wrong. I was such easy prey; I cringe when I think back to those days and what I escaped.

I thought about the previous summer when my mother sent Connie and me to Newark to see a movie that she had seen when she was young. It was a love story, *Magnificent Obsession*, starring Rock Hudson and Jane Wyman. This was an adult movie and not appropriate for two girls ages twelve and thirteen, but I knew my mother really wanted to get rid of us for the afternoon. She gave us enough money for bus fare and the movie. I was never afraid to go to downtown Elizabeth, but I had heard so many horror stories about Newark and all the crime that happened there that I would never have gone there alone. It was scary enough going to Newark with Connie. It was an old theater, with high ceilings and red carpeted floors. There were only a handful of people at the matinee. We could sit wherever we wanted, so of course, we wanted to sit in the balcony, and of course, we were the only ones in the balcony. As we sat watching the movie, Connie started giggling and nudged me to look over to the exit ramp. A man stood right under the exit light, stroking his penis and staring at us. I was terrified, but Connie was laughing. I suggested that we move down to the regular seating, but I worried about how we would get past the man. I also thought of telling the usher, but when I looked again, the man was gone. I couldn't concentrate on the movie for fear that he would come back. When the movie finally ended, I was anxious to leave but afraid that maybe this man would follow us as we walked out to wait for the bus. I wished I had stayed home. Connie always made fun of me if I showed fear of any kind, so I didn't want to let her know how terrified I really was. Luckily, we walked out of the theater without a problem; the sun was extremely bright as we stepped outside, and I felt a sense of relief when the bus pulled up in front of us.

East Brunswick was a breath of fresh air for me. The first person we met was Margaret, who was our age and lived directly across the street. Margaret, like me, was going into the ninth grade in the high school in the nearby town of South River. Margaret gave us a lot of information about the area, and we became friends. I was excited to have a fresh start in a new school.

A week before school started, Daddy gave Connie and me money for new school clothes. It wasn't much, but he gave us what he could. Money was going to be much tighter since we no longer had the extra income from renting rooms. Daddy was still driving the old Dodge, which was now nine years old. Besides dealing with the loss of rental income, Daddy had to deal with my mother's poor money management. Daddy was still paying off a five-year loan for the siding that my mother bought for that big house in Elizabeth. She would often buy things that we did not need, and since my father had a steady income, she could always put whatever she wanted on credit, even if my father knew nothing about it. There were also fines that he had to pay when she wrote bad checks. She signed his name to these checks, the bank cashed them, and he had to make good on them. Daddy had managed to keep his excellent credit rating in spite of my mother. He was a very responsible money manager and always saw that the bills were paid, finding ways to squeeze by even when there was little left.

Connie and I walked the mile or so to South River to do our school shopping. It was quite a hike, but we were young, and to us, it was fun. There were no shopping malls like there are today. The one ladies' clothing store on the main street was small and had little to choose from. When it was time to shop, I missed downtown Elizabeth and all its choices.

School started, and Connie and I fit right in and made friends easily. I continued to make good grades, while Connie concentrated more on having fun and didn't do as well. We had to walk several blocks to the highway to catch the bus to school. The ride was fun; there was a group of us who rode the bus together. Even on brutally cold and stormy days, whatever we did was fun for us as long as we had a group to do it with. There were two sessions of classes, and ours started at ten fifteen. Bart was in the fourth grade, and the elementary school was within walking distance of our new house. Only my mother found our new location to be inconvenient. The distance between our house and the nearest stores made it much less convenient for her to buy her liquor, especially in the winter. However, nothing was going to stop her. She would trudge through the woods a couple of miles to the liquor store, dragging Margie along with her.

Daddy was now employed by the 3-M Company, and he was no longer required to work different shifts. He was offered the day shift permanently because he had seniority coming from Irvington Varnish. He suggested that my mother apply for a job at his company because money was tight, and they needed the extra income. After my mother got a job, life for all us improved. My mother was sober more often, and most nights, she would fix dinner, and we would all eat together. She had her own money now and did her more serious drinking on the weekends. She could buy her own supply and hide what she needed for the weeknights. Many times, she went to work hungover, but Daddy was always bragging about how lucky 3-M was to have her and how smart she was to catch on to her new job so quickly. I remember Friday nights; it would be dark by the time my parents got home after stopping at ShopRite to buy groceries. In East Brunswick, there were no local bars for Daddy to hang out in.

Margie was four now, and Bart was nine. Daddy was the only real parent that we had, and he took almost total responsibility for Margie. She would wait for him to come home each night, often on the swing he built for her in the backyard. My mother was too busy drinking and working to have any concerns about our needs. My parents no longer sat together in the dark drinking, and the bar scene was now a thing of the past. Our lives would not be called normal by most people's standards, but I attributed all the small but positive changes from my mother's new job to the end of the bar visits to the prayers of the people who came from the church in Elizabeth and prayed with my parents. However, I knew enough from experience not to expect even these small changes to last very long.

3-M provided a picnic for its employees each year. It was a family event with games and entertainment for the kids. It was a nice fall Saturday when we all piled into the car, looking forward to a day of fun and good food. There was a pavilion, a band played, and the beer flowed freely. I can only assume that Daddy was aware of the problem inherent in "free beer," but my mother insisted on going. Taking my mother to this picnic proved to be a huge mistake. Connie and I played some of the games, ate hot dogs and hamburgers, and were having a good time. In the meantime, my mother found the pavilion, found a table, and drank until she was sloppy-drunk. While she sat on the bench, she pissed right through her clothes, all over the floor. Then she started ranting loudly about how my dad was supporting girlfriends in apartments while she was going without. Connie and I were so embarrassed; we told Daddy that we should get my mother into the car and go. However, my mother started fighting and yelling that she was staying, and he couldn't make her leave. Some of

Daddy's friends helped him to get her in the car. I knew that the ride home was not going to be pleasant. We rolled down the windows in the back, trying to snuff out the smell of beer and urine as my mother continued to yell. When Daddy stopped at a traffic light, my mother opened the car door, got out, and ran into the woods. Daddy pulled over to the side of the road and went after her; I thought he should just leave her there and let her find her own way home. He struggled with her, and she fought back. She wanted him to stop at a liquor store and get her a six-pack on the way home. I hated her; I hated who she was, and I wished there was some way for us to get rid of her—not for just during that one trip home but forever. Her insane drunken behavior had gone on too long, and we had no choice but to put up with it. One thing I was sure of, I would not be going to any more 3-M picnics.

That spring, Bart wanted to play Little League baseball, and Daddy agreed to be a coach. Daddy always liked baseball, but I never got the feeling that he enjoyed his involvement with Little League. I believe he saw coaching as more of a drudgery than a pleasure. I knew he would rather be hanging out in a bar, having a few drinks, talking to people, and playing a game or two of shuffleboard. Daddy was a social person; he loved being around people, especially drinking people. He could talk to anyone about anything and got along with everyone. He missed what he considered "fun." His life looked so sad to me. I could feel his unhappiness and discontentment.

I was having fun at school and had lots of girlfriends. The Friday night after school started, there was a football bonfire in South River. I had never been to a bonfire, but I was going to this one with my girlfriend Gerry. It was about a mile walk to South River, and I always found the walks to be a fun way of getting to know my new friends better. According to these new girlfriends, I was way behind in the boyfriend area, or they were way ahead of me. We were all fourteen. I often wondered if there was any real truth to their stories since some of them were hard to believe. The bonfire raged high and wide, and the warmth from it felt good against the cold night air. Gerry met up with a boyfriend, and that left me by myself, so I just hung around until it was time to go home. I didn't have to be home at any certain time. I based my schedule on whatever time my girlfriends had to be home, and I used my friends' rules as my rules.

One day after school, I was invited to go for a ride with Gerry, her boyfriend, and his friend. I was not sure whether I should do this, but Gerry assured me it was safe, and we were only going for a ride. I slipped into the front seat, hugging the door. Gerry and her boyfriend sat in the back. The car was pretty cool; it was blue and had skirts over the back wheels with red-and-yellow flames painted on them. I was introduced to the driver, Harry Jackson. I was still not sure about this arrangement, but I went along with it. Both these guys were older than us. Harry told me that he was eighteen and had graduated from high school the previous June. He said he had signed up for the Navy and would be leaving at the end of the summer for boot camp. As I began to relax with Harry, we started to have a fun time. We were not gone long, and on the way back, Harry dropped me off first, even though Gerry's house was before mine.

A few days later, Harry drove to my house and asked me if I wanted to go to the Dairy Queen for an ice cream. He was very much a gentleman, and we became friends. After that, he began to come over a few nights a week. He was always decent and respectful toward me. He took me over to his house one night and introduced me to his mother. I was extremely shy, felt awkward, and barely said a word. I liked Harry, and I knew he liked me. My mother told me years later that my dad didn't like it when I would go off with Harry Jackson, but he never said anything to me about it.

That fall, Harry left for boot camp. Soon after he left, I got the first letter from him, and we wrote back and forth for the two months or so that he was gone. At the end of October, he was supposed to come home on leave, and I was anxious to see him. When a few days passed and I hadn't heard from him, I thought of every possible and impossible reason why. However, the next night, just as we finished dinner, a knock came on the back door, and it was Harry. I was thrilled to see him. He asked if I wanted to go to the drive-in movie with him, and of course I did. Harry was home for two weeks. Some days when school got out, I would be surprised to find Harry waiting for me outside the school. He would give me a ride home, and we would go into my house, turn on the stereo, and sit at the dining room table and talk.

When the two weeks were up, Harry was off to Texas. His parents came and picked me up to go along for the ride to the airport. It was the first time I had met his dad. Harry was all dressed up in his Navy uniform. He and I sat in the back seat with a cooler of beer, and Harry drank as we rode. This was the first time I had seen him drink; I hated the smell of it, and I wished I hadn't come. We arrived at the airport, and as we walked to his gate, he acted sillier than usual, and he had a stupid smile pasted on his face. I noticed how short he was, maybe 5'6" or 5'7". As he left, he attempted to kiss me on the lips. This embarrassed me because his parents were watching. He stood and waved as he reached the platform before entering the plane, and we all waved back.

After that, I lost interest in Harry. We still wrote back and forth, and at Christmas, he sent me a pretty white sweater decorated with pearls. I think he was a nice guy, but at barely sixteen, I was just too young to be tied down to a boyfriend, especially one who wasn't around. My girlfriends were all going to the dances, and I missed our fun together. I didn't think that it was right to keep Harry as a boyfriend while going out with my girlfriends to the dances. What would I do if I wanted to go out with someone else? I didn't feel good about stringing Harry along when I really wasn't willing to wait for him. I wrote Harry a letter and told him that I no longer wanted to be his girlfriend. He never wrote back. I saw him a few times after that, but I was too embarrassed to talk to him. Maybe I felt as if I owed him more of an explanation, but whatever the reason, that was the end of it. Of all the boyfriends who came and went, Harry treated me the best.

My mother had been at her job at 3-M now for almost a year. One morning, she left with Daddy as usual, but when I got home from school, she was already home, in bed and asleep. Daddy came home at his usual time, and I could hear him asking her questions about what happened at work. She had had a few drinks by then, and her comments were much louder than Daddy's. I soon heard that my mother had been fired. Daddy told me later that there had been too many complaints from other workers that she was meddling in their affairs and causing trouble. She had also come to work with a hangover too often. My dad was well-liked and respected at 3-M. He worked with a lot of guys who had known him for many years; some had started at Irvington Varnish when he did. I don't think anyone, even the long-term coworkers, knew the extent of my mother's problem, even after the picnic fiasco. Daddy never asked for help; he just handled everything on his own. I always wished my father would divorce my mother so we didn't have to put up with her abuse. She was the reason there wasn't enough money. She was the reason I was embarrassed to bring a girlfriend home. I imagined that a life without my mother would be a life of peace, free of anxiety and worry. I thought that if my father was not willing to divorce my mother, at least he should send her away someplace to get sober. She had gone to Marlboro, a mental health hospital, once when we lived in Elizabeth, but after the second week, she begged Daddy to sign her out and bring her home. He did what she wanted, and nothing changed.

Eventually, I stopped asking my father why he never asked for help; I knew he was never going to change. I could tell that Daddy was miserable. He went to work every day, never missing a day. He would never go to a doctor when he was sick, never buy new clothes for himself. He lived in his work clothes. One time, when he was sick with the flu and wasn't able to go to work for a couple of days, Connie and I were so worried that we called a doctor to come to the house and see if he was okay. I magnified my father in my mind as a hero, a god of sorts. Daddy had an enormous coping ability and endless powers of resilience, but he also had crippling misconceptions about life. He was unwilling or maybe unable to look at the situation, change direction, and create a better life for himself and for us. In the end, his way of life would prove to be a cowardly compromise.

Sometimes on Friday nights, Daddy would just disappear, and I would find him down in the basement sitting in a corner in the dark. I knew he was drinking, and this was where he hid. "Why are you down here?" I would ask.

"Oh, just thinking," he would say.

"Why don't you turn on a light? Do you want me to turn on a light for you?"

"No, just go on. I'll be up soon." I knew he wanted to be alone in his misery, and I felt sad for him. He struggled to keep us all afloat. He bailed my mother out of all her jams, never knowing when the next crisis would occur. I worried about him, and I wished he could be happy, but darkness dominated his life.

My mother was home all day now. Without her job, she had little access to money. This made it difficult for her to drink, but it by no means stopped her. I remember my mother offering me a cigarette one day while I was sitting at the dining room table doing my homework. When I refused, she insisted that I "just try it." I still refused. I knew by now that her various proposals were never for my benefit. I later figured out that her plan was for me to be addicted and therefore supply her need. I was lucky to have learned at an early age not to trust my mother.

Christmas season came, which usually triggered a drinking binge. A few weeks before Christmas, the tree was up, and Christmas gifts were already bought and under the tree. My mother left one day, and we didn't know where she was for more than a week. Connie said she saw our mother in New Brunswick begging a vendor for a hot dog. I asked Daddy if my mother was coming home, hoping he would say no. But he said not to worry, that she would come home eventually. On Christmas Day, we opened our gifts. I got a paint-by-number set, and I spent all Christmas Day working on my painting and watching television. That was the happiest Christmas that I could remember; it was peaceful, with no drunken rampages. About two weeks later, my mother suddenly stumbled through the door, dirty, sloppy, and hungover. I was home with Bart and Margie since school was still out for the holiday. I hated the sight of her because our time of peace and quiet was over. I was always glad to get back to school; it was a safer place for me.

American Bandstand was the hottest show on TV for the teen crowd. The show's host, Dick Clark, was our hero. One day, a flyer came around at school advertising a bus trip to Philadelphia to appear on the *Bandstand* show. The bus would leave after school and return that evening. I had some babysitting money that I had been saving, and I had enough to go. My girlfriends and I all loved *Bandstand*; we knew all the local Philadelphia kids who were on each week, and we followed the dance contests, who won and who didn't. The day of the trip, the bus was parked in front of the school, waiting for the bell to ring. It was about an hour and a half ride to Philadelphia, and we arrived just as the show was starting. Dick Clark looked just as he did on TV, young for his thirty years. The regulars on the show looked the same also, and it was incredibly exciting to see them in person. I loved every minute of it. We all got to dance, knowing that those watching TV at home could see us since the show was live.

The three years that I lived in East Brunswick were the best years of my childhood. I still had the same problems and worries, but I also had lots of fun and great friends. I visited a Methodist church in South River a time or two, but I was no longer seeking relief through religion as I had when I was younger. I saw myself as having more choices as I got older, and it was always at the happy times that I stopped praying and seeking.

During those relatively peaceful years in East Brunswick, we did have one fire caused by my mother smoking in bed. It was never safe to live in our house with my unpredictable mother in residence. Many times, I was invited to spend the night at a girlfriend's house, but none of them were allowed to spend the night at my house. However, I no longer tried to talk to Daddy about it; I began to accept the situation because in my mind, the battle for a normal childhood had been lost. I now began to focus on finishing school and leaving my family home. I was now in the eleventh grade and would be graduating the following year.

Connie, however, would not be graduating. Daddy had a habit of always referring to Connie and me as "the girls." I hated that cliché, mostly because it suggested that Connie and I were alike. If Connie got into trouble, it was never something Connie did; it was "the girls" who did it. I was having enough trouble with my own identity; being Connie's sister added another layer of difficulty. The older we got, the more unlike we became. Connie was a drama queen. She craved attention and would stoop to any level to stand out in the crowd. I kept a low profile, got good grades, and had plenty of friends. Connie enjoyed embarrassing me in front of my friends; her humor was always at someone else's expense. She could be quite brutal with the hostility that she cleverly disguised as humor. I made it my policy never to let her know much about me because she could use any information as a weapon. Connie didn't care about school and didn't get passing grades. When she didn't get enough credits to move up a grade, she and I wound up in the same homeroom. I could then see for myself how her lack of respect for authority and outspoken fearlessness made it difficult for teachers to control their classrooms. After the school had had enough of her rebelliousness, she was expelled. She always had to have the last word, and when they told her she was expelled, she shot back that they couldn't expel her because she quit.

Connie got her driver's license as soon as she turned seventeen. Daddy did not know what he was in for when Connie got her license. She was always borrowing his car, and he never knew where she was or when she would be back. If you heard a tow truck coming down the street in the middle of the night, it was probably Connie. She often ran out of gas and had to be towed home. Daddy seldom raised his voice, but he knew he could no longer afford to let Connie borrow his car. After Connie left school and got a job as a waitress, she had enough money to buy her own car, an old Ford convertible. It was a real rattle trap, but it took her back and forth to work and out with her friends on the weekends. She had a lot of fun with that car. Once, she drove to the drive-in movies with several of us squeezed into the trunk. After driving through the ticket line and paying only for herself, she pulled into an inconspicuous parking place and, as it got darker, opened the trunk and let us out. Another day, as she was driving with her friends down Route 18, the hood of her car flew off and landed in a tree. One of her friends had to climb the tree and retrieve the hood. These things only happened to Connie. She worried about nothing; she had lots of friends and lots of fun. Her fearlessness was a gift and a curse at the same time.

One night, Connie invited me to go for a ride with her to Jamestown, a nearby town. I knew that she had a steady boyfriend who lived in Jamestown, but she didn't tell me that our ride to Jamestown was for the purpose of seeing him. We rode through Jamestown, up and down the main drag, until she saw her flame, a big Italian guy named Phil Sisciera, standing in front of the pool hall. I then learned that the two had planned to attend the drive-in movies, and Phil soon figured out what to do about me. I heard him say, "Oh, I know lots of guys. I'll get one to go with her." The next thing I knew, this tall guy with a ten-gallon hat came out of the pool hall and got into the back seat with me. So far, I had kept my cool, but this wasn't going to work for me.

"I'm not going to the drive-in movie. You can just take me home," I said.

After some discussion that I couldn't hear, Phil looked at me and said, "Charlene, you're with us, and while you're with us, you're going to have to do what we do, so we are all going to the drive-in movie. If you don't like it, well, too bad." I hated both Connie and her boyfriend; now I was stuck with this cowboy dude in the back seat.

He better not try to touch me, I thought as I hugged the door on my side, all the while trying to figure a way out of this. When Phil drove to the Jamestown drive-in movie, it was full, and I was glad. Plan B was the East Brunswick drive-in, which would be closer to home, so maybe I could somehow figure out a way to escape. I said nothing as Phil drove, running his big mouth all the way. I kept trying to think of someone I could call to come and get me. When we got to the drive-in, it was dark, and the movie had started. I could sense the dude moving closer to me when he took off his hat and placed it in the back window.

As soon as Phil turned the car off, I announced that I had to go to the bathroom and would be right back. Once I was out of the car, I walked to the phone booth next to the concession stand. Luckily, I had some change in my pocket. I sat down on a bench and thought about who I could call. My girlfriend Margie came to mind because she was a good friend who had access to a car. I slid into the phone booth, looking each way to see if the coast was still clear before I called Margie. "Margie, this is Charlene."

"Oh, hi," she answered.

"I am in a real predicament and need your help," I blurted out.

"What's wrong?"

"I'm stuck at the East Brunswick drive-in with my sister and her boyfriend, and they've fixed me up with a cowboy friend of his. I was wondering if you could give me a ride home. I can walk down to the entrance out by the highway and wait for you there. Please help me," I added, with desperation in my voice. There was a short pause.

"Why doesn't your sister just take you home?" she asked.

"Because she doesn't care. She's with her boyfriend and won't to help me."

"Okay, I'll leave now and be there in about fifteen minutes. Wait at the entrance." I was thrilled. I hung up the phone, looked around me, and immediately walked as fast as I could out to the entrance. I wasn't there very long when Margie drove up, and I hopped into her car. I loved my girlfriends; they were true friends and were always there when I needed them. The next day, Connie asked me how I got home, and I told her. She said that the cowboy dude was mad and complained through the whole movie.

Oh well, too bad, I thought to myself, smiling under my breath.

There were teen dances on Saturday nights, and I didn't miss too many of them. One of my girlfriends had a skirt that her mother had made for her. Everyone in our crowd loved it and wanted one just like it. My friend's mother told us that the skirt was simple to make, and if we bought the pattern and fabric, we could each make our own. The skirt was straight with a slit on each side. When we started making these skirts, the hardest part was the buttonhole on the waistband. We solved the problem by using a safety pin instead of a button. Our tops would cover the waist anyway. We would gather together at someone's house on Saturday and make our skirts to wear to the dance that night. Since we still had our old sewing machine, I could have worked on my skirts at home, but sewing was more fun with my friends.

I had let go of my need to mother and protect Bart and Margie because I was too busy. There was always a party, dance, or sleepover that I was invited to. Very few of us had boyfriends; we just liked to go to the dances and hang out where other teens hung out. South River High School was directly across the street from a place called Terry's. Terry's was the place, before school, after school, and for lunchtime. It was small with a lunch counter, a jukebox, and a telephone booth. We all packed in there like a bunch of sardines, breathing room only. The jukebox blasted the latest new *Bandstand* songs as we waited for the school bell to ring. The bus let us out a block or so away, and it was on to Terry's to meet the rest of the crowd. These were some of the most fun-filled days of my life so far. Looking back, even though I screwed up a time or two, I was a pretty good teenager, and my girlfriends were also. Without the guidance I picked up from my friends' parents, I would not have had any direction, so I am grateful to my friends and their families for helping me through the teen years.

One of those rare Charlene-screws-up days started one morning when a classmate approached me as I got off the bus in South River. This classmate lived in South River only a few blocks away from the bus stop. As we turned the corner toward the school, she suggested that instead of going to school that day, we skip school and go to her house instead. She egged me on, telling me that no one was home, and we could have fun. "Come on," she pleaded. "We can just hang out, watch TV, and talk. It'll be more fun than going to school." I told her I was afraid of getting caught. She assured me that wouldn't happen. She said she had done it before and never got caught.

"Where are your parents?" I asked.

"My parents are divorced. My sister and I live with my mother, but my mother works in the daytime, and she has already left."

"What about your sister?" I asked, trying to weasel out of her offer.

"She will be at work all day also. Don't worry," she assured me, "it will be okay. We'll just spend the day together at my house. No one will know we were ever there." It sounded inviting, rebellious, and far from anything I would normally do, so I agreed. Once we got inside her house, she told me about her family problems, and I began to feel more at ease. She said her sister's wedding plans were called off at the last minute because of a disagreement with her mother. The sister and mother did not speak to each other, even though they lived in the same house. Anyway, it sounded like a rather small problem compared to what I had to deal with. Of course, I did not divulge any of my family problems but just listened to her. The time seemed to pass quickly, and she asked if I wanted a sandwich for lunch. As we ate at the kitchen table, she said her mother would soon be coming home for lunch, so we would have to go up into the attic and hide until she left. This kind of worried me, but I did as she said. After she pulled down the stairs to the attic, I followed her, lugging my books and coat with me. We sat on the rafters, and she told me not to talk. A minute or two later, the sound of a key in the front doorknob made me sit up and hold my breath. This attic deal was a scary addition to the original plan; I feared her mother would find us. To add to my fright, there were massive spiderwebs and beehives hanging everywhere. I was afraid that if I moved, they would soon be nesting in my hair. We could hear her mother downstairs, moving around, turning the water on and off, and opening and closing the refrigerator.

I kept thinking, *How did I get myself into this mess?* I wished I had just gone to school. Finally, the front door opened and closed, and I heard the key go back in and the lock click.

"She's gone," my friend said. "We can breathe again."

We had no sooner climbed downstairs when the doorbell rang. *Oh, no,* I thought. "What now?" My friend instructed me this time to stay in a bedroom closet.

"I will get rid of them," she said as she quickly slipped on a pair of pajama bottoms and ran to the door. It was the truant officer. I was terrified! "Are you home sick today?" he asked.

"Yes, I am," she said as she sniffled.

"Are you Judy?" he asked.

"Yes, Judy Taylor," she said.

"Okay," he said, "just checking." He left; I could tell she was good at this. My friend called to me to come out of the closet; the coast was once again clear. It was now almost two thirty, time for school to be dismissed and finally safe for me to leave. I feared that a truant officer might be watching her house and waiting for me, so I left out the back door and cut through the backyards instead of walking down the sidewalk where I could have been seen. I came out on a side street to get to my bus stop. I was the first one at the bus stop, and I just knew someone would notice that I hadn't been in class and ask me where I had been, but no one did. When the bus pulled up, I stepped on quickly and took a seat. I felt ashamed of what I had done and didn't want to be noticed. When the bus finally let me out at my stop, I breathed a sigh of relief. I was thankful to be home that day, and I never skipped school again. I never told anyone about that day, ever.

Now and then, I would get a babysitting job and earn extra money, which I would use to see a movie or buy something for myself. I never asked Daddy for extra money because I knew he was barely scraping by and had no extra to give me. Once, I made the mistake of using my babysitting money to buy a bottle of lilac cologne that was something like 80 percent alcohol. I left the cologne on my dresser, and one day while I was at school, my mother drank it. She filled the bottle up with water, thinking I wouldn't notice. I noticed, but it did no good to confront her; that would just increase her hostility.

Connie and I were busy with our friends, our social life, and school activities. Bart and Margie were not as lucky. They never went anywhere. Life was better for Connie and me only because we were old enough to come and go as we pleased. We were all on our own one way or another. It was truly a game of survival, and Bart and Margie had the worst of it because of their ages and lack of choices.

When I wanted to earn more money than I could earn babysitting, my girlfriend Margaret and I got jobs at W. T. Grant, a small department store on Route 18. We were scheduled for a few hours after school and some Saturdays. My station was in the curtain department. I hated the curtain department. It was my job to keep the curtains straight and folded, with the sizes in order. It was a boring job, with few customers to break the monotony. I was constantly watching the clock, trying to look busy standing around and wishing I had something to do. I earned about $8 a week. Daddy had to take me to work and pick me up. I wanted to quit so bad but stuck it out since I had agreed to do it.

One weekend, Daddy was invited to play poker with some friends. He seldom went out anywhere after we moved to East Brunswick. He loved to get together with a group of guys, have some drinks, and play poker. Anything that had to do with gambling and drinking was his game. As luck would have it, one night, his card game was raided, and he and his friends were arrested. He had to appear in court and pay a fine, and I could tell he was worried about it. This news just delighted my mother, who enjoyed anything that would diminish Daddy in our eyes. I was working the night of Daddy's court hearing, and I would never forget the evening he stopped by to tell me about it. While I was straightening up a display of curtains, I could hear footsteps behind me, and when I looked up, there was Daddy all dressed up in a coat and tie and his old overcoat that I hadn't seen in years. I could see the sadness in his eyes. "Hi, Char," he said.

"Hi, Daddy, where are you going?" I asked.

"I had to go to court about the poker game."

"Oh, how did it go?"

"I had to pay a fine, that's all," he said as if it were no big deal. I knew he had no extra money for a fine since he was barely keeping his head above water. More than money, he lacked companionship, someone to share his thoughts and feelings with, but he had no one. I think that was why he came to tell me, but he never knew how bad I felt for him. I listened, but I couldn't make things better. I know today what I didn't know then, and that was the fact that he always had the ability to change his world and his defeated life. He needed to make a move in the right direction and learn that he had choices. Hanging out in bars and getting invited to poker games would not lead to the good life. Happy people are not in bars; defeated, miserable people are in bars. I know now that real strength can only be found in admitting we need God's help. I believe that God was always calling my father through the pain in his life, but nothing got his attention enough to change his thinking. He refused to give up his faulty beliefs, and despite all the gifts he had, he lived his life in darkness. That night, he waited for me to get off work, and we rode home together.

Chapter 7

Rebellion and Courage

After that, Daddy decided to give up the struggle of trying to keep us afloat in a nice, middle-class lifestyle, and he told us he was selling the house. We would be moving to Freehold, closer to his job. He felt the need for a social outlet, friends to hang out with, and a place to socialize. He wanted something more than going to work every day just to survive. My mother was a burden all by herself. In addition, Margie and Bart depended on him to take care of them. Most nights, my father would come home, clean up the kitchen, and try to put together a meal for Bart and Margie. My mother would be drunk and abusive as he worked. Connie and I were busy and found ways to be gone most of the time. We were not happy about the news of moving away from our friends; we hoped that the house didn't sell quickly so we could stay longer. When June arrived, school was out, and the house went up for sale. I would have to finish high school in yet another school.

In the summer of 1959, I was invited to go on vacation with my girlfriend Shirley. We had been friends most of the year and had fun going to the dances and hanging out at her house. She was an only child and had just about everything. Every summer, her parents took her on vacation, and she was allowed to invite a friend. This year, I was the friend, and we were going to Wildwood for the entire last week of July. Wildwood was *the* place for teens in the summer, and I could hardly wait to get there. Wildwood had a great boardwalk, and a different singing idol was there every weekend. Ricky Nelson, about the hottest thing going at the time, was booked for the week we would be there. His hit song was "Garden Party." Shirley and I went swimming in the ocean every day, ate out each night, and after dinner, we hit the boardwalk. Teenagers were everywhere; boys would whistle at us and flirt with us. I didn't want that week ever to be over, and I will never forget either the vacation or the joy of having good friends like Shirley.

When the house sold, Daddy told us that he was not going to buy another house. I asked a lot of questions about what kind of a place we would be moving to but never got any real answers. One weekend, Daddy told me that he had rented a place in Freehold and wanted to know if I wanted to take a ride with him to see it. Of course I did. I couldn't wait to see the new place, and I wondered what the high school would be like. "We will be living right in town, so you will be able to walk to school," Daddy said in a happy tone of voice. My thoughts raced back to how he assured me that East Brunswick would be better since we would be so far away from any liquor stores. One thought that kept going through my mind was, *If I can walk to school, then you can probably walk to the local bar, and Mommy can walk to the local liquor store, and none of this change will be better for us, but it sounds as if it will work just perfectly for you and her.*

We arrived in Freehold, a clean-looking small town. On Main Street, I noticed the courthouse, stores, banks, pizza places, bars, and the Freehold Diner. As we turned onto Center Street, we passed rows of old houses which had large porches that sat too near the sidewalk. Daddy stopped a few blocks down Center Street and parked in front of what looked like a group of row houses. I thought to myself, *You've got to be kidding. We are moving here?* A barbershop sat directly across the street with the candy-striped column spinning. There were eight duplexes, and my father used his key to enter the right side of the first building. It smelled of new paint, and the floors were newly painted a stone-gray color. The living room was a small room with double windows that faced Center Street. On the other side of the hall were the dining room and kitchen. Off the kitchen were an attached shed and a backyard that provided parking for the tenants. We walked up the stairs to the second floor, which contained two bedrooms and a bathroom. On the third floor were two additional bedrooms. This was a very old duplex, and the only closet in the entire place was a small closet in the dining room. "Where will we hang our clothes?" I asked.

"Don't worry," my father said. "I'll get some hanging racks for each bedroom." So this was it. This was where we were moving to from our nice house on Coleman Place. I hated it, but complaining would not have helped. The lease was already signed, and our house was already sold. We walked out through the front door onto the porch, three steps down, and we were standing on the sidewalk. As Daddy locked the door behind me, the neighbor in the next duplex came out. Daddy said in his most happy-go-lucky voice, "I want you to meet my daughter. Charlene, this is Mr. Brown. He goes by Brownie. He is our new neighbor. One of Brownie's daughters lives on the other side of our duplex, and another one lives in the end duplex."

"Hi," I replied. We got back in the car and headed down Center Street. When we got to Main Street, Daddy turned right instead of left.

He said, "I want you to see the high school." This was a very big regional high school that enrolled kids from many neighboring towns. The school was a brick building that covered a whole block. The grounds were manicured. The school looked impressive and inviting, and I thought about all the new kids that I would meet. I had already attended two different high schools; another one shouldn't make any difference. I began to think that maybe it would be fun. However, I didn't want Daddy to think that I was happy about the move. When it came to the old duplex and my parents' access to bars and liquor, I could smell disaster in the new arrangement.

Moving day consisted of endless trips back and forth. Daddy bought three pieces of linoleum to put down in the kitchen, living room, and dining room to cover the painted wood floors. He also bought hanging racks to put in each bedroom for makeshift closets. We threw out a lot of our old furniture, and Daddy bought a new living room sofa and chair. Of course, we brought the old dining room suite, which had been with us as far back as I could remember. If it could talk, it would have been able to tell the whole story and more. Bart and Margie had the two third-floor bedrooms; on the second floor, Connie and I shared one bedroom, and my parents had the other one.

Daddy was excited about this move. He loved Freehold. Not only was it a horse-racing and gambling town, but it was less than five miles to work. Daddy had no trouble finding the local bar. Gus's was just a few blocks from Center Street, and besides being a bar, it had the best pizza in town. I could tell that Daddy was happier. He now had a place to hang out, play some shuffleboard, and socialize with friends. Gus's also served as a place to make connections for a Friday night poker game. Daddy loved to go to the track on Saturdays; he loved to gamble and be around other guys who shared his passion.

Connie kept her job at the East Brunswick Diner. Audrey, her boss, invited both Connie and me to stay at her house through the summer. That summer, I spent a great deal of time on a bus back and forth between East Brunswick and Freehold. While Connie worked at the diner, I ironed for Audrey. It was a good trade-off for me. Audrey and her husband had a beautiful home, and when the ironing was finished, I could take a dip in their pool in the backyard.

My mother loved Freehold as much as my dad did since she found that getting her liquor was much easier. Daddy had given up on trying to "get ahead" as he always put it and just accepted the unacceptable situation and made no attempts to change anything. Margie and Bart had no homelife, with their parents either gone or drunk. By the time school started, Bart was in middle school, and Margie was in the first grade. They pretty much fended for themselves. None of us went hungry, but when Margie came home for lunch each day, there was usually no one there to fix her lunch. Her teacher would send home notes telling my parents that Margie needed someone to help her get dressed properly for school. Daddy always gave the note to me since he thought that should be my responsibility. I knew it made him angry when I ignored his attempt to shift more of my mother's responsibilities to me, but when he realized that I wasn't going to do it, he took it on himself.

I began twelfth grade that September at Freehold Regional High School. I expected to fit in as well as I had in South River, but that just didn't happen. I was the new kid, and everyone was already involved with their own friends and cliques. I eventually made a few girlfriends, but they were not true friends like the ones I had in East Brunswick. One good thing was that I was no longer seen as Connie's sister. I was now Charlene. Freehold Regional had half sessions, and my school hours were 7:30–1:30. I never missed school because it was a place to go every day and forget about what was going on at home. My mother had found a job in a nursing home. Her jobs never lasted more than one payday, but for the time being, she was gone most of the day. I liked coming home in the afternoon to an empty house. It was peaceful and quiet, and I could concentrate on my homework.

Each time my mother had a new job lined up, she would ask Daddy for money to get a new uniform and shoes to get her started until she got paid. I always wished he would tell her no, but he just said nothing, pulled out his wallet, and gave her what she asked for. She could no longer work as a registered nurse because her license had lapsed and could not be reinstated. There had been too many complaints about her work, and she had gotten fired too many times. In between jobs, she stayed home, got drunk, and smoked packs of cigarettes. As far back as I can remember, my parents' mattress was full of burn holes, some down to the springs, and my mother's arms and chest were covered with scars, all from the ashes she carelessly allowed to drop. A glass of water always sat on the table next to her bed so she could douse any small burn hole before a real fire ensued. The house was always a mess, meals seldom cooked, or clothes washed. I was now looking forward to graduating and thinking about how to escape to somewhere else. Anywhere else looked better than where I was.

As I struggled through my last year in high school, there were many times that I wanted to quit. I was tired from lack of sleep because of the many nights my mother would be up raving all night long. One night, as I walked into my bedroom, I caught her just as she had tipped up a bottle of Mennen's Skin Bracer, guzzling it down, her face twisted from the taste and green all over her lips. She knew I saw her. It was a moment when I remembered that I truly hated this woman. Daddy was no help; however, in spite of his unchanging actions, I could see his attitude toward my mother changing. They seldom spoke to each other anymore.

One morning, as I sat at the kitchen table drinking a cup of coffee, my mother poured a cup for herself and joined me. Her old worn dirty housecoat laced with cigarette burns was draped around her. I watched her as she drank her coffee and smoked her cigarette. Her face looked old, much older than it should have. Her index finger and middle finger were yellow from the nicotine that would no longer wash off. As she put out one cigarette, she would quickly light up another. She was unable to sit still, always moving, rocking as if music was playing, but it wasn't. Her pinkie finger and ring finger twitched nervously as she held her cigarette between the other two fingers. Her constant movement was the result of drinking excessively for so many years, which had taken a toll on her nervous system.

The neighbors on the other side of our duplex were a youngish couple, Tex and Marion Vineyard. Marion was Brownie's youngest daughter. Dotty Burge, the oldest daughter, lived in the end side of the last duplex. Tex and Marion didn't quite know what they were in for when we moved in, but they soon found out. Tex was a tall guy who spoke with a kind of Southern drawl. He worked at Anheuser-Busch, but he was frequently either laid off or at home nursing an injury. As he sat on his front porch, he would stop me as I walked by, wanting to talk. Although I didn't want to talk to him, I would politely stop anyhow. He was full of funny stories about things he had done; I just mostly listened, and he talked. Marion worked at the courthouse downtown. Nights when my mother was up all night ranting, they would bang on the walls, yelling for her to shut up. One day as I was coming home from school, Marion stopped me. "Could you please ask your mother to be quiet at night so we can get some sleep?" she asked. I said I would ask her. Trying to explain would not have done any good because no one would have understood the insanity we had to live with. Asking my mother not to rant and rave at night would have been similar to asking a rat to stop gnawing.

On September 29, 1960, I turned seventeen. The first thing I did was take the test to get my driver's license. Daddy had finally traded in the old Dodge and bought a used 1956 Ford. After he felt I knew how to drive well enough, he would allow me to drive his car to the dance on Saturday night. I loved the dances. My new group of girlfriends all smoked, and they were always egging me on to smoke with them. In order to fit in with the crowd, I eventually succumbed to the pressure. It was a wrong decision, and I knew it.

That Christmas, Aunt Bea and Aunt Ellen sent us Christmas gifts as they usually did. I was really surprised when I opened mine and received something that I really loved, a pretty pair of shorty pajamas. They were light pink and trimmed in lace. I carefully stored them in my dresser drawer, saving them in case I was invited to a sleepover with my girlfriends.

Dating for me was difficult. I didn't want any decent guy to see where I lived or, worse yet, come in and see what really went on. So far, I had never had a drink of alcohol. I wanted a nice boyfriend but had not met anyone who would fit into my life as it was. I was fearful and extremely insecure. Life had dealt me a bad deal, and I had no clue how to change it. I never thought about going to church or praying anymore. Daddy told me never to go to church; he said that there was no value in it, and they were just out to get my money. He also said that religion was an insult to his intelligence. I thought back to when I lived on Wyoming Avenue and how prayer helped me then. It was all different now because I was so much older, but I know now how much prayer would have helped me as a teen. Daddy also advised me to stay away from men who didn't drink. His exact words were, "Stay away from men who don't drink. A man who doesn't drink cannot be trusted. If you are going to date someone, be sure he is someone who can hold his liquor. After all, look at all the trouble I've had with your mother." Even though I trusted Daddy and his logic sounded reasonable, it was not. I wanted to please Daddy because I saw him as the only one who cared whether I made right or wrong decisions. However, I still believed in God, regardless of what my father told me. I was greatly conflicted. I wanted my father to be wrong about God, but I wanted to believe that he was trying to give me good advice because he loved me. Today, I know that there is nothing loving or caring about a close parent-child relationship when it serves the needs of the parent rather than the child. It took me many years to figure out that Daddy was manipulating my life to accommodate his drinking. Daddy's influence on my life and his part in the wrong choices I eventually made were based on his twisted view of the world, men, and religion.

Connie and I knew early on that attending the prom or having a wedding were never going to be options for us. I had given up those expectations long ago. Daddy could never afford such luxuries, and we knew better than to mention wanting them. Also, I would have been embarrassed for a guy to come to our duplex on Center Street to take me to the prom. Those things were for the kids who came from nice families and had nice homes and sane parents. That simply was not us. We were not in the white-picket-fence category.

Early spring was generally cold in New Jersey, but now and then, there would be a nice warm day. On one of those days, as I walked home from school, I noticed people sitting on their porches. The air had the smell of spring in it, and I loved feeling the warmth from the sun. As I came closer to Center Street, I noticed a rope draped across the street. I walked around the rope, and as I turned the corner, I saw a large fire truck parked in front of our duplex. I knew right away what was going on. Firemen were working, going in and out, moving our living room furniture out to the front porch. Lots of people had gathered around to watch. I walked up to our front steps and saw my mother sitting in Daddy's easy chair, which had been moved out to the middle of the porch. Of course, she was drunk, and she wore a dirty nightgown and a duster that hung open and exposed too much of her bare skin. I heard Daddy call my name, and when I looked around, I saw him and Connie standing in the crowd. "How did you find out about it?" I asked.

"They called me at work and told me to come home," Daddy answered. I asked him whether we could go in to see what we had left.

The front door stayed open as the firemen went in and out, and I could see that it was very smoky inside. The Jackson Street grammar school children were walking past on their way home from school. They stopped and looked, and if they asked my mother what happened, she answered in a slur of words that could not be understood. Her mouth was full of foul language. Luckily, I don't think the children understood what she was saying, but I knew because I was used to hearing her tirades.

The sun was just going down when the firemen started packing up their equipment to leave. The front door was still open as we all walked past my mother to assess the damage. The air in the duplex was so thick with smoke that it was almost nauseating. I went directly upstairs to my bedroom, where everything I owned was either wet, scorched, or smoke-damaged. My bed and dresser were ruined, as well as all my clothes on the clothes rack, and the new pink lace pajamas I had been saving in a drawer. I was angry that I had again been victimized by my mother; I learned that she had started the fire while smoking in my bed. I can only suppose that she wanted a fresh bed that was free of burn holes for her nap. I wanted to scream and yell and insist that someone step up and put a stop to this before we all died, either because of another fire or whatever else she might do to us. However, I did not have enough emotional strength left to start complaining, and I already knew what Daddy would have said. "We're going to be fine. You're making a big deal out of nothing." I wondered what his idea of a big deal was.

I slowly walked back downstairs, trying to keep composed. Daddy and Connie were sitting at the small table in the kitchen, but I didn't want to join them. I hated how they sat there laughing and making small talk, never considering what we were going to do or where we were going to live. I glanced out the front door that was still open because of all the smoke. My mother sat in the same chair, rattling on like the drunken fool that she was. Daddy always tried to tell me about how smart she was, what a great nurse she was. Yeah, right. I just never answered him when he said those things. I walked back into the kitchen. "What are we going to do now?" I blurted out.

"Everything in my room is ruined," I said with obvious anger in my voice.

"Don't worry, everything will be all right," Daddy said.

"Well, not if everyone sits here and does nothing," I snapped back.

The phone was on the wall directly in the back of where Daddy sat. I picked it up, pulled the cord around into the dining room, and dialed the Freehold Police Department. "This is Charlene Haynes. I live at 37 Center Street. We had a fire here today because my mother was drunk and smoking in bed. She is still drunk and sitting out on the front porch using foul language. My family and I will have to find a place to live for the time being. Please send someone to come and get her. There is a possibility that our neighbors will help us, but not as long as she is with us." As I tried to continue, my voice began cracking, and I knew I was losing my composure.

"I'll see what I can do," said the voice at the other end of the phone. I hung up, unable to say another word. No one seemed to notice what I had just done. I doubted that the police were going to come and get my mother, but minutes later, to my surprise, a police car pulled up in front of our duplex. The police officer exited the car and walked up on the porch. I looked away as he spoke to my mother. When I looked back again, he was helping her out of the chair and walking her to the waiting car. I saw him put her in the back seat and close the car door, and then I walked out to the front porch and watched as the police car pulled away from the curb. I could not have been more grateful for their quick action. Watching her leave gave me a renewed sense of hope.

I went back into the kitchen, looked at Daddy, and said, "She's gone."

"What do you mean?" he asked.

"The police came and got her." He just looked at me and said nothing. I repeated, "I called the police, and they came and got her." I knew he was glad that I did his dirty work for him.

Tex came to the front door and walked in. He was amazed at all the smoke and made a remark about how hard it was to see through it. "How did this happen?" he asked.

"My mother was smoking in bed in my room. She was drunk, and the mattress caught on fire."

"Where is she?"

"She's gone. They took her to jail."

"Do you have a place to stay?" he asked.

"No, we don't know yet what we are going to do."

"Let me go and check on something, and I will be right back," he said. He was back in just a few minutes. He suggested that Connie and I come and stay with him and Marion. Daddy, Bart, and Margie could stay with Dotty Burge and her family. Daddy started saying that he didn't want to intrude on anyone, but Tex insisted that we were welcome, and they were glad to have us. I knew the only reason the offer came was because Tex knew my mother was safely in jail. I didn't blame any of them for feeling this way because we didn't want her either. Besides, for now, we would all be able to get a good night's sleep and not have to worry about any ranting in the middle of the night or anyone drunk and smoking in bed.

Both of these families did all they could to make us feel welcome. Dottie Burge made lunches for Bart and Margie, and she made sure they had clean clothes and got to school on time. She had dinner ready for them at night, and they were happy to be there. It was crowded since she had two kids of her own, but they made room, and Bart and Margie were grateful to have a safe place to come home to each night, as was Daddy. Tex and Marion were just as accommodating. They bent over backward to make sure Connie and I had all that we needed. Marion cooked dinner each night, letting me help her get it ready. I didn't miss a day of school.

The fire on Center Street made headlines and was plastered all over the front page of the Freehold newspaper. Everyone in town now knew our names and the details of the fire. The next week, the landlady came over with her insurance adjuster to assess the damage. She told Daddy that it would be six to eight weeks before we could move back in, and it was obvious that she wasn't happy with us. I'm sure if she had known the problems that came along with us, she would have found a way not to rent to us in the first place.

My gym teacher made an announcement in class asking my classmates to bring in donations of clothes for me. Her request caught me off guard, and even though I knew she meant well, I was embarrassed. I hated the idea of handouts. The next day, there were bags of new and gently used clothes that my classmates had brought in.

Each Friday when he was paid, Daddy gave me money to buy new clothes. One Saturday, he even took me to the Eatontown Mall and let me pick out a brand-new outfit. It was spring, and I picked out a lilac skirt and blouse to match. I had never had anything that nice; I knew it looked good on me, and I wore it a lot. In spite of his weaknesses, Daddy was a fixer. He always tried to fix what my mother destroyed.

I was happy staying with Tex and Marion, and they seemed to enjoy us being there. It was a relief to me to not have to worry about the rest of my family, and I was able to relax for a while and concentrate on my schoolwork. Marion had an ironing board that was quite ancient. Trying to figure out how to set the thing up was a challenge, and Connie and I would have laughing spells over that ironing board. Like Daddy, Connie was quick and witty with her remarks. However, Connie's bold and fearless humor was often a disadvantage to her. This was one of those times. One night at the dinner table, Tex was telling us a story about when he was growing up in Kansas. "I thought you were from Texas," Connie said.

"No, I grew up in Kansas."

"Well then, why does everyone call you Tex?" she asked. When he didn't answer, she said, "Don't you think that since you are from Kansas, they should call you Kan instead of Tex?" As the conversation kept going, I could sense that Tex was becoming more and more annoyed by her remarks and by his inability to take control of the conversation. The tension was hot. Marion and I just listened, hoping it would soon end. Tex suddenly stood up from the table, walked to the door, and left, slamming the door behind him so hard that the windows rattled. Connie felt that she had won her matching of wits with Tex; it was a game that she was good at. She knew she had gotten the best of him, but she had gone too far. She now felt uncomfortable staying with Tex and Marion, and she told Marion that she was going to find another place to stay. Marion tried to convince her to stay, saying that he would get over it, and it would be all right. The next day, Connie found a room to rent on Jackson Street just a block away. She packed up her things and left before Tex got home from work the next evening.

This was getting even better for me. Tex and Marion gave me a key to their duplex so I could get in after school. Their house was always clean and neat. When I told Marion that I was working on my term paper, she offered me the use of their typewriter. I was the happiest that I had been for as far back as I could remember. The incident with Connie was never again mentioned. Sometimes, Connie would come by to visit me, but not when Tex was home. I enjoyed her visits; she was funny, and we laughed about everything, including the fire. I was amazed at how that fire turned into a welcome change for me and allowed me the opportunity to enjoy my last couple of months of high school. I now had new clothes, a nice place to live with people who were glad that I was there, and my mother was safely in jail. Daddy told me that my mother had appeared before a judge and was sentenced to three months in jail. I assume that the charges had something to do with her drunk and disorderly conduct on the porch or her reckless endangerment of her family and everyone in the neighborhood of duplexes. It was my mother's bad luck and her family's good luck that the judge she drew was the same judge who had taken away her nurse's license and was well aware of her character. My mother had previously been before this judge for drunk and disorderly conduct and for stealing liquor. For me, my mother's jail sentence meant three months of peace and quiet and worry-free living. However, I was well aware that the three months my mother was to be in jail would end sooner than I wanted it to.

The weekend following the fire, Daddy let me use the car to go to the dance with my girlfriends. The world somehow felt better, and I had a surge of uplifting energy. Kathy Hannon and I had talked before the fire, and we had our plans in place for the dance that night. The radio played my favorite songs as I rolled down Route 9 toward Lakewood to pick Kathy up. We loved these dances. The music was played by a DJ, and when the slow songs played, the strobe lights came on, and bubbles floated through the room. I thought I was pretty cool joining the others when they gathered in little groups to smoke cigarettes. Until recently, I was the oddball, the only one who didn't smoke, but joining in made me feel as if I was one of the crowd. The dance was over at eleven. Kathy and I thought it was fun to race to the car and see who could get there first. I quickly started the engine to get the heater going. I pulled out onto Route 9, and as I drove through Lakewood, a car pulled out from a side street and blinded me with its bright lights. As I tried to avoid hitting the car, I veered off to the right, lost control, and hit a tree. Neither Kathy nor I was hurt, but Daddy's car was wrecked. The police were quickly on the scene, asking questions about what happened. The police officer asked us where we lived and called another officer to come and take us home. While we were leaving, a wrecker came and towed Daddy's car away. I hoped this would be a slow ride home as I agonized over how to tell Daddy.

By the time the police car finally pulled up in front of Dottie Burge's duplex, it was almost 1:00 a.m. I knocked lightly on the door and waited for someone to answer. When the door finally opened, Dottie stood in front of me in her bathrobe. I whispered, "I'm sorry to get you up this late, but I need to see my dad."

"Upstairs in the bedroom to the left." I tiptoed slowly up the stairs, but every step creaked as I put my weight on it. I hated to do this; I wanted someplace to hide, but I knew I had to face up to it. I also knew it couldn't wait until morning. I turned into the room on the left, where I found Daddy asleep. I touched him, and he opened his eyes slightly.

"What's the matter?" he whispered.

"I had an accident. No one got hurt, but your car is wrecked." I said it as gently as I could.

"Where is the car?" he asked.

"It was towed away. I hit a tree, but no one was hurt," I repeated, trying to emphasize the good part.

"Okay, go on to bed. We'll talk about it tomorrow." I crept back down the stairs quietly, locked the door behind me, and walked over to Tex and Marion's duplex. I put the key in the doorknob, slipped upstairs, and went to bed.

How I wished this had never happened! I berated myself unmercifully for causing Daddy any more trouble than he already had. However, it was Daddy's upbeat, forgiving spirit that took my focus off our hopeless situation. His message said, "You never give up no matter what." Daddy had unusual endurance, and he was always calm and cool under pressure. He never reacted, got mad, or yelled; he just took it as it came. I loved that about him. In many ways, Daddy was an exceptional human being. He had an exceptional work ethic and was as faithful to his employer as he was to his family. What Daddy lacked was courage; he was unwilling to take a risk or step up to make difficult changes. He worked at fixing everything after it happened instead of doing what he could to prevent it. As I grew older, I came to realize that Daddy was never really interested in changing his life. He liked Freehold, the local bar was close by, the racetrack was always hopping, and he had friends to play a game of poker with on weekends.

The insurance company informed Daddy that his car was totaled; he had to finance a used Chevrolet that was not nearly as nice as the Ford. It was quite a while before I asked to borrow the car again. I settled down at Tex and Marion's and concentrated on finishing my term paper. Tex offered to drive me to the dances on Saturday nights, if I could arrange a ride home. On these occasions, Tex would always ask if I wanted to drive. "Well, of course I want to, but remember what happened to my dad's car," I would say jokingly. "I'll be in the passenger seat watching you, so I'm not worried." Of course, I never asked him to pick up any girlfriends; they were on their own now. A few nights a week, I would walk over to Dottie Burgess's house to visit with Daddy, Bart, and Margie. Daddy would tell me how our duplex was coming along and when we might be able to move back in. Even though I liked staying with Tex and Marion, I wanted us to all be back together again. I was concerned about my bedroom since that was where the fire started, and all my furniture had been ruined. Daddy said he would take me shopping, and I could pick out a new bedroom suite. Except for the car accident, this was a happy time for me.

One day after work, Daddy came by and gave me an envelope and instructed me to drop it off at the jail after school the next day. He said it was money for my mother's cigarettes. I took the envelope and said nothing. I knew he was passing this off on me because he didn't want to do it, but I couldn't understand why he cared if she had cigarettes. His concern for her annoyed me. Wasn't it her smoking that caused the fire? I not only didn't care if she had cigarettes, I hoped she would stay in jail. Nevertheless, I did as he asked. The next day after school, I walked to the courthouse. The building was old and had a musty smell to it. I saw an officer standing along the wall and asked where the jail was located. He directed me down a flight of stairs to the basement and down a long hallway. At the end of the hallway, a lady officer sat at her desk. She smiled warmly as she said, "Can I help you?"

"Yes, I just wanted to drop off this cigarette money for Ethel Haynes."

"Are you a family member?"

"Yes, I'm her daughter," I said reluctantly.

"Oh, well, I'm sure you would like to visit her while you are here," she said, still smiling.

"No, I'm in a hurry. I can't stay. I just want to drop off the money," I said politely.

"Oh, you should see her while you are here. It'll just take a minute for me to bring her down." I was annoyed by her tone of voice and persistence. I didn't want to see my mother; I had nothing to say to her. Why couldn't this woman just let me make that decision? I already told her I didn't want to see my mother, and I felt trapped by her pushiness.

I was seething inside as I followed the officer down another long hallway. The floors were square tiles, every other one black and white; I kept focusing on the floor as we walked. We turned a corner, and there was a folding chair that sat against the wall and a large screened door directly across from it. The door was layered in screening panels all going in different directions so I could not see through it. "Have a seat here. I'll go get your mother."

As I waited, I thought again, *What am I going to say to her?*

Suddenly, my mother's voice echoed from behind the screen door. "Hi, Char, how are you doing?" she whined in a sweet, loving voice, so nauseating that I could barely recognize that it was her. I couldn't actually see her, even though I knew she was standing directly behind the screen. She was just a vague image, but we could still talk.

"I'm okay. Daddy gave me some money for your cigarettes. I dropped it off at the front desk."

"Oh, good! I've had to roll my own since I've been in here," she continued in the same pitiful-sounding voice that I had absolutely no sympathy for. I felt no love for this woman as I realized once again that everything was about her—her comfort, her needs, her life. Did she have any clue what she had done to her family? Did she care? The more I heard her voice, the more I hated her. I wondered how Daddy could even consider her need for cigarettes when we were camped out with neighbors. I wanted to scream as loud as I could; I wanted her to know I hated her and that I wished that she would die in jail.

Instead, all I said was, "Well, I have to go."

"Okay," she replied.

"Tell Bart and Margie I'll be home soon." I didn't answer her but just turned the corner and walked back down the hallway. As I passed the lady officer, she looked up and smiled at me. I didn't stop. I was glad to be out of there. I had done as Daddy asked, and I never had to go back. I felt a kind of freedom as I came out the front door and walked down the steps to the sidewalk. My mother was safely locked up, and I had a good life with Tex and Marion. It was a moment of extreme gratitude.

As graduation became more and more of a reality, I began to look forward to it. The next few weeks flew by as I stayed busy studying for all the year-end exams. I finished my term paper, and I knew I would be graduating with my class. I was relaxed and happier than I had been in a long time. One evening, Daddy came over to tell me that our duplex was finished, and we would be moving back in the following weekend. Daddy and I walked next door to see how things looked. I was amazed when we walked through the front door at how different it was. All traces of smoke were gone, and the smell of fresh paint made the place seem clean and inviting. I looked forward to moving back in. Daddy took me shopping for a new bedroom set and said I could pick out whatever I wanted. I chose a set with a bookcase headboard and a matching triple dresser. It was a light shade of wood with a grayish tint to it. It had been a long time since I had so many new things. I loved Daddy for all his efforts to go the extra mile without ever a word of complaint.

The following Saturday, Daddy and I worked all day moving back into the duplex. My new bedroom furniture was delivered. We sorted through all our clothes and threw out what had been ruined. I did the wash while Daddy cleaned out the refrigerator. It was springtime, and the air had a new smell to it. I thought about how lucky I was as I worked, hanging each piece of clothing on the line. I was so grateful for this day, mostly because I knew we were safe. With my mother still in jail, there was no worry about her coming through the door unexpectedly. Daddy and I shopped for groceries; I cooked dinner that night, and we all sat down to eat together. We were grateful that we had all survived yet another crisis, even though we knew it would not be the last one. As the days went on, the mood in our house was light and loving. Margie, Bart, and I sat around the table, talking and even joking about the fire and how we all managed to survive. We reconnected with one another, and we loved it when Daddy joined in with us. He was very funny, and we would spend what seemed like hours laughing and having a great time. Sometimes, Connie would come by, and her quick wit just added to the fun. I was sure that our laughter could be heard for blocks away, and Bart and I often wondered if people who came from sane families had as much fun as we did. We all knew that my mother's release date must be approaching. We never spoke about it, but we all knew that our fun-filled and worry-free days were soon to come to an abrupt end; we just didn't know the exact day. This time for us was a gift. Daddy even offered me the car to go to the dance that next weekend. I would never have asked him for it, but since he offered, I accepted. I was much more conscious of being careful, and I no longer suggested picking up my girlfriends.

I remember one day when Daddy came in after work with a new pair of shoes for himself. As I watched him put on his new shoes, I could feel the weight of his dreadful life. I felt sad that this kind man would, once my mother returned, continue to be deprived of simple pleasures like a clean set of work clothes or a hot meal in the evening after work. He was as dependable as my mother was undependable. He paid the bills and bought the groceries. Daddy never had new clothes; he wore his work clothes wherever he went. He never, ever complained. Each morning, he would fix himself a cup of coffee, boil two eggs, eat, and go off to work. He was entitled to a week's vacation each summer. He spent his week sitting in front of the television in his work clothes. In the afternoon, he would go down to Gus's place, hoping to find someone he could talk to and have a drink with. On the bright side, Daddy had lots of friends and plenty to do. Every now and then, he would take a day off from work and spend it at the Freehold Track. Daddy was never a foolish gambler, but he loved both the challenge and the environment.

If I had any concerns about Daddy's well-being, he would assure me that he was happy. That never made any sense to me, and my dad's unspoken message was that it was not okay to acknowledge feelings. He made light of all the drama at home: just forget about what happened yesterday and don't live in the past. In other words, do as he did, and act as if what was happening wasn't real or painful. Most important, he taught us not to express our pain to anyone. My father taught me that denial was a good tool to use in order to cope with life's problems and avoid unpleasant truths. I had lots of hard lessons yet to learn, one of which was that escaping reality was not possible. On the eve of graduation, I was going to start out in life without the self-confidence and realistic coping skills I needed in order to make good decisions for myself. My father's philosophy of denial and silence left me vulnerable to anyone with a kind face or a nice smile who seemed willing to listen to me.

Spring in New Jersey was a welcome change after so many months of bitter cold and short dark days. Bart was now almost thirteen, and Margie was seven. After school, we would sit around the table and do homework and talk. One afternoon, as we sat at the table, the doorknob turned. We all stopped and looked up at one another; we were caught off guard. When I heard the first step hit the hard floor, I knew it was her. She turned the corner into the dining room, and there she was, big as life. She had already been drinking. Our mother walked around the table, pulled up a chair, and joined us. "Did you just get out of jail today?" Bart asked.

"Yes, this morning," she replied, with a slight slur to her words.

"What's jail like?"

"Oh, I met the loveliest people there. They didn't belong in jail either." She proceeded to tell Bart about the other wonderful ladies, who came from terrible families like hers and who, just like her, were unjustly arrested. She got up, started to walk unsteadily, holding the buffet for support, and turned the corner and went up the stairs to finish whatever she had in her bag. I hated the thought of her being back home. Our party was over, and we knew it; it was now back to the old life we had temporarily escaped.

That night, when Daddy got home, I had made dinner. My mother strolled down the stairs and into the dining room to make sure everyone knew that she was back. I put the platter of meat and potatoes on the table just as she turned the corner. She took the first seat at the table and helped herself to a large portion of the steak, making sure there was not enough left for the rest of us. I told Daddy I wasn't hungry and went up to my room. I hated her; I wished she would just die or go away and leave us alone. But I knew for a fact that nothing was ever going to change in my parents' home. I needed to make my own plans; I had been convinced for years that any place I went would be a better place than where I was. However, I was also too young and immature to know how to escape without making a bad decision that I would soon regret.

A Kirby vacuum cleaner salesman came to the door one day, and my mother invited him in to give her a demonstration. In spite of the fact that all the floors in our duplex were linoleum and we had no rugs, she bought the four-hundred-dollar vacuum cleaner using Daddy's credit. She had bought useless items many times in the past, and Daddy would get stuck paying for them. However, this time, when Daddy found out about the vacuum cleaner, he called the company and told them that they could come and get their merchandise because he was not paying for it. I was glad to hear Daddy put his foot down and stick up for himself. Daddy's refusal triggered a drinking binge for my mother, and she ranted and raved for days about how badly she was treated and how she was denied things that she deserved to own.

We all made extra efforts to make sure that my mother didn't have access to any money. We had to hide our purses, wallets, or whatever we might have had whether it was a dollar or a pack of cigarettes. She sometimes resorted to taking back groceries that had not yet been opened. It did not matter what we did; she found ways to manipulate, steal, or lie to get what she needed. My mother did sober up long enough to find a job, and this job happened to have a few perks for us. The job was in a nursing home in Englishtown, about twenty miles from Freehold. The good news was that the job included a room so that she would not have to worry about transportation back and forth. Reverend Bickerstaff, the owner and manager, was a kindly large black man. He was aware of our most recent fire, and he knew the problems my mother had. Because he was badly in need of nurses, he thought he could help her, and she could in turn help him. I don't know the whole story, but I do know that I was delighted to hear that she was going to be living at the nursing home. I was also aware that in time, she was not going to be able to hold up her end of the agreement without getting drunk and causing a major problem of some kind. Of course, I said nothing and was grateful for any relief for us.

In the days leading up to starting her new position, my mother kept telling me about this great arrangement that she had maneuvered. On the day she left for Englishtown, she soberly packed up some of her things as Daddy waited to drive her to the nursing home. It was a Sunday afternoon, and she would start her job the following day. I always felt sorry for my mother when she was sober. She was a likable person, and her sober days brought back thoughts of how she used to be years earlier. I wanted to feel something for her other than sympathy, but I just didn't. The blackness of her life and all the pain she caused still outweighed any smile or kindness she tried to exhibit. I wanted to love her as I did when I was very small, but I knew that trusting her was nothing more than setting myself up. Her seemingly right intentions never turned out to be any more than lies. I kept my distance from her, always fearful of disappointments that I could count on.

Although this nursing home job seemed like a perfect solution to our problem, I was not surprised when less than a month later, Reverend Bickerstaff called to tell us that my mother had set fire to the room he provided her. He asked that we all come up to the nursing home for a meeting with him. It was a Saturday morning when we met the reverend in his office at the nursing home. He was an oversize man and had an oversize office with a large desk that took up most of the room. Large bookcases lined the back of the room on each side of a window that was covered with heavy drapes. He asked us all to sit down, and he started talking about my mother and the trouble he was in because of the fire she had started. He liked my mother but acknowledged that she had a serious problem, more serious than he had anticipated. He spoke about her getting help. I knew that she wasn't going to agree to get help because she was sure that she didn't have a problem. According to her, it was us who had the problem. In her paranoid vision, if we would just treat her better and stop depriving her, she would be okay, and none of this would be happening. Daddy explained to Reverend Bickerstaff that my mother had been in for treatment and had been in AA but that she always came to the conclusion that she did not have a drinking problem and therefore stopped going.

Reverend Bickerstaff's final decision was that my mother could work at the nursing home but could not live there. He then prayed with us, and as he did, the tears streamed down my face uncontrollably. I could feel the reverend's compassion for us. We were children trying to survive life with parents who saw nothing wrong with drinking and were not willing to change. Although Daddy was clearly the stronger of the two, his beliefs in many ways matched my mother's. Looking back, I believe that it was the prayer that triggered my crying spell. God was a source of relief for me, and tears were the way I acknowledged the truth of our situation; that afternoon, I allowed the effects of the trauma, hopelessness, and pain that I had held in for so long to leak out. Bart and Margie kept asking Daddy why I was crying, but I was so traumatized that I couldn't talk. Daddy didn't want to or couldn't deal with my emotions. If he had said anything, it would have been, "Oh, come on now. You're making a big deal out of nothing," but this time, he just ignored me. I knew it wasn't okay to cry, and Daddy was uncomfortable being around me when I expressed the pain we were all in.

Chapter 8

A Trap, Not a Way Out

In June 1961, I graduated from Freehold Regional High School. I was proud of this accomplishment because it had been such a struggle to get that far. I didn't know at the time that I would be the only one of the four of us to graduate, but that was how it turned out. The graduation was held at the Freehold Racetrack. My mother was wasted that day, but Daddy came home early to attend the graduation ceremony. I wore a white cap and gown with my first pair of spike heels. I remember how I loved the smell of the warm June air as I sat in my seat waiting for the event to begin. I glanced at the sun shining on the grass as the shade closed in on it. The FRHS band played. I knew that Daddy was proud of me for sticking it out and graduating. I stood up when my name was called and did my best to walk across the uneven ground with those spike heels, praying all the way that I would not fall and make a scene in front of all those people. It seemed like a mile to the podium, but I finally arrived, and I smiled as I was handed the diploma. I turned toward the audience and felt truly deserving of this rolled-up piece of paper as everyone applauded. This ceremony boosted my almost nonexistent feelings of self-worth.

There were a lot of graduation parties, and a boy from one of my classes came over and asked me if I would like to go to one of them. Since ours was a regional high school, a lot of the kids came from other counties, and since I had only attended for one year, I didn't know many of them. I was also afraid that there would be drinking that I did not want to get involved with, so I declined. There were no parties, gifts, or celebrations for me. Of course, my mother had no clue that I had even graduated. I didn't expect more from her, and I was glad she didn't come to the ceremony. Even if she had been sober that day, I would have feared her causing me some kind of embarrassment. Graduating from high school was something that I had accomplished despite my family situation. It had not been easy, and there were days I wanted to give up, but I was glad that I stuck with it. I give a lot of the credit to Tex and Marion, who took me in and provided me with the tools I needed to succeed in school.

Connie ran her car into the ground, and I was not surprised when it suddenly died. She came home one Sunday evening with her latest boyfriend, Phil, and asked to borrow Daddy's car. It was late, and Daddy was already in bed. Connie kept begging, and he kept telling her no. She promised over and over again to be back in time for Daddy to get to work the following morning. Connie never gave up; she could be obnoxiously demanding, and her persistence usually paid off. Daddy finally gave in and gave her the keys. I doubt that Daddy knew that Phil was waiting downstairs for her. None of us knew Phil; we only knew that he was in the Marines and was from Elizabeth. We surely didn't know that he had gone AWOL or that he and Connie were planning to elope.

The next morning, Connie was nowhere to be found. Daddy got dressed for work and ate breakfast as usual. He never mentioned his missing car; he just picked up the phone, called a taxi, and went to work. This went on all week. When I asked him when Connie was supposed to return, he said he had not heard from her. What annoyed me was that she never acknowledged others' needs, only her own, and we already had a mother who played that same game. Finally, on Sunday, Connie came back, married and pregnant. I wanted Daddy to get angry with her for her disappearing act, but as usual, he said nothing. I think that after a week of taking a taxi to work, he was just glad to have his car back. It was understood among all of us that as long as Phil was stationed at a nearby base, Connie would continue to live at home with us.

In the summer of 1961, John Fitzgerald Kennedy was the hot new presidential candidate. JFK was young and smart. He was not only attractive but had a charming personality that appealed to the American people. Daddy liked to watch the political debates on TV, especially those between Kennedy and Nixon. He thought that Kennedy was way smarter than Nixon, and he liked Kennedy's Irish sense of humor, which in a lot of ways matched his. Nixon never smiled and always appeared to be nervous and sweating, while Kennedy was always cool and relaxed. Kennedy's wife, Jackie, was very attractive; she dressed like a model and was the envy of women everywhere. Their lifestyle of power, money, and perfection was hard for me to imagine, and the world was intrigued with them.

Daddy would sit in the living room in one of the easy chairs, with his container of beer on the floor hidden between the right side of his chair and the sofa, where he was sure my mother couldn't see it. Every now and then, when he knew she was out of sight, he would reach for the container and enjoy a few swallows. I would watch with him as he explained all the political strategies to me and answered all my questions. Daddy seemed to know something about everything. He was up-to-date on world affairs, and I admired that about him.

I was looking for a job. I had a high school diploma but no real skills for the work world, and Freehold was a small town with little opportunity. Connie had the perfect solution for me. She was leaving the Speedy Diner on Route 9 to take another job, and I could have her old job. She would be there for two more weeks and could train me as a waitress. I wasn't excited about being a waitress; it had never occurred to me to emulate Connie in any way. I wanted to work in an office, but Connie had it all worked out with her boss. I knew that if I rejected her plan, I would have been the butt of her unrelenting humor. For that reason and because it was available, I agreed to do what Connie wished. Fear was always the driving force that caused me to go along with what others wanted. I didn't have the security within myself to do my own choosing. I also had no adult I could consult about my future. I don't know why I no longer felt my special connection to God. I began to think of God as someone who used to help me when I was a child, but I was an adult now, no longer stuck, and able to fly if I wanted to. Emotionally, I was still that small child, begging Daddy to come home and save me. I still was in desperate need of God, but not desperate enough to seek as I used to.

Connie and I went to the diner one afternoon to meet with the owner, John Dailey. The Speedy Diner sat on a corner directly on Route 9, just a few miles from Freehold. The restaurant didn't look like a typical diner with the silver metallic trailer look but looked like a regular restaurant. This was a new business for John Dailey, a large Irish man in his fifties who had a background as a cook. John came out from the kitchen as we walked in, and he looked like a cook with his white clothing and large apron. He motioned for us to sit down in a booth, and he would be out to join us. We ordered a Coke as Connie spoke to some of the incoming customers and introduced me. John soon was sliding into the booth with us and making small talk. He and Connie talked about things going on at the diner with different customers. He suggested that I start on Monday morning at 5:30 a.m. and work until 1:00 p.m. because that was their busiest time.

I wasn't sure I would work out as well as Connie. She was an experienced waitress and had the outgoing personality and confidence that I did not. After working as a waitress for two years, Connie was tough, seasoned, and not intimidated by off-color remarks. She had always been much more mature than I was, gutsy, bold, and afraid of nothing. Even though I felt I was not right for this job, I was willing to try it, but I would later regret this decision.

Connie and I worked together for the first two weeks so she could show me the ropes. Connie knew all the customers—the truck drivers, the state troopers, and the other groups of guys that came in regularly. Even my dad's friend Arnie, whom we knew from our old apartment house in Maplewood, stopped in one morning when my dad told him Connie and I both worked the morning shift at the Speedy Diner. I hadn't seen Arnie since I was six years old. I often found myself in the midst of a lot of off-color joking, but I just ignored it, kept busy, and didn't join in. I left that up to Connie and John Dailey, who were into it and enjoyed that sort of thing. They would try to involve me, but I wouldn't budge.

After the first two weeks were up, I was on my own. The tips were pretty good, and of course, I opened a savings account and saved most of my money. I also paid Daddy $20 each week for my living expenses. It wasn't long before I had saved enough to put a down payment on a car. With Daddy's savvy ability to haggle with the car dealer, I was able to buy a 1959 Chevrolet Impala. It was long, sleek, black, and what was called a hard-top convertible. This car was nice, nicer than anything I had ever dreamed of. Daddy had it financed under his credit and worked out a plan for me to pay him each week.

Now that I was sporting this hot new car, all the jokes at the Speedy Diner were related to my car, and John Dailey had fun discussing me and my car with the regulars. I didn't respond to the joking, but at times, I had to keep myself from laughing at some of their remarks. It was less funny when John got carried away and the jokes about me included off-color remarks that were not only embarrassing but demeaning. Since I didn't respond while it was going on and never complained. I guess he thought I was okay with the jokes. I should have spoken up, but I was afraid of losing my job, and I was too young to know how to handle it. I especially hated when the whole counter would be lined up with a group of guys from the local car dealer, and John would say, "Her birthday is coming up. I think I will give her a good Gruen" [a Gruen was a fancy watch; "a good Gruen" was supposed to sound like "a good screwin'."] Of course, they would all laugh, and I would act like I didn't hear them, just keeping busy and ignoring their remarks. Then he would continue with, "Now that she has a new car, she doesn't care anything about me. I try to get her to come back in the evening, but she's too busy out dancing and drinking at the local bar." None of this was true, and I don't know whether the customers thought it was. There were some regulars who did not join in, and I tended to cater to them. I thought they knew I was uncomfortable with the jokes. Looking back, I realize how disrespectful and demeaning the jokes were, and I wish I had the self-confidence to stick up for myself, but I did not. Besides, I was catching on and realized that the entertainment at my expense was part of the job. I also knew that as long as I didn't respond, they wouldn't reach the full potential of their fun. Some days I wanted to quit, just walk out the door, and never come back. This environment was not where I belonged any more than my home environment was. I had become well aware that I needed to find another job.

On New Year's Day 1962, Daddy was invited to a friend's house for a Christmas drink. He took Margie with him, and someone took a picture of Daddy with Margie sitting on his lap and Daddy's glass of cheer sitting on the table in front of them. In the photo, Margie looked cute; she was eight years old and wearing a new sweater she got for Christmas. Daddy looked worn, weathered, and worried. Time and stress had clearly taken its toll on him. This photo presented a clear picture of the trauma at home; my father's face was a portrait of struggle and sadness, and only we knew how severe it was. Since I was working now and had some extra money. I had fun buying Margie new toys and clothes. Also, that Christmas, Daddy had suggested that we go shopping together for my Christmas present. He wanted to buy me a new winter coat, so we drove to Sayreville, a neighboring town that had a strip mall, and went into a ladies' clothing shop. The coat I liked was black; it had a fox collar and draped beautifully. When I put it on, I felt like a million dollars. The price tag was $125, and I could see the joy on Daddy's face as he paid for the coat. Daddy always amazed me with his ability to come up with that much money; he must have had a good day at the track. You could not help but love this man for his ability to endure and his attempts to make it up to his children for their terrible homelife. Daddy was a giver, and he always paid his own way, took nothing for himself, and never ripped anyone off. I loved that coat. Wearing it made me feel pretty, polished, and sure of myself. I wore it for many winters and carefully stored it in the summer months. It was a gift I would always remember.

Although I hated the early morning hours, I was getting better at the waitress job. However, I always knew that it was temporary and nothing more than a dead-end job. It would never provide for me a way to move out and be on my own. Even though I was always hoping to find something better, nothing ever seemed to materialize for me. The turmoil at home continued to get worse. One night, Bart and a couple of his friends were sitting at the kitchen table playing cards. Daddy's game was poker, so he joined in to show the boys how to play. Daddy took some change out of his pocket and explained to them how to play and how to bet on each hand. The boys were having fun, and Daddy was having just as much fun. My mother had been drinking but was not exactly wasted, and this in-between state was always a danger zone. She kept walking through the dining room, making slurring remarks to my dad, but he paid no attention to her. I knew she couldn't stand to hear my dad laugh or think that he was enjoying himself. There was not going to be a shred of happiness in our house as long as she could do anything about it. She made a couple of remarks about how gambling was against the law for minors, and when they continued to ignore her, she put on her coat and walked out the front door. They were glad to be rid of her annoyance and were happy when they heard the door close behind her. The game went on, but it wasn't long before she was back. She was obviously quite proud of herself as she marched in with a police officer. She had gone down to the police station and told them what was going on and insisted they arrest Daddy for "gambling with minors." Daddy was highly embarrassed. The officer stood there, explaining in front of these young boys that what they were doing was against the law. Daddy, in his humble way, explained that he was just showing the boys how to play, that he was not taking the boys' money, and they meant no harm. I hated the smug, gloating look on my mother's face when she brought Daddy down. The officer finally said that he would give my dad a warning this time, but if it were to happen again, he would be arrested. Daddy had been humiliated in front of my brother and his friends. Needless to say, the game was over. Daddy picked up his change from the table, and the boys left. I hoped my dad remembered the incident when my mother sobered up and started asking him for money to start another one of her new jobs.

I could see Daddy's attitude toward my mother slowly changing, and he didn't defend her as he had before. Her tirades about her family's ill treatment and how she deserved better had been replaying for as long as I could remember. Her theme was always Daddy's failure as a provider and how she had to do without because of him. However, this time, when she complained, "I haven't had a new coat all winter," he dared to talk back: "Why do you need a winter coat? You spend the winters in jail." I was always glad to hear my father refute her abusive remarks. We all knew the truth, but there was no way to reason with her. Alcoholism is a way of self-destruction that does not allow for any logic or reason.

Daddy was now part of a group of Freehold guys who played poker regularly on Fridays or Saturdays, rotating from one house to another. Daddy loved these games. It gave him a place to go, a life, and something fun to do after he had worked all week. My mother was still working at the nursing home, and she was allowed to stay there on the weekends when she was on that shift. We all looked forward to the weekends when she was gone. This particular Saturday, it was Daddy's turn to have the game at our house, but as luck would have it, this was not my mother's weekend to work. Just the thought of that worried me, but she was sober that day, and she did not seem to know about Daddy's plans. Daddy gave me some money and asked me to take my mother out to eat at a local diner and then drop her off at the nursing home in Englishtown. I hated when Daddy asked me to do anything with my mother because she always caught on when anything out of the ordinary went on that involved her. But Daddy knew I would always do what he asked. He also knew the poker game could not go on with her there. Even if she was sober, she would insist on playing with them. She could never stand for Daddy to enjoy himself; that was just not going to happen. She could always find some clever way to ruin his fun for him.

I asked my mother if she would like to go out to get something to eat with me, and she agreed. However, it was unusual for me to invite her out to eat, and I sensed that she was smelling a rat. Nevertheless, she got dressed, and we left. This was the first time she had been in my car. We made small talk as I drove to a local diner. Since it was still quite early and not crowded, we were quickly seated. We discussed what we wanted off the menu, and I told her to get anything she wanted because I would be paying. "What made you all of a sudden decide to invite me out to eat with you?" she asked.

"I wanted to give you a ride in my car so you could see how nice it was," I answered while studying the menu.

"Why did you want to take me out to dinner?" she asked again.

"I just thought it would be fun. I was hungry. I was coming anyhow and thought you would enjoy coming along." Our food came as I kept trying to change the subject with no luck. Finally, I said, "Why can't you just sit back and enjoy the meal?"

Smoking was not a problem in 1962; it was accepted that you could smoke anywhere at any time. My mother's cigarettes were extremely important to her; she had to have her cigarettes. At the diner, she never put her cigarette out and ate as she smoked. Her hands moved nervously, and she was unable to sit still. By the time we left, it was dusk. I pulled out of the parking lot and drove in the direction of Englishtown. "Where are we going?" she asked.

"To the nursing home so you can do your weekend shift," I said as if she should have known it.

"I might not be scheduled this weekend. Why didn't you tell me earlier you were taking me to the nursing home?"

"I thought you knew where we were going," I replied as we pulled into the parking lot. Nothing more was said about it, and when I pulled up in front of the nursing home, she recognized a few patients sitting out front. As soon as the car stopped, she got out of the car and walked over to speak with them. I didn't look back, just took off and drove home. All the way home, I felt that I should have been up-front with her, and I was annoyed with Daddy for involving me. Why did I always have to get included in his dirty work? Then I remembered that he did deserve to have a few hours at home to play poker with his friends if he wanted to. After all, he went to work every day, and he paid the bills. I knew that without him, we would be sunk. Did he not deserve to enjoy an evening with his friends, without being annoyed by her?

I took my time driving home. I walked in the front door and turned into the dining room; Daddy and three of his friends were sitting at the table playing poker. All of a sudden, I heard my mother's voice from upstairs. I looked at Daddy and said, "How did she get here?"

"I don't know. She arrived about ten minutes ago."

"Well, I didn't bring her back."

My mother started ranting and raving from upstairs; she had clearly been drinking and was right about at her high-wired stage. She was in prime form to make as much trouble for Daddy and his friends as she could. The poker game continued, and the men ignored my mother and paid no attention to anything she said. I felt bad for Daddy because I knew that she was not going to let up until she destroyed the game. How she destroyed the game was a new low, even for her. Our duplex's heating system was designed so that the heat vent on the first floor was in line with the vents on the second and third floors. My mother stood over the vent on the second floor and pissed down the vent, big-time. The man seated next to the vent in the dining room, right in the line of fire, got hit pretty hard. His glasses fell off his bald head, and his cards fell on the table. It was a sight you might see on comedy TV, but in our house, it was real-life drama. At first, the others thought she had poured water down the vent, but soon the truth was apparent. She accomplished what she had set out to do; the party was over. This story was a great source of fun and laughter for us years later, when we would get together and talk about the things that went on under our roof that no sane person would ever believe.

Dates from the Speedy Diner were plentiful. The problem was that they were with what I considered "older men." I simply wasn't interested in men in their thirties because I was eighteen years old. One man I met at the diner was from the Chevrolet dealership where I had my car serviced. It was convenient for this man to pick up my car from the restaurant and return it whenever I needed service. He offered to do this, and he would encourage me to tell him about any concerns I had about the car's running condition so he could check it out for me. I did notice a particular noise when I made a right turn, so the man from the dealership suggested that I bring the car in after work that day so he could drive it and I could point out the problem. He also suggested that I come back to the shop around seven o'clock, after closing time, and he would put the car up on the lift and look at it at no charge. He did find the problem, and when he was finished, he asked me if I would like to go to a local restaurant and get something to eat with him. Feeling that I was safe with this "older" man, I agreed. As we ate, I was caught off guard when he asked if I would be interested in going out on a date with him. Without hesitation, I said no! I knew he wasn't happy with my answer. I tried to explain that I was way too young for him, but my words seemed to infuriate him. I was still very naive about the ways of the world, still a virgin, and had barely dated anyone.

A few days later as I arrived for work, John called me into the back and told me that the guy from the dealership had been in earlier and was telling the whole restaurant that I had been out with him. He had even bragged about what a great lover I was. I was horrified! "Did you go out with him?" John asked.

"Absolutely not! He's too old for me to go anywhere with. He asked me for a date, and I told him no! That must be what he is mad about." I was in a state of shock that this guy would do such a thing to me. I hated adults; they were liars, liars, liars.

"Oh, so you did go out with him," John insisted. "He told a very different story about what you two did together."

"He is a liar," I said, my voice louder and very angry. I walked out to the counter, shaking from our conversation. I felt victimized; I wanted to quit, walk out the door, and never come back. A few people came in, and as I got busy, my tension eased. John continued to bring the man's story up to me, but I refused to discuss it anymore. A few days later, John called me into the back. As he talked to me, he put his hand on my butt and asked me if it felt good. I started crying, grabbed my coat, walked out to the front door, and left. I cried all the way home. I didn't know what to do. I couldn't tell Daddy; you just didn't discuss things like that with him. I needed out; I needed to escape. I hated my life.

I stopped on the way home and picked up the local Freehold paper to look for another job. There was little opportunity in Freehold, and I could not find anything in the paper that was suitable for me. I didn't know where to go or what to do. Asking for help was not an option because who would I go to?

The next day, I went to work as usual, and no more was said about the incident. I had no doubt that when I walked out, my message came across clearly because John told me that an old friend of his was coming in to help during the lunch shift. I figured that she was really coming to replace me, but I didn't care because I was going to look for another job. Kay came in that afternoon, and I liked her the moment I met her. She had worked for John a few years back when he owned another diner in Plainfield. She was mature, married, and had two children. John had hired her to work nine to two, school hours, since she had a family to deal with. Kay was a safety net for me. There was no off-color nonsense or teasing going on while she was there. I no longer got my car serviced at the Chevrolet dealership, and the guy who told the lies about me did not come back in while I was there. I never again went back into the kitchen where John was; I just spoke to him through the opening ledge where he left the food. These changes gave me a solution to my employment problem for the short term.

As my mother's addiction escalated, she became more and more preoccupied with herself. Her needs, her comfort, and her life were of the utmost importance. As always, she had no awareness of the needs of those around her. Everything she didn't like about her life was Daddy's fault, even down to her bed, which she claimed was just too uncomfortable. Of course it was uncomfortable; it was full of burn holes, some of which were huge. She decided to sleep in the bed on the third floor.

One Saturday when she was very drunk, she waddled down from the third floor, picked up the phone, and called the police department. In her slurred and hard-to-understand words, she asked the person on the other end if they would give her a few days' lodging at the jail. I don't think they could understand what she was asking, and she finally hung up. As she started her climb back upstairs, I smelled smoke. I told Daddy, and we went up to the third floor and found that the mattress was smoldering. The third floor was thick with smoke, and it was hard to breathe. Daddy yelled for me to go down to the second floor and insisted that he could handle pulling the mattress down himself. Somehow, he managed to drag the mattress down the stairs with much effort and struggle. Luckily, the bathtub sat at the bottom of the stairs, and he was able to douse the mattress in the bathtub. Daddy was gasping for breath, and I was terrified that he would pass out. He kept bending over, trying to get a breath of air. I asked if I could help him, but he insisted that he would be okay; he just needed some fresh air. I opened the windows in my bedroom, and he finally stopped gasping and started breathing normally again. I wanted to scream, *Why, do you put up with this? Will it ever end? Why does she have to live at our house?*

    I had long been traumatized by this environment of never-ending confusion. The smog of our house was filled with hate, abuse, fires, filthy language, and the stench of alcohol. I was becoming more and more intolerant of my mother's abuse, and with no end in sight, I wanted out. As a result, in the years ahead, I succumbed to quick and wrong decisions that seemed reasonable in my desperation. Marriage to a relative stranger, which I soon saw as a solution, was nothing more than a trap filled with long-term negative consequences. I did not think about how my choices would affect me ten years down the road. I was looking for any escape that would put an end to my suffering and give me relief for the moment. With my limited ability to reason, the now was all that mattered, and I was foolishly willing to jump in headfirst and hope for the best. I had seen several of my girlfriends get married, and it worked out well for them; they were happy, treated well, and were content. The desperation I felt inside was my downfall. The girlfriends I speak of came from families who loved and supported them. I had no such support, and if marriage didn't work out for me, there was no help, no coming back; it was final. I was still willing to chance it. If I had some way to know the price I would eventually pay, I would never have even considered an impulsive marriage. My advice would be to think carefully about any decision in your life that screams of desperation because it is probably a trap. Nothing is urgent; nothing needs to be done right away. There is no such thing as a last chance.

    Connie's husband received new orders and would be stationed in Virginia Beach, Virginia. Their baby was due in August. Phil was able to acquire base housing, and as soon as the baby was born,

Connie would be joining him. Connie was happy, knowing that she would soon be leaving Center Street and the trauma that went with it.

The hottest movie of 1962 was *Splendor in the Grass*, with Natalie Wood and Warren Beatty. I loved this movie and could have watched it a hundred times. It was a love story about love and loss, based on an excerpt from a poem written by William Wordsworth.

I think I was drawn to the movie because it was about family dysfunction. Both the movie and the words from the poem provide a strong message about coming to terms with the past, picking up the pieces, and looking ahead. I must have known that these lessons about dealing with the past and moving on were ones I would face eventually.

The possibility of going to college never crossed my mind. I didn't know anyone who went to college, and I believed that higher education was only for those who came from privileged backgrounds. My girlfriends from high school either landed a job or got married and had a baby. That was the way it was. Getting married and having a baby was acceptable, and whether you got married first or got pregnant first didn't really matter.

I kept telling myself that I was an adult now—no longer stuck, free to fly, to go anywhere I wanted. The problem was fear; it takes a lot of courage to release the familiar and embrace the new. I knew that I could do this but was extremely fearful and much too insecure to leave. As bad as my life was, it was what I knew. I needed strong encouragement, someone to hold my hand. Life so far had been pretty brutal, and I feared getting out and finding myself in a worse place.

One Saturday night, a girlfriend and I went out to Earle Base, a Marine base that I had never heard of before. In order to get through the guard post and onto the base, you had to know someone there. My friend had been to the club before and had a name she used to get us through the gate. I had no clue what to expect, but once we were inside the building, the base club looked similar to any club, a friendly atmosphere with a bar, pool tables, dartboards, and a TV. There was a second large room with tables and music playing. It wasn't long after we sat at one of these tables that a few guys came over and introduced themselves to us and asked if they could join us. My friend agreed since she did all the talking. One of the guys went to the bar and came back with a pitcher of beer and glasses for everyone. As the glasses were filled with beer, we were laughing, dancing, and having a fun time. Our new companions were Jimmy Minor, Jimmy Diaz, and the others names I do not remember. Minor was from Atlanta, and Diaz was from New York City. I hated the smell of beer, but I joined in with the crowd and sipped along as we talked and danced. I had never done anything this risky before, but the beer helped me to let down my guard and relax. I sat next to Jimmy Minor; I liked his Southern accent, and he was cute. He was Irish like me, and he had blue eyes, a nice build, and he was friendly. Diaz was entertaining; he told stories about growing up in the city, and he acted out his stories. We laughed a lot that night and had a good time. At the stroke of midnight, I insisted that it was time to go home. They all teased me about leaving so soon, trying to egg me on to stay longer, but I told my girlfriend that I was leaving, and if she wanted to stay longer, she would have to make other arrangements. Minor asked me if I would be coming back. I answered, "Probably." He suggested that if I wanted to get back on base, I could use his name at the guard post.

The base became a regular Saturday night pastime for us. I met some new girlfriends and had fun with them. Drinking beer had also become a regular routine for me; it was a way of allowing myself to fit in. I thought I was an adult because I was eighteen years old, but growing up as I did, I had never emotionally matured and was still very much a child. I can now see clearly how the drinking changed my thinking and destroyed my ability to make good decisions for myself. I was blending into and following the crowd instead of choosing for myself. When I drank, I became relaxed and lost all ability to determine right from wrong. I found myself acting on impulse, doing things that I never would have considered had I not been drinking.

Jimmy Minor and I began to see each other off base as well as at the dances. I had the car, so we would sometimes go out to eat or go to a local bar to drink and dance. When he suggested that we stay in a hotel for the night, I went along with his request. Some days, he was on duty and couldn't leave the base. On those days, I would drive to the base, and he would come out and sit in the car with me. He talked a lot about his family back in Atlanta, and his Southern accent added to my attraction to him. On a few occasions, he became quite jealous when I talked with or about another guy. I took that as a compliment and liked the fact that he was threatened by the thought of losing me. I saw his jealousy as one of the signs of love; little did I know what it really meant.

I invited Jimmy to my house one night to see where I lived. I explained about my mother so he would be prepared and there would be no surprises. Daddy was home when we arrived; I introduced them, and of course, Daddy with his gift for gab made Jimmy feel comfortable. Daddy was interested in Jimmy's service experiences and his family in Atlanta. My mother was upstairs, asleep, and I was quite worried that she would get up and begin one of her tirades, but that didn't happen. Jimmy met Bart and Margie, and it was a pleasant visit.

On our way back to the base, we stopped at the ShopRite. As we walked in together, the guy from the Chevy dealership who had told the lies about me was walking out. As we passed, I looked him straight in the eye, took Jimmy's hand, and kept walking. I was so glad that I had the opportunity to look him straight in the eye. It felt powerful. I never saw him again. He should have been ashamed of himself, but I'm sure he wasn't.

Those days were the most pleasant that I remember of my time with Jimmy. He treated me well, and he was personable and well-liked. We made plans to take a weekend trip to Washington, DC. Jimmy had been stationed in Quantico, Virginia, before he relocated to Earle Base. He liked Washington, DC, and told us about all there was to do there. It was springtime, and the cherry blossom celebration was in full swing. We wanted to include Jimmy Diaz, so I called a high school girlfriend, told her our plans, and asked her if she would like to come along to be with Diaz. Even though she had never met him, she agreed, and we were all set. Planning this trip was also a wrong decision for me. I had never done this kind of thing before, but the drinking changed my mind as to who I was and what I believed was right for me. I justified my behavior by telling myself that I was tired of being the oddball, tired of being left out. In reality, I was lowering my standards and allowing the world to decide my path. It was a wrong path for me, and I knew it. I was ashamed of what I was doing, but after a beer or two, the shame was gone.

It was early Friday evening, and I was all packed and excited about our trip. My mother was drinking that day. The two Jimmys arrived, and I invited them in as I got all the last-minute things taken care of. My mother was sitting in the living room easy chair when they arrived, and I had no choice but to introduce them. I knew she would show them what a fool she was, but it was a worry that I had no control over. She didn't budge from her chair in the living room as she attempted to make conversation with them. It was quite obvious that she was drunk, and I wished there was some way to hide her presence. I quickly got my bag together and was ready to leave. Jimmy always drove my car when we went anywhere together, and I liked it that way.

Washington, DC, was all I was told it would be. There was plenty to do and great places to eat. We woke up Saturday morning to a beautiful spring day and strolled through the streets, enjoying the scenery and the cherry blossoms, which were in full bloom. Jimmy talked a lot about his family. He told us how his mother lounged around the pool all day and got her hair done on the weekends. His dad, he said, looked a lot like Robert Mitchum and in his younger days sold moonshine. His dad was a millwright; he was employed by Chevrolet and had been for many years. They were a very close-knit Catholic family, and he had two brothers and two sisters. He was the second oldest, and his older sister was already married and had a little girl named Kathy.

Sunday afternoon, we packed up for our trip home. As we got closer to the Freehold area, I turned the radio to the local station, and Freehold was in the news. The closer we got to Freehold, the better I could understand what was being said. We were all shocked to learn that there had been a fire in one of the restaurants on Main Street. Since the businesses were all attached, the fire burned a whole block of stores. The first thing I thought of was where my mother might have been. Surely, she didn't start this fire! We finally reached Freehold and drove through Main Street to see the damage firsthand. Four businesses in a row were gutted—the pizza shop, pharmacy, five-and-ten store, and a restaurant. No one had been hurt, but it was a sight to see.

A few weeks after that, we planned a trip to New York City, Diaz's hometown. Diaz needed another date, so I asked my girlfriend Mabel if she wanted to come along. Mabel had graduated from high school with me. She agreed, and off we went. When we got to New York City, Diaz first wanted to stop by and see his mother. I suggested that Diaz do the driving since he was familiar with the area, and I was not. He grew up in Harlem, after his parents had emigrated from Puerto Rico when he was a baby. When we got to Diaz's neighborhood, the only parking was on the street in front of the apartment building. We walked up several flights of stairs, with Diaz leading the way. When we arrived at his apartment, he used his key to let us in. He introduced us to his mother, who did not speak English. We all sat down in the living room, and Diaz kept communicating with his mother in Spanish. Eventually, Diaz and his mother went to a back bedroom to visit Diaz' brother. "Is your brother sick?" I asked when Diaz returned and sat down with us.

"He is a heroin addict and is having a bad day," he explained. "This is a rough neighborhood, and he got caught up in it." I felt bad for Diaz and his mother. "That is why I joined the service, to get out of here before I got involved too."

I thought to myself, *Everyone seems to be trying to escape something. I'm not the only one.*

"The service has been good for me," Diaz went on. "It has given me a chance to see another view of the world and helped me to grow up." We all laughed about how "grown-up" he really was. The truth was that none of us were grown-up; we were all still kids trying to find our place in the world. I felt as if I was the only one who could really understand Diaz's home situation and feel the pain he must have grown up with. As we left, Minor talked about how he hated the service. He was not grateful for it and complained about how they mistreated him in boot camp and made him do things that he didn't want to do. He went on and on about how when his four years were up, he would never consider signing up for another stint but would be on his way back to Atlanta. The two Jimmys had grown up with entirely different experiences.

Diaz and Mabel eventually got married and had a baby. Last time I ran into them, they had bought a farm in upstate New York and seemed happy. Mabel told me that Diaz treated her well and was a faithful husband and a loving father. I was happy for both of them.

As the next month approached and I had missed a period, I suspected that I was pregnant and made an appointment with a local doctor. This was before the home pregnancy tests that we have today. The doctor's diagnosis was that he suspected pregnancy but could not confirm it until I had missed three periods. When I told Jimmy about it, he suggested that we take a ride to Elkton, Maryland, where we could get married without a waiting period. That was the place where Connie and Phil had married also. We found our birth certificates and picked out two simple gold bands. We did not tell anyone about our plans; I was very nervous about eloping, but on the other hand, I was enjoying the secrecy of it. I also felt a sense of shame for getting pregnant out of wedlock; I knew it was wrong, wrong for me anyway. Even so, I told myself that I loved Jimmy Minor, and his youthful good looks appealed to me. Sometimes his conversations were immature and even childish, and it would not take me long to realize that this was not love. The marriage was no more than me once again ignoring what was best for me in order to comply with what someone else wanted. I had already lost myself, and it was difficult to know the right way to go. The drinking was my first wrong decision, which allowed me to relax and be led by evil impulses and misguided will. When true love comes, it comes in its own way and in its own time. You cannot make it happen. I was in denial and had no way to separate truth from reality. Nevertheless, I was determined from the outset to do my part to make this marriage work. I intended to be a responsible parent, a faithful wife, and to give my child a better life than my parents gave me. However, I was on a wrong path, and as long as I stayed on that path, life would screw up the best of my intentions.

Jimmy and I were married on May 2, 1962. I wore my two-piece lavender dress, the same one I wore when I graduated from high school just a year earlier. We drove to Elkton, Maryland, a small town with "Get married today" signs everywhere. It was such a simple process and lasted no more than fifteen minutes, after which we received a certificate showing that we were now Mr. and Mrs. James H. Minor. When we arrived home, Daddy had just come in from work, and I waited until Daddy had sat down in his easy chair. Jimmy stood next to me as I proceeded to tell Daddy what we had done. He said, "You did?" with a startled look on his face. I knew he didn't really care what I had done. "Well, congratulations!" he added while reaching for his checkbook in his back pants pocket. He shook hands with Jimmy and handed him a check for $25. That check was not much but was all he could afford to give us on such short notice, and it was all that we ever received from anyone. Jimmy called his family to tell them the news that Jimmy had married a "Yankee" of all things. I was sure the news shook up Atlanta's phone lines for at least an hour or so.

We settled in on Center Street, and Jimmy adjusted to my mother's tirades with great tolerance. I made an appointment at the base for an examination, and the pregnancy was confirmed, with a due date in December. We were both excited! If it was a boy, Jimmy wanted to name the baby after his father, James Lee Minor. A girl's name would be my choice. As Jimmy and I became more comfortable with each other, I realized that there was another side to him. His stories about his family and especially his mother began to drain me of energy, and he seemed to be way too enmeshed with them. Each story portrayed the Minor family as quite the perfect group, not only rich but also flawless. We planned a trip to Atlanta so that I could meet this group of elites that I had heard so much about. Jimmy told me that his mother was having a hysterectomy in July, and she wanted him to be there when she went into the hospital. I asked for the date of the surgery numerous times but never got any specific day that this would happen. I wondered how we could plan to be there if they couldn't tell us when the surgery would be. I didn't press the point, but I probably should have.

We finally made plans to leave for Atlanta the last week of June. I found it very strange that Jimmy still couldn't give an exact date for his mother's surgery. The facts about this whole event were far too sketchy. As we sat at the dining room table talking about our trip, Connie stepped in and asked Jimmy what kind of operation his mother was having.

"A female operation," he answered.

"You mean a hysterectomy?"

"Yes," he said hesitantly.

"What day is she supposed to have it?"

"I'm not sure." I just listened as Connie put him on the hot seat because I knew she would get to the bottom of it. Connie was relentless; she would keep it up until the truth was told.

"How come you don't know when she is scheduled to have the operation?"

"Well, the reason I don't know is because she is pregnant, and the baby is due at the end of June. After the baby is born, they will schedule the hysterectomy."

"Oh," Connie replied, "now that makes more sense."

"Yeah, she wants me to be there when the baby is born." I knew Connie would keep on until she dragged every ounce of truth out of him. Neither Connie nor I could understand why he had so much trouble telling the truth and why he tried his best to tiptoe around the fact that his mother was pregnant. I felt that maybe he was too embarrassed to tell it as it was; after all, this was her sixth child, and she was a grandmother.

This incident was just the beginning of Jimmy's subtle but deceptive ways that would grow bigger and more deceitful over time. I began to wonder what else he was hiding from me.

Chapter 9

False Promises

We left for Atlanta the last week of June, driving my car that had now become our car. I was excited and looking forward to seeing Atlanta. I had wanted to visit Atlanta since I looked the city up in our encyclopedias back when we lived in East Brunswick. I had admired the pictures of Atlanta, which made the city look as if every season was summer, with flowers growing everywhere and masses of people coming and going. I had many reservations about Jimmy's stories about his family. I wondered how much of what he told me was actually true, but I was now on the way to finding out. Going by Jimmy's stories, I pictured his family living in a Southern Antebellum-style house surrounded by no less than an acre of land, with a kidney-shaped pool next to the covered patio in the backyard. Their place would surely put Center Street to shame. I knew little about Southern customs, but I was determined to fit in; I was going to love Atlanta as much as Jimmy did. We made conversation on the way, and as we drove through the Carolinas, Jimmy pointed out to me how the soil changed from dark brown to red clay the farther South we went. He said that was how you know you were in the Deep South, by the color of the soil. He also told me to remember that in the South, black people were referred to as niggers. He warned sternly, "That is what you call them in the South. Remember that."

"Why do you call them niggers?" I asked.

"Because that is what they are," he answered.

"And what are we called?"

"We are white, but they are not really considered people in the South."

"Why not?" I could hear the annoyance in his voice as I continued to press him.

"They have a smaller brain than we do. They are not as intelligent as we are." I could feel his attitude and his real thoughts coming to the surface, more boldly than I had heard before. I didn't like his attitude, and I knew he was wrong. However, I kept it to myself, let it go, and changed the subject.

As we got closer to Atlanta, Jimmy asked, "You didn't believe all those things I told you about my family, did you?"

Uh-oh, here we go, I thought. Somehow I was expecting this. "Like what?" I asked.

"Whatever I told you so far about my family was just a line."

"I'm confused. You mean about the big house and your mother lounging around the pool? About your dad who looks like Robert Mitchum and always has a car for you to drive when you come home on leave? None of this is true?"

"No, that was just a line."

"I still don't understand. So instead of saying it was a lie, you are calling it a line? What is the difference between a lie and a line?" There was a long silence; I knew he was annoyed that I was questioning his warped thinking.

"A line is just something you tell a broad to impress her."

"Oh, so in other words, you didn't tell me the truth about your family, and now that we are almost there, you want to set the record straight?"

"Yeah, you could say that." I began to realize how little I really knew about Jimmy Minor and his family. Now we were close to the final showdown, and I was about to see for myself and make my own determination as to the truth versus the lies. I didn't believe there was any such thing as a line. Besides, he told most of these lies to me after we were married, when he was no longer "trying to impress a broad." I felt very troubled by all this. I knew that time would tell more of this story, and I feared what could be ahead for me. I was anxious to see with my own eyes who these people really were. Maybe meeting them would also give me a clue as to who my new husband really was.

At about 4:00 p.m., we arrived at the "Southern plantation." We pulled up in front of a fairly run-down house that sat close to the street and had a rickety front porch in bad need of paint and repair. As we proceeded through the front door, Jimmy's mother, pregnant and barefoot, greeted us with a hug. She seemed nervous, and she insisted that I sit down. I sat on the sofa, and she plopped into one of the chairs. A minute or so later, a sister came in with a baby. I knew that this was Jimmy's older sister Margaret and his niece Kathy. Next came Jimmy's two brothers, Jack and Mike. Jack was a year or so younger than Jimmy, and Mike was a young boy around nine. The only ones missing were his dad and his sister Theresa. Theresa was in high school and had not gotten home yet, and the dad was on the late shift at the Chevrolet plant and had already gone to work. These were all exceptionally good-looking people. They were friendly, and their chatter filled the room. I kept quiet, just sat there, watching and listening to their odd language. Several fans were going, and there were extension cords lying across the floor that kept the fans running. Margaret sat her baby, Kathy, on the floor. She was a pretty little girl, not quite two. As Kathy toddled across the floor barefoot, she stepped on the extension cord. The fans slowed down, almost stopped, then started again when she stepped off the cord. Margaret was the loudest of the group and hovered over her mother, asking her questions about her health, did she feel okay, had she called the doctor today, etc. Margaret looked over at me and said, "She is really not in good health."

"Oh, really?" I replied, not knowing how else to respond. My first thought was, *If she has five children already and is a grandmother, why would she be having another baby?* I didn't dare open my mouth. Thoughts of my own mother, who had Margie when she was nearly as old, flashed through my mind. The difference was that my mother was not exactly a sane person. The thought came to me, *Could this woman also have a problem that caused her common sense to fail her?* In time, the pieces would become clearer.

Jimmy and Jack were talking as Jimmy tried to get caught up on all the latest news. Mike stood by, hoping for some attention. They spoke about Jack's girlfriend, Diane. Her name came up quite often in the conversation, and I could tell that Diane was not a favorite. I just listened to see if I could learn more about these people. I wanted to see and hear for myself since I no longer felt any confidence in Jimmy telling me the truth. The plan was that Jimmy and I were going to be staying at Margaret's house. It was getting late, so we finally said our goodbyes and left. Margaret lived in a nice area of all-brick homes. Her house was small but neat, clean and very nice. She had an extra bedroom ready and waiting for us. When I was introduced to Margaret's husband, Kenneth, I quickly realized that he was the mastermind behind the nice house. Kenneth was young, sharp, and obviously knew how to handle his money. He had graduated from high school and worked for Delta Airlines. Neither Jimmy nor any of his siblings so far had finished high school. Jimmy had quit and joined the service, but at least the service had taught him something about discipline, a quality which eventually would prove to be in somewhat short supply in the Minor family.

That night when we were alone, Jimmy explained to me that the family was in the process of moving. He said the house they would be moving into was, as he put it, a "damn dream house." Well, this sparked my curiosity. He explained that his dad had had back surgery, had been out of work for a while, and they were just getting back on their feet. The next morning, we went back to visit his mother and meet his dad. As we walked in, his dad was standing at the stove, cooking. He now took care of the cooking since his wife was pregnant and not in good health. He was tall, and his round blue eyes had sort of a bug-like look to them. James smiled as Jimmy introduced me. He spoke with a slurring accent that I had trouble understanding unless I listened carefully. I wasn't sure what to call either of Jimmy's parents. Jimmy told me their names were James and Frances, so that was what I called them. During breakfast, there was an inordinate amount of talk about what I liked to eat, and I admitted that I had never had grits but was willing to try them. After breakfast, we went visiting, and I enjoyed driving around the various neighborhoods to see what they looked like. I liked Atlanta; it seemed easy, laid-back, and casual. The weather stayed the same each day, hot and sunny. Air-conditioning was still a luxury. You could get some relief in a movie theater, hotel, or a restaurant, but most houses were not equipped. Air-conditioning had not yet become an affordable option for most people.

A few days later, the family moved into the "damn dream house." This house was located on McDonough Boulevard, directly across the street from the Atlanta Penitentiary. It was a large old house with big rooms and high ceilings, which made it much cooler inside than outside. It was much larger than the run-down place they were moving from, but it was quite a stretch of the imagination to consider it a "dream house." The Chevrolet plant was only a block away, so it was convenient for James to walk back and forth to work. The only vehicle they had was an old work truck, which stayed parked on the dirt right outside the back door.

Jimmy and I spent all that day visiting with his aunts, his mother's five sisters. We arrived back at the "dream house" late in the afternoon. James had cooked dinner, and the family all gathered around the table. The chatter went on, and once again, the family proved to be obsessed about food. They asked me about what kind of food I ate up North, what kind of meals my mother cooked, etc. Of course, I fudged the part about my mother. "We eat the same things you do," I said.

"What about grits?" they asked.

"Well, they sell them in the stores, but I had never eaten them until I came here," I replied. The youngest, Michael, watched me closely and noted everything that I did, said, or ate. He was still recovering from the previous morning when I put some milk in my hot tea.

"I saw her put milk in her tea," he blurted out. "Eeewww." I tried to join in the conversation by asking my own questions.

"I noticed restaurants here that advertise catfish and hush puppies. What are hush puppies?" I asked.

"What?" they all replied loudly at the same time. "You've never heard of hushpuppies?" They all chattered about my question, looking at one another with twisted faces as if I were some sort of a freak.

"I'll tell her," Jimmy jumped in, as if to rescue me. He explained not only what hush puppies were but how they were made and how good they were. "Tomorrow," he said, "we will go out for catfish and hush puppies."

"Okay, that sounds good to me." I felt less uncomfortable with the group, and for a short period, I felt that Jimmy was on my side. These people had some kind of a hang-up about food, who ate what, and how much, blah, blah, blah. I couldn't understand why they were so interested in this subject or why any of it mattered.

I looked forward to the next day when Jimmy and I would be going out for catfish and hush puppies. I wanted to be away from the busyness of the family and have time for us to talk alone. As we got on the road, Jimmy suggested that we stop first at his high school friend Richard's house, which was on the way. After we pulled in the driveway, Jimmy said for me to come also, and we both walked up to the front door and rang the doorbell. Richard's new wife, Bobbie, whom Jimmy had never met, answered the door. She was pregnant, due any day now, and she and Richard were living with his parents. It turned out that Bobbie was the only one home, and she invited us in. She told Jimmy all about Richard, what he was doing, when they got married, etc. She suggested that we come back later when Richard would be there. "We are on our way to eat catfish and hush puppies," Jimmy said. "Would you like to come with us?"

"Oh, okay," she said, "but I don't have any money with me."

"That's okay," Jimmy insisted. "It'll be my treat."

I was annoyed with his unexpected invitation, but I didn't say anything. I didn't want this girl to come with us; I wanted it to be me and Jimmy. As I suspected, she and Jimmy did all the talking, and they yakked on as if they had known each other for years. She told him all about her pregnancy and spoke of things in detail that you would not generally tell someone that you had just met and didn't know very well. I just listened. I was embarrassed by some of what she felt it necessary to tell, like tales from her doctor visits and how her pregnancy made her feel in different parts of her body. As we arrived at the restaurant, she and I both slid into one side of the booth, and Jimmy sat across from us. Every now and then, I would glance at him to make eye contact, but he was so engrossed with Bobbie that it didn't seem to matter whether I was there or not. I tried to change the subject by mentioning the food, but nothing I did seemed to matter. I felt disrespected, ignored, and hurt that he would allow her to monopolize the conversation during what I had been looking forward to as a time for us to be together. Little did I know then that my being disrespected and ignored was how it was always going to be in our marriage.

When we drove back to Richard's parents' house, Bobbie suggested that Jimmy call Richard so we could make plans to go out together to eat or see a movie while we were there. I was never so glad to hear a car door close as when Bobbie finally got out. I wasn't excited about going anywhere with them, and I was hoping this would be the last I would have to be around her. I did wonder about Richard and what kind of a person he might be. It was still early afternoon as we drove back to "mother's." She was sitting out on the front porch, which was the best place to sit in the shade in the late afternoon. There were trees in the front yard that hung over the porch, and every now and then, I could feel a breeze. "Mother" was glad to see us and asked Jimmy all about Richard and his new wife. It was obvious that she wasn't crazy about Richard. Jimmy went in the house while she and I sat and talked. Frances was a heavy smoker, and she puffed on her cigarettes as she talked. "I wish that Jimmy would stay away from that Richard," she said.

I replied, "I haven't met him yet, but they're supposed to be making plans for us to go to see a movie tonight." Jimmy soon came out and said that he had spoken to Richard, and we were all set to go to the drive-in that evening. Theresa walked up and sat down with us. I enjoyed listening to her talk, and she was a cute girl. Jack and Diane came out to join us also. They all chattered, and I just listened, unless I was asked a question. I suppose that my accent was as different to them as theirs was to me.

By now, I was ready to get back on the road to New Jersey. Frances's baby was already two weeks late, and we had been there almost a week. I found Jimmy's relationship with his mother to be quite overbearing because of her unrelenting need for him to be there when her baby was born. Jimmy finally had to call, get his leave extended, and request that his check be mailed to Atlanta. Now the focus was on when his check would arrive because we were running out of money. I was feeling very antsy to get going back to New Jersey.

Frances was in the backyard spraying a patch of grass as we came out to leave for the movies. There was little grass in the backyard; most of the yard was dirt. Her hair was pulled tight to the back with a rubber band around it. As we got in the car, Jimmy remarked to me in an odd, nostalgic tone of voice, "Isn't she sweet. She looks just like an Indian princess, doesn't she?"

"Uh huh," I replied. His statement caught me off guard, and I didn't know Frances well enough to reply to her son's assessment. His mother and I had spent a lot of time talking on the porch. Sometimes I had trouble understanding all that she was saying, but for the most part, she had been friendly. I didn't dislike any of his family, but I felt as if there was more to this group than they were allowing me to see. I felt there was an odd attachment between Jimmy and his mother, but I also knew that they were putting forth their best efforts to impress me.

Richard and Bobbie came out when we pulled into their driveway, and Jimmy introduced me to Richard. He was tall and good-looking with a million-dollar smile. Bobbie acted different now that Richard was there; she was quieter and had little to say. I was not looking forward to being with them, but it turned out to be a pleasant evening. The movie was good, and there was little conversation. On the way home, Bobbie said she wasn't feeling well.

As we pulled out of their driveway, I mentioned to Jimmy that I felt we had been in Atlanta long enough, and I was ready to get back to New Jersey. "I have to stay until the baby is born," he snapped back rudely. I couldn't understand why this was so important, unless this was his baby she was having. None of this made any sense to me.

I was getting a strong feeling that expressing my thoughts was always going to be a source of contention between us.

"But we don't know when that might be," I replied.

"We'll wait until I get my check. If nothing happens by then, we'll leave." I was relieved that he was agreeable, even though it wasn't what Mother wanted.

The next morning, Richard stopped by to tell us that their baby had been born. He said they had a healthy baby boy. Jimmy's mother asked him what the baby looked like.

"Like he had a smashed-in face and bulging eyes," Richard replied with a smirk on his face. Frances and I went out to the porch. She was annoyed by Richard's statement, and I agreed that it was very crude. His rough statements detracted from his good looks.

"That is why I don't like him," she said. "He's not the kind I want Jimmy hanging out with. Jimmy isn't like that. He loves babies. You see how he loves Kathy, Margaret's little girl, and he will be just as crazy about y'all's too." As she spoke about her children, it soon became obvious to me that they were all held on a pedestal, and it was the spouses who were flawed.

Just then, the mailman came, and there was Jimmy's check. I was thrilled and went in to tell him and to suggest that we leave the following morning. He didn't answer me, so I assumed that that was the plan. We had been there almost ten days now, and I was antsy to get out of there. The next morning, July 3, we said our goodbyes. When we arrived home to New Jersey, Jimmy called, as promised, to let his family know that we had arrived safely. He was told the good news that his mother was in the hospital, that she had had a baby girl that morning, and all was well. For some reason, I felt relieved that we were already home when this event occurred. I still felt it odd for his mother to "need" Jimmy to be there.

I had quit my job at the restaurant, so Connie and I were home all day. This made for a better environment for Bart and Margie. We cooked dinner every night, did the washing, and kept the house in order. Phil's mother lived in Elizabeth, and when Phil had leave, he and Connie would stay at her apartment. Phil came from a large family and had many aunts and uncles. When Phil's family had a wedding shower for Connie, she got many nice things. She shared some of her gifts with me because in some cases, she had received two or three of the same item. Phil's family also gave Connie a baby shower, and when her baby was born at the end of August, she had everything she needed and more. Now we had a baby in the house and another on the way. However, Connie didn't hang around too much after her baby was born; she went back and forth to her mother-in-law's, sometimes for weeks at a time.

One evening when Connie was with us, we were all gathered in the living room. Connie was feeding her baby. My mother had been on a drunken spree, ranting and raving, and we kept hoping she would give up and go to bed. However, my mother unexpectedly put her coat on and walked out the door. We were all relieved when she left, but about an hour later, a police car pulled up in front of our duplex. This was always cause for panic because we never knew what it might be about. A police officer walked up on the porch with my mother, opened the door, and let her step in ahead of him. "I picked up your wife downtown. She's drunk, so I brought her home," the officer said, addressing his message to Daddy as if he were doing us a favor.

"What the hell is this, you pick up any other drunk off the street, and you haul their ass to jail. You pick her up and bring her home? We don't want her here. Take her to jail." My mother was in the dining room, yelling her obscenities in the loudest possible voice. The officer walked into the dining room, handcuffed her, and took her to jail. I loved it! Daddy had never done anything that bold before. I was so glad to see him stick up for himself and for us. We had had a long day of her, and it was such a relief to know that we were free of her for at least a few days. There was no peace with her there, drunk or sober.

By the time their baby was six weeks old, Phil received orders to be stationed at Virginia Beach. Phil went on ahead and had an apartment waiting. Daddy helped Connie pack up, rent a U-Haul trailer, and move all their furniture and belongings to Virginia. I soon realized that I could no longer afford my car. The payment and insurance were more than the small amount that I received from the government. I never did know how much Jimmy received; he never shared that information with me, and I never asked. Daddy and Jimmy spent one Saturday in Pennsylvania at the largest car dealer in the Northeast, shopping for another car. When they arrived home, my car had been traded in, and we were now the proud owners of some type of Plymouth. The only thing good about this car was that it was paid for. Other than that, it was a piece of junk.

There was a nice lake with a sandy beach on Earle Base that the enlisted men and their family and friends could use. Jimmy suggested one Saturday that I drive to the base and meet him at the lake. When I arrived, he was sitting on a towel, talking to some girl, and I felt that I was intruding. He had little to say, ignored me, and kept talking to the girl as if I wasn't there. The last time I had this feeling was in the restaurant with Bobbie. I was clearly sensing that there was something strange going on. Jimmy still felt free to talk to other women, and I was also learning that I could not predict when or why his anger would flare up. All in all, I was having a hard time figuring out his odd personality. Daddy liked Jimmy, and he invited him to go to the Freehold Track one Saturday. Jimmy talked about the fun they had for weeks later. Daddy's sense of humor and his relaxed demeanor always made it fun to be around him. Jimmy was impressed with Daddy's willingness to talk to strangers as if he had known them forever. Sometimes we would walk down to Gus's, order a pizza, and sit around and talk. Daddy knew all the guys that hung out there, and he liked introducing me and Jimmy to his friends. Daddy and Jimmy would drink a pitcher of beer, and I would have a Coke. I never again had any desire to drink, pregnant or not.

Jimmy and I looked forward to the day he would get out of the service. Jimmy talked about us moving to Atlanta, where he had plans to get a job on the police force. I introduced Jimmy to my friends Kathy and Jimmy Weaver, a young married couple who lived on South Street. I had met Kathy one day at the Freehold drugstore while I was still in high school. They had their own place, and they would invite Jimmy and me to come over and visit them. One night, Weaver and Minor made plans to go to a local bar and shoot some pool, and Kathy and I stayed at their house. She was now pregnant with their second baby. The next time I talked with Kathy, she mentioned that her husband would never be going out with Jimmy Minor again. "Oh, why?" I asked. "Did something happen?"

"It was just that after drinking a few beers, Minor kept picking fights with older men at the bar, trying to get them to go outside with him. It was always old guys, men he knew he could beat." What she said worried me because Jimmy's personality kept showing signs of disregard for others. By now, I was aware of his warped thinking, and although it worried me, I ignored it.

That Christmas, Jimmy surprised me with a diamond wedding and engagement ring set. He said he wanted to give it to me since all we could afford when we got married were the gold bands. He told me how he had put the set on layaway and paid on it a little at a time until it was all paid for. This impressed me. It was at these times that I would gain some confidence in Jimmy's commitment to this marriage. I justified in my mind that although he had some issues, he was a good person and just needed more time to mature.

Daddy's baby gift to me was a new crib. Jimmy helped Daddy put it together and set it up in our bedroom. I had been buying a few baby items all along and had enough to manage a newborn. A week or so before my due date, Jimmy came home from the base with a gallon container of ammonia. When he brought things like this home, I didn't think about the fact that he was stealing from base, but he was. He set the large bottle in the corner of the kitchen and began to tell me that it was a special kind of ammonia that only the government could produce. "It's completely odorless," he claimed.

"Are you sure?" I asked.

"Yeah, I'm sure. I use it to clean at the base all the time. Come over here and take a whiff."

"No, I don't think so."

"Oh, come on," he insisted, holding the bottle up with his hand on the cap. He walked closer to me, lifting it up, holding it closer to my face.

"Here, just take a big whiff." He removed the cap and moved the bottle under my nose. I took a small sniff and immediately started gasping for air and almost passed out. Jimmy was laughing hysterically as I gagged and continued to try to get my breath. I held on to the wall and walked out onto the front porch, hoping the fresh air would help me. When I came back in, coughing but somewhat recovered, Jimmy was still laughing and bragging about how he had fooled me.

Two weeks later, on January 8, 1963, our baby, James Lee Minor, was born. He was perfect, healthy, and I felt blessed. I can still hear Jimmy out in the hall on the telephone telling his mother that her first grandson had arrived. I could hear the air of excitement in his voice as he gave her all the details. Three days later, I was on my way home, and I could hardly wait to show my baby off. That morning, I dressed little Jimmy in his new baby-blue outfit with bunting to match. I got dressed, put on some makeup, and slipped into my black coat with the fur collar. I carried the baby; Jimmy carried the suitcase and diaper bag. As we walked up to the nurses' station to check out, one of the nurses remarked that I looked way too young to have a new baby, and I smiled proudly at her comment. It was a cold, gray January day when we left the Patterson Army Hospital in Eatontown, New Jersey, and more snow was in the forecast for that day. As we rode home, I noticed the dirty old snow all piled up on the sides of the road. At nineteen, I had little memory of ever being a child. I had thought of myself as an adult for most of my life, and now I had a baby to prove it. I hoped it didn't snow again before we got home. Something told me that this was the beginning of a very long winter and a long hard road ahead.

A few weeks later, Jimmy and I ventured out with the baby for the first time to visit with Kathy and Jimmy Weaver. I wanted everyone to see our beautiful new baby. Kathy's family was Catholic, and they had all their children christened in the Catholic church. Jimmy talked to the Weavers about how important it was to him that little Jimmy be baptized Catholic. Kathy's mother said that since she was active in her church, she could make all the arrangements. She offered to be the "godmother." I didn't know anything about Catholic traditions, so I let them make their plans. I had never heard of such a thing as a godmother, but I guessed it was something common in Catholic circles. Kathy's mother was a very responsible person, and it was because of her that I trusted the process. She bought little Jimmy a white satin christening outfit. The following Saturday, she came over, dressed the baby, and we all went down to the church. Jimmy had brought a friend from the base to be a witness. At about 11:00 a.m., the priest held little Jimmy, all fussy and squirming in his satin outfit. The priest asked us all questions. He wanted to know who the parents were, who were of the Catholic faith, and who were not. Suddenly, he handed the baby to me and said, "I will not christen this baby this morning. The father of this baby and this witness have been drinking. You will have to come back another time when there is more respect for this important event." I knew Kathy's mother was embarrassed. I was embarrassed. The men chattered on about the priest's comments as we all left. Little Jimmy and I were dropped off at home while Jimmy and his buddy went to a bar to spend the rest of the day.

One day, Jimmy caught me off guard with the news that his parents were coming for a visit in two weeks. They had some kind of fear of flying and would be coming by train. I was not opposed to their visit, but as usual, my mother was a nagging worry because her drinking, ranting, and raving episodes were not dependent on whether we had company or not. Neither did she care whom she mistreated or embarrassed. I knew there was nothing I could do to control the situation; I would just have to hope it worked out okay. Jimmy's parents arrived on a Friday night. Daddy, James, and Jimmy went down to Gus's for a couple of beers, and Daddy shared with me later how difficult it was to make any conversation with James. It was difficult to understand anything that he said because his words came out in grunts and slurred words. In addition, his head and arms kind of jerked while he talked, so I wondered if he had some kind of disability. I kept my questions to myself since I knew it would only cause an argument if I mentioned his father's speech to Jimmy. The next morning when Jimmy's parents got up, James asked for a glass of buttermilk with a raw egg in it. Frances translated James's request for me. Since I didn't have any buttermilk, he wanted the raw egg by itself in a glass so he could drink it. I asked Frances if I understood him correctly, and she assured me that was what he wanted.

James and Frances had a rented a nice car and suggested we all go for a ride that afternoon. Daddy came along, and Jimmy drove. First we went to Earle Base so Jimmy's parents could see where Jimmy was stationed. Afterward, we stopped at a restaurant in Long Branch for dinner, James's treat. Early that evening, Jimmy's parents left to catch their train back to Atlanta, and I let out a sigh of relief. We had made it through the weekend with no ranting episodes and no fires.

When little Jimmy was only a few weeks old, it was apparent to me that I was going to be caring for this child with little if any help from his dad. Jimmy Minor did not change diapers or feed babies. He believed that was women's work. Jimmy had a clear idea in his mind as to what was his responsibility and what was mine, and anything that involved a baby was not his job. Margie was almost ten years old now. She hung around me and helped me with the new baby. She had been abandoned by both parents, and I was the only adult around for her. Bart was now fifteen years old. He was growing tall and good-looking. Bart had my dad's quick wit; he was funny, entertaining, and very popular in Freehold.

The first signs of my mother's serious health problems, caused by years of alcohol abuse, were now beginning to surface. She was in her fifties; her health was failing, and her body was rejecting the alcohol. Now when she drank, she would become violently ill, sometimes vomiting blood. The bathroom door was directly behind our bedroom, and we could clearly hear the misery she was in. Jimmy would mention how he couldn't help but feel sympathy for her and wished she would get well. His words surprised me because her abusive ranting had extended to him and his Southern ways. I liked his concern for her and thought it showed there was goodness in him. Maybe his sometimes warped personality wasn't so bad after all. I truly wanted to believe that deep down, Jimmy was really a good person. As for my mother, she was now experiencing the early symptoms of the slow and painful death that was to come. Her body was telling her to stop drinking, and although she didn't stop drinking altogether, she would stop for longer intervals, giving her body some time to heal. As a nurse, she must have known all along what the future consequences of her drinking would be, and by now, the symptoms were too obvious to ignore.

That spring, Connie moved back home. She was pregnant with her second baby. Phil was soon to be out of the service, and they were going to settle in Freehold. In September, their new baby, Michael, arrived. Now the duplex was again full of activity; it was crowded, but we managed. I knew Connie's presence was just temporary, and she and her family would soon be getting their own place.

Any communication Jimmy had with his family was directed to the base, and his line of communication with them did not include me. I wasn't too surprised when he told me that Jack and Diane had gotten married, were expecting a baby, and were living with his parents. Jimmy suggested to me that since he would be getting out of the service the following June, that I go to Atlanta and stay with his parents until he was discharged. His exact words were, "M'er and Diddy [Mother and Daddy] would be honored to have you stay with them." He suggested that we drive down together, and he would fly back. That way, he could leave me with the car, and I would have a way to get around. After struggling with this "suggestion" for a while, I decided to go. I was willing to jump in and figured any change would be for the better. How wrong I was.

It was fall when we packed up the car and left for Atlanta. Jimmy told his mother we would be there the day after we were actually to arrive so he could "surprise" her. She was surprised, all right; they were doing some serious cleaning, and the house was in a mess. Little Jimmy was eight months old; Jack and Diane's baby, Cindy, was six months old; and Frances and James's youngest child, Sheri, was fifteen months old.

I was set up in a bedroom which I shared with Theresa. The room had two twin beds and was large enough for the baby crib. After each meal, Diane's job was to clean the kitchen. Diane was always working, doing dishes, or cleaning. It was clear to me that Frances didn't like Diane, and she was treated like domestic help or like an unappreciated stepchild. Diane didn't seem to let it bother her. I felt she was afraid to speak up for herself and knew Jack would never support her if she did. Frances dominated; she ruled, and all her children bowed down to her every whim, right or wrong. At this point, I didn't know the ropes, but I was learning.

There had been some changes to the "damn dream house" since Jimmy and I were there the previous summer. A serious plumbing problem had surfaced, and there was no running water in the kitchen sink. The bathroom also had a problem with a constant leak, and a thin layer of water floated on the concrete floor. So be sure to put on your shoes or, better yet, boots if you need to use the bathroom. The bathroom was now the only source of running water, so in order to do any cleaning, wash dishes, or whatever, water had to be drawn from the bathtub. Since I received a small allotment from the government, Jimmy and his mother set an amount that I was to pay for little Jimmy and me to stay there. Up until now, I had no idea that I would be paying room and board to live at the "dream house," but Jimmy and his mother did not share that part of the plan with me until I was safely moved in and had no choice but to comply. After I paid Frances, there was little left for anything else. As usual in my life, going along with someone else's plan was guaranteed to leave me feeling used, lied to, and taken advantage of. However, this visit did serve me well in other ways. I learned what kind of family I would be dealing with and gained a clear picture of who they really were. The Minors were completely different from the picture Jimmy had painted for me, right down to their financial status, and this move of mine was nothing more than a plan to help Jimmy's parents with their need for extra income.

Jimmy caught his plane back to New Jersey the following weekend. The Minor house was always busy with babies, people, and chatter. The evening after Jimmy left and the babies were asleep for the night, Frances invited me to sit in the living room with her so we could talk. She told me about how brutally her husband had treated her throughout their marriage. She started with his unfaithfulness and how he ran around with younger women while she was left at home to raise the children. One story was about a trip to Florida, during which James had attempted to push her out of a moving car. Another time, he had broken her jaw. I listened intently to the horrors she was telling me and became worried that I might be in for the same thing. She assured me that Jimmy would never do those things to me because he hated how his dad treated her. She talked about how James would leave her home alone when he went out to do his womanizing. She said Jimmy would stay up late at night, sit and talk with her, and try to console her through each ordeal. This was when Jimmy bonded with his mother as her surrogate spouse. As I knew all too well, there is nothing loving about a parent who uses their child to fill in the void left by a wayward spouse. This behavior toward a child ends up damaging that child, and Jimmy was no exception.

My most significant problem with Jimmy's family was the behavior of his baby sister Sheri. She was a biter, and none of the other babies were safe around her. She would quietly sneak around and wait for opportunities when a head was turned and bite the baby so hard that blood surfaced. If I heard a scream from little Jimmy or Cindy, I knew what had happened. I kept Jimmy with me all the time. It was not safe to leave him alone or take an eye off him if Sheri was in the house. Although Frances said that she didn't like it, she made it plain to Diane and me that it would be our responsibility to keep our babies away from Sheri. Her baby was never ever going to be disciplined, the reason being, in her words, "because I had such a hard time having her." I did my best to keep Jimmy safe. I wouldn't put him down unless I sat on the floor with him. One day, I had laid him down for a nap, closed the bedroom door, and sat on the sofa in clear view of the bedroom door. All of a sudden, I heard a blood-curdling scream and ran to the bedroom. Sheri had quietly opened the door when my head was turned, sneaked in, and bit Jimmy on the back, right through the crib slats. After that, I hung out in the bedroom at naptime while Jimmy slept. I had decided to come to Atlanta because of the safety issues at Center Street, but this house was no safer than where I had been. I was becoming resentful that Jimmy had encouraged me to make this wrong decision.

My evening talks with Frances continued sporadically, and I was learning a lot. I soon realized that it was not only Diane that Frances had a problem with, but she didn't like Kenneth either. She didn't think that either of them were proper mates for her outstanding children. Was I supposed to think that she thought I was okay? The problem with Diane was that she didn't appreciate how hard Jack worked, and she was not taking proper care of "Jack's baby." Kenneth's sin was not treating Margaret as well as she deserved. I tried to stick up for Diane since she appeared to be the mistreated stepdaughter who could do nothing to please the wicked stepmother. Diane was always working while everyone else sat around and watched TV or did whatever they pleased. Sometimes she would have to hold Cindy with one arm while she cleaned up with the other. Frances quickly informed me that Diane just looked as if she was always working because she worked so slowly and that Diane could have done the work in less time if she had done it correctly.

Once Frances blurted out, "I have a nigga that irons for me. Her name is Flossie. She comes every other Wednesday." I was taken aback by this statement and thought about Jimmy's stated prejudice toward black people on our first trip. I knew that the South was known for its racial prejudice, but hearing such a bold statement jolted me. Frances was comfortable about referring to Flossie as a nigger, but I thought it was a hateful way to describe this lady who was coming to work for her. Frances went on to tell me how she hated it when Jimmy joined the Marines because she feared that he would not be fed or treated well. She told me about how he had gotten involved in a few fights while stationed in New Jersey. He had been locked up, and she and James had to wire money to bail him out. This must have been before I met him. Jimmy had never told me about any previous fights or arrests, but I didn't let on to Frances that I was learning about my husband's history for the first time. I was certainly getting an earful, and I wondered why I had earned the privilege of sitting in the living room and hearing the scoop. Did she like me better than the other spouses? I doubted that.

Frances's sister Dorothy lived a few blocks up McDonough Boulevard. Frances and Dorothy were, as Frances called it, "not speaking." She told me that if I were to take little Jimmy on a walk in his stroller that Dorothy was not to see him. I was quickly figuring out how this group worked. Frances held all the power, and if she was on the outs with one of her relatives, the other family members were not to speak with that relative until amends were made and they were back in good standing with each other. Such nonsense!

The day Flossie came, I noticed that she addressed Frances as Ms. Minor just as Diane did. This sounded so odd to me. This black lady had to address Frances with respect while Ms. Minor referred to Flossie as a nigger. Somehow, this didn't sit right with me, but I knew I had to be careful because I was the oddball, and I was staying at their house. It was obvious to me that these people were lacking in more than an education. They had an air about them that reeked of unearned superiority. I soon learned that their prejudice was not limited to blacks. "Yankees" also did not measure up. The Minor sense of superiority was no more than a figment of their twisted imagination, and they were pitifully delayed in their thinking for the year 1963. Flossie ironed in the TV room right off the kitchen. She had a can that sat on the ironing board that she spat into every once in a while. I was told that it was a snuff can, but I wasn't sure what snuff was. I soon learned what it was by observing rather than asking questions. I was not asked to do any work while I was there, probably because I was paying for the honor of living in the dream house. Each evening before James went to work, Frances cooked a nice meal. She prided herself on her cooking. I was constantly questioned about what kind of meals my mother cooked and whatever dish I invented that my mother supposedly made. Frances would always reply the same way, "I wish I could get by that easy." Her constant need to question me about food and meals annoyed me, and who ate what and how much continued to dominate much of the conversation. This was all such nonsense to me. I would offer to help with the cooking or the dishes, but I was always told that it was not necessary. They had a routine, in which Theresa watched Sheri while the meal was being prepared, and Diane did the dishes afterward.

Little Jimmy was now nine months old. He was smart, full of energy, and just learning to walk. I had to watch him more closely now since he was curious and wanted to get down and explore. Frances paid no attention to her grandchildren; it was not obvious that she was the babies' grandmother, and little Jimmy had no clue who she was.

The only phone the Minors had was in the living room. Frances would spend hours on the phone in the daytime, especially after her husband went to work. One day as I was walking down the hallway, I overheard her on the phone saying, "Could you invite her over to your house for a day? I need to get rid of her. I can't stand her being here under my feet all the time. She's getting on my nerves." I had stopped before she could see me so she didn't know that I heard her. As I walked out to the front porch, I could hear her saying, "Well, go on now and do what you've got to do, and I'll talk to you later." A few minutes later, the phone rang. "Charlene, it's for you," she yelled to me. I wondered who would be calling me in the middle of the day. I picked up the phone and said hello.

"Hi, this is Margaret. How are you doing?"

"Okay," I replied.

"I was wondering if you would like to come over to spend the day with me tomorrow," she continued.

"Does Kathy bite?" I asked.

"Oh, no, you won't have to worry about little Jimmy being bitten while you are here." I agreed to go over because I was as glad to be out of there for a day as Frances was to get rid of me. I was quickly catching on to their schemes, dishonesty, and the real reason I was there—to stay out of the way and help with the finances.

One Saturday night, James and Frances dressed up and went out on the town, and Theresa was left in charge of Sheri and Mike. The next day, James and Frances didn't get up as usual. I asked Diane what was going on with James and Frances, and she said that they had been drinking. "What do you mean?" I asked.

"Every once in a while, they start drinking and go out dancing." The drinking and dancing routine continued for the next few days. Frances was a sight to behold, all dressed up, staggering into the TV room with her crooked lipstick, glassy eyes, and slurred speech. I wouldn't have missed that for the world. Theresa complained to her dad that she needed to get back to school. Frances and James stayed home the next day, hugging, kissing, and pawing all over each other. I kept my mouth shut and looked the other way as if I didn't notice. That night, they dressed up again and took off for the honky-tonk.

It took a few days after that for them to recover. It was at this time that Diane and I had a chance to talk. Since she and I were both the intruders, we had a lot in common. I always learned a lot from Diane because she had been an eyewitness to the goings-on and conversations that I was not privy to. The Minors liked to talk about being devout Catholics, but no one ever attended church, and their values and morals did not seem very solid to me.

Eventually, the parents sobered up, and things got back to the usual routine. Frances and James decided to fill up their freezer. They bought a pig and had it slaughtered, cut up, and wrapped. When they bought meat this way, they bought it all. Frances said that every part of the pig could be eaten. She fried up what she called cracklin'. This was some kind of fat that she also used to make corn bread. The pig's head was put in a large pot filled with water on the stove, and as the water boiled, the steam whistled up out of the pig's snout, and his ears stuck up straight on the corners of his hairy face. It was a sight I had never seen before, and I wondered whether Frances was planning to have pig head for dinner that night. However, I didn't ask any questions for fear of offending the cook. I was relieved when Frances put the pig's head in a large glass jar for Flossie to take home on the bus to feed her children. I was overtaken with the kind of generosity Frances showed her "nigga" that day.

A little over a month into my life at the dream house, I was certain that I was not staying until June, but I needed a reason to leave without making it look as if I wasn't grateful "for all they did for me." I had to think up something acceptable. Since Christmas was coming, I told Frances that I had planned to go home for Christmas. It sounded good, and I felt it would work without causing any rift. I called Jimmy to let him know that little Jimmy and I would be back in December. I started packing up my clothes and mailing them to Center Street. I was discreet with my process, but I knew that anything I left there I would never see again. I was worried about leaving my car, which was now giving me the freedom to drive to the post office to accomplish my secretly permanent getaway.

One incident that made me want to hurry my departure date had to do with Sheri swallowing a pill from a bottle I had secured in the top drawer of my dresser. My pill, which had been prescribed for a previous bladder infection, ended up turning Sheri's diaper red. Theresa was supposed to have been watching Sheri, but Frances was furious with me instead. She started lecturing me about how medication should never be left in a dresser drawer and how little Jimmy could have gone into that drawer just as well, so I'd better get used to making sure things were out of reach. I was kind of amused when Frances tried to imply that the incident was somehow my fault because between her and Theresa, they couldn't keep up with Sheri. I knew that the real reason Sheri got into the drawer was that no one was watching her, and she needed constant supervision. Little Jimmy was watched very carefully because if I didn't pay close attention to him, he would be savagely bitten. I looked forward with more and more anticipation to getting out of there. I kept a calendar in my drawer, marking off the days until I could leave. It was also a comfort to know that I would never live with them again. The message to me was now clear. The lies, the dysfunctional family, and the abuse of power were all staring me in the face and should have given me enough information to run in the other direction before I became any more victimized by them. Even though I knew this entire marriage was all wrong for me, I was bound by fear. My insecurities were stronger than my ability to turn my life in another direction.

Even though I had my doubts about Jimmy and his family, I loved Atlanta. The weather was delightful. I had been there through most of the fall, through beautiful sunny days and cool nights, and it was now the end of November. Little Jimmy started to pull on his ears as if he could have an ear infection, so on November 22, I took him to the base to see the doctor. As we drove to the base, the regular program on the radio was suddenly interrupted, and the news was reported that the president, John F. Kennedy, had been shot and killed in Dallas, Texas. My mind wandered to the times Daddy and I sat through the Kennedy-Nixon debates. I thought of John Kennedy's smile and how he always seemed so relaxed and at ease. He was too young to die. Then there was Jackie, how I envied her life, and how she seemed to "have it all." Now in an instant, life as she knew it had been shattered. I held tight on to little Jimmy. I still remember the wind blowing through my hair and how I tried to keep the hair out of my face as we walked up the long stairs to enter the medical building. On the way back, all the radio stations were flooded with the news, and when we arrived back at the dream house, the TV was blaring with all the details. We all crowded on the couch over the next few days to see and hear the latest. On November 22, they had arrested the assassin, Lee Harvey Oswald, and we watched two days later as Oswald was being escorted by police and detectives to the county jail. Suddenly, BAM! a shot came from nowhere, and Oswald dropped. It was hard to believe what we were seeing. We later found out that Oswald's killer was Jack Ruby, a Dallas businessman. We were all in a state of shock, united in our disbelief. I never thought I would experience an assassination of a president in my lifetime. I thought these were things that happened in history but not in today's world. I worried that the assassination would somehow have an impact on the airports, and I would not be able to leave as I had planned. I wanted to talk to Daddy because he would know if my worry was valid or not. On November 25, the funeral of President John F. Kennedy, an all-day event, was televised. That evening, I called home and talked with Daddy, and he assured me that the planes would fly as scheduled. I could hardly wait to get back home.

A week or so later, a large bed was put up in the TV room for Michael. Frances said that Michael was happier when he could watch TV in bed. The two youngest Minor children, Michael and Sheri, were spoiled and pampered beyond what was reasonable. They ran the show; they made the rules, and they would never be disciplined for any reason. With only two weeks left before I would be out of there, I had no doubt that my time at the dream house was nothing more than a financial deal, arranged to accommodate Jimmy's parents. I suspected that my time in Atlanta was also designed to give Jimmy his freedom to see other women and carry on as he had before he met me. I began to wonder what Jimmy Minor had been doing in New Jersey while I had been gone. Now and then, I thought about how he had presented this deal to me as a wonderfully loving opportunity and how his parents would be so honored to have me in their home. Yeah, right! By the time I left, I knew that the extra money was the only thing they were going to miss about me.

My worries about leaving my car in Atlanta were over one day when I put it in gear, and it would not move. The transmission was gone. Happily, the day I had long awaited had finally arrived, and I packed up whatever things I had left that I could fit into my suitcase. I had never flown before, and I was somewhat terrified. However, even though all sorts of fears went through my head, nothing could have stopped me from getting on that plane. It was a cold, overcast day in Atlanta that morning. I wished the sun would shine to ease some of my fear of flying, but it didn't.

The plane was full, and it departed as scheduled. Once we were in the air, the pilot spoke reassuringly over the intercom, and I decided to relax and enjoy the flight. Little Jimmy fell asleep on takeoff and did not wake up until we were landing in Newark. I felt lucky to be on my way back home. I knew it wasn't much of a home, but it was with people whom I loved and who loved me. I knew I would never go back to Atlanta unless I had my own place to go to. I was never going to fit into the Minors' way of thinking. Even though none of them were educated, they held onto a misguided belief that their Southern heritage and whiteness somehow made them superior. I never understood why their "superiority" mattered to them so much.

I gave a sigh of relief when the plane silently touched down. I had a window seat, and I could see snow falling every so lightly. I never loved the sight of falling snow as much as I did at that moment. As we taxied toward the terminal, I could see a crowd of people watching the plane from the ground. Daddy was unmistakable in his bright-red wool coat that stood out amid the crowd. We had always teased him about the coat, telling him that he looked like Santa Claus in it. Daddy didn't care; he just wore whatever anyone gave him and then wore his clothing for years and years. The red coat had been given to Daddy by his brother Ferd a few years back, probably after Ferd noticed that Daddy needed a warm coat.

Newark Airport was relatively small compared to Atlanta. There was no walkway that attached to the terminal, and I thought it would take forever before we were actually able to stand up and exit the plane. Little Jimmy was growing impatient and wanted to get down. The line finally started moving, and then I was stepping onto the landing platform on our way down. I held Jimmy, diaper bag on my shoulder and the other hand on the railing for support. The air smelled clean, blowing snow that was now falling harder. As I reached the last step, Daddy walked over and took little Jimmy from me. Jimmy was all excited to see his Pop Pop. We hugged and kissed Daddy. I never thought I would ever be this grateful to be back home. I could feel the tears coming, but I managed to keep my composure because I knew that my crying would only make Daddy uncomfortable. He simply did not know how to handle emotions, whether his or anyone else's.

Connie and Phil were now settled in an apartment in Freehold. Phil had landed a job at 3-M as a pipe fitter, a skill he had learned in the service. Connie shared with me that while I was in Atlanta, she had run into Jimmy one night, and he was out with another girl. She asked me not to tell Jimmy that she had told me, and I didn't. However, I had suspected that kind of behavior from him before she ever told me. I had asked myself why Jimmy had suggested that I go to Atlanta, once it became obvious that it was not to make things better for me or little Jimmy. I had figured out that Jimmy wanted to get us out of the way so he could get back to his womanizing lifestyle and at the same time furnish his parents with some extra cash. I was learning that Jimmy was not only untrustworthy but selfish. Little Jimmy and I were of little importance to him, and his behavior and character kept telling me that I had made a terrible mistake getting involved with him in the first place.

Little Jimmy was now eleven months old. He was a handsome baby, smart and full of energy. He was walking very well now and had already started repeating words. He would say "bye-bye" to everyone when we were leaving. He loved Daddy, and he would get all excited when he was invited to ride in Pop Pop's car. His vocabulary increased quickly, and he would talk in sentences very plainly well before he was two. Even though I believed that Jimmy loved his son, he spent little time with him. He was never willing to be inconvenienced, and the baby was my job, not his.

The afternoon of Christmas Eve 1963, snow had started falling, and Jimmy and I walked the few blocks downtown to do our Christmas shopping. It was fun walking downtown, where the streets were all decorated with wreaths laced with red-and-green ribbons. Christmas carols echoed as the snow began to fall more heavily. We shopped at the Ben Franklin five- and ten-cent store and picked out a few toys for little Jimmy. We laughed about how poor we were and how we didn't even own a car. The streetlights came on as it got darker. We walked home, slipping and sliding, playing in the snow and having fun together. When we were having fun like that, it was easy for me to forget about the negative, thinking that it was all just temporary, and in time, Jimmy would change. I really didn't want to admit that I had made such a poor choice. We had a delightfully beautiful child, and I wanted everything to work out for us.

One afternoon Connie, Phil, and Daddy were sitting at the dining room table, talking. Phil was holding little Michael, who was just a few months old, and Jimmy and I were in the kitchen arguing about something. Jimmy had drunk a few beers that afternoon and was advertising it. At one point, Jimmy blurted out angrily, "You're my wife, and you will do as I say."

As Jimmy walked through the dining room, Daddy spoke up, "Hey, you don't talk to her that way."

Jimmy was furious. "I'll talk to her any way I want."

"Oh, no, you won't. Not while you live here."

"She lost her rights when she married me," Jimmy continued, showing what an ass he was. The atmosphere became tense. Phil handed the baby to Connie and stood up at the table. Jimmy was no match for Phil; he was cornered, and he knew it. He left in a hurry, slamming the front door behind him, and then he picked up a snow shovel off the front porch and threw it against the door. Daddy ranted on about how he never knew of a Southerner who could drink, and Jimmy Minor was no exception.

Jimmy's hitch in the service was finally coming to an end, and there were only a few months left until he was, as he called it, "a free man." I knew he wanted to go back to Atlanta; I also knew that Atlanta offered more opportunity than Freehold did. Nevertheless, I was fearful of leaving because of Jimmy's behavior and the extreme ups and downs of his moods. One thing I was sure of was that I did not want to live anywhere near his family. The day of Jimmy's discharge, he came in and set his seabag down in the middle of the living room floor. He told me he was going out to celebrate, and he left as quickly as he arrived. Once he was gone, I looked through his bag. I came across a letter from a former girlfriend that he had hooked up with when I was in Atlanta. He may have still been involved with her for all I knew. In the letter, she expressed her love for him and talked about when his divorce would become final. This divorce was news to me. When Jimmy arrived back home, I confronted him with the letter. "You had no business going through my bag," he complained.

I insisted, "Tell me about this pending divorce that I have just learned about."

"Give me the letter."

"No, I'm keeping it. I might need this as proof of what has been going on."

He argued, "It's none of your business."

And I yelled back, "Oh, yes, it is. It's very much my business." He was caught, and he knew it; I had the letter in my hand. Jimmy pulled up the ropes on his seabag, threw it over his shoulder, and left for the airport. He was going home to see Mama.

I spent the next few days and weeks reading and rereading the letter. Somehow, I was not all that surprised. I thought about things his mother had told me about Jimmy. I looked at him as another one of her children who could do no wrong and had never been disciplined if they did. She had worried that he wouldn't be fed right in the service, and I had felt at the time that there was something wrong with that statement because she was not talking about a three-year-old who needed his mommy. I knew that Jimmy's mother was going to be a problem for me because it didn't matter who her children chose to marry; they were never going to suit her. Her hatred and prejudice were becoming more obvious to me, and I knew I would never measure up to her qualifications, any more than the other in-laws had. There was as much wrong with his family as there was with mine; it was just a different kind of wrong. I didn't know when I would hear from Jimmy again. As I sorted out all the facts, I was leaning toward not going to Atlanta. I had made a poor decision, and I wanted out of this before I got into it any deeper. I knew it was not going to be easy to get child support for little Jimmy. I had no money and no job, but the fear of going to Atlanta with no protection was a heavier burden.

After a few days, Jimmy called and brought me up-to-date about the "family." They had moved. They had managed to purchase an older home that needed some work, and they were planning to fix it up. I wondered if it had working plumbing but didn't ask. Jimmy told me that he was looking for a job and would send me some money. Jack and Diane were still living with the family, now in an unfinished attic. Jimmy and I continued to communicate. I would mostly write to him since calling was expensive back then; besides, I wanted to do what I could to avoid his mother. Someone later told me that when Jimmy would receive one of my letters, his mother would give it to him and stand over him while he read it. As she stood watching, he would then tear the letter up into tiny pieces and throw it into the garbage. I knew that this was Jimmy's way of giving me the privacy and respect that a wife deserved. Jimmy's mother must have been highly annoyed by his actions. I know she was just dying to read my letters in order to find out what was going on between us. Her meddling would always remain a source of contention.

As the weeks rolled by, I was faced with another problem that might throw a monkey wrench into any possible choice that included leaving Jimmy. I started to suspect that I might be pregnant. I prayed that it wasn't true and tried to figure out how this could have happened. I had used birth control without fail and was so very careful. However, all my wishing and hoping did not change the fact that I was pregnant. Oh my, what was I going to do now? Connie suggested that I go to the welfare agency in Freehold, tell them the situation, and get some help. I walked downtown to the welfare office, but the lady I spoke with was both unsympathetic and arrogant. She told me that my situation was my own fault, and I needed to figure out a way to support myself and not lean on welfare. I left in tears. As I walked home, I couldn't stop crying, shaking, and wanting to scream. When I reached Center Street, I turned down one of the side streets and walked for blocks through the streets until I could calm down. I knew that no matter what, I would never ask for welfare again.

I presented the news to Jimmy and suggested that he come back to New Jersey and get a job. We talked on the phone, and many of our conversations were less than agreeable. He was always angry, as if everything was my fault. I suggested that we just go ahead and get a divorce. "Okay, if that's what you want. I'll take little Jimmy, and you can have the new baby."

"Oh no! It isn't going to work that way."

He refused to come back to New Jersey. I asked about his previous plan to join the Atlanta police force, and he said they weren't hiring. I later found out the truth that the police force wouldn't accept Jimmy because of his previous arrest record. Jimmy insisted that a good job was forthcoming since he had lots of applications pending. He told me about one job that sounded very good, but it was not an option for him since it was in Stone Mountain, about twenty-five miles from his mother's. "What's wrong with that?" I asked.

"Oh, it's too far to commute."

"Too far from what?"

"Too far from 'the house,'" he said, annoyed with my question. I knew this was about what his mother wanted instead of what was best for us.

I tried not to focus on the negative situation I was in. I knew I wouldn't be able to deal with two babies, living on Center Street without any money, and worrying about my mother's behavior. I also knew it would be a battle to get any consistent child support from Jimmy Minor. His next call was less than a week later to let me know that he had landed a job with Fisher Body, a division of the Chevrolet plant where his dad worked.

He was calmer and suggested that if I was willing to come to Atlanta, he would rent an apartment for us. He said that he wanted me to come. I told him that I would have to call him back to let him know. I was so fearful about this move. I spoke with many friends about my fears, hoping I could make a wise decision and not just jump in without thinking it through. I was told more than once that I could always come back if it didn't work out. That advice sounded reasonable, but I worried that it was never going to be as simple as it sounded. The idea of our own apartment was very inviting to me because I so badly wanted a safe place for little Jimmy. The stress of a new baby on the way was a gnawing worry, so I decided to go and hope that things would somehow work out for us. I was prepared to do my part, although I had a lot of fear about how I would be treated.

Chapter 10

From Bad to Worse

In June of 1964, Daddy drove little Jimmy and me to La Guardia Airport in New York, and we boarded a plane bound for Atlanta. As I kissed Daddy goodbye, I thought about Bart and Margie and worried about how they would get along fending for themselves. I had an uneasy feeling about leaving, not only for Bart and Margie but for myself as well. It was a beautiful day, and little Jimmy looked so precious in his new sailor outfit that a friend had given him. The flight was as smooth as silk, and little Jimmy was asleep as the plane climbed into the air. In Atlanta, we were the last to exit the plane. I waited as everyone else went ahead. It was finally our turn, and as we walked down the bridge to the concourse, I could see Jimmy ahead, waiting for us. It was a grand reunion, and little Jimmy was all excited to see his daddy. We got into the car Jimmy had bought recently, and as we drove to the new apartment, Jimmy told me about the furniture he had bought. He was as anxious for me to see the apartment as I was. He told me how lucky we were to get an end apartment because those were at a premium, and everyone wanted them. We finally arrived at Wellswood Apartments, and Jimmy had his key out before we got to the front door. It was a simple apartment but clean and neat. It had two bedrooms and a bath upstairs and a kitchen, living room, and a small playroom downstairs. After I got unpacked and settled, Jimmy suggested that we take a ride to his mother's to see their new house. I was a little antsy about this, but he said the family would all be there to welcome us back. I was surprised when Frances made a big deal out of little Jimmy as we arrived because she had paid so little attention to him when we lived with her.

I hoped this would be a new beginning for all of us. I wanted to get along, be friends, and not start off on the wrong foot. I wanted to forget about the months I had lived with Jimmy's family, put the experience behind me, and start over with a good attitude. Having my own apartment and my own space was going to make living in Atlanta much easier. The house Jimmy's family bought was nice. It needed updating, but all the plumbing worked, and it was in pretty good shape. It was a large older house, all brick with a large covered front porch that spread across the entire length of the house. Frances suggested that we sit out back on some lawn chairs that were positioned under a large-shade tree. Margaret was there, pregnant again and due two months after I was. Diane also came out and sat with us. I let little Jimmy run and play, but I should have known better since Sheri was there, and she was still undisciplined and now had the teeth of a two-year-old. It wasn't long before I heard little Jimmy scream; Sheri had bitten his hand so hard that it broke the skin.

James, who had been working in the garage, came out, grabbed Sheri, popped her on the behind, and told her to go into the house and stay there. Sheri let out a loud scream and stood on the back porch, carrying on as if she were being killed when James continued to deny her access to her mother. Sheri was used to getting her way, and that was probably the first correction she ever had. When it became clear that James was not going to let Sheri come back out, the screaming got louder, and Frances started squirming in her chair. She and Margaret looked at each other as if they were both in pain. "I just hate that she got whipped," Margaret said in a pitiful voice, directing her comment to her mother as if they had both seen a severe beating. These two were two peas from the same pod. Margaret didn't care what her mother did, said, or believed; she automatically agreed with her. I often wondered how Margaret would have felt if it had been her child who was getting bitten. I was enjoying Frances's discomfort to the max. Diane and I glanced at each other, catching an instant of eye contact, and I knew she was salivating in the pleasure of it all as well. Neither of us made any comment. Jimmy also said nothing, but I was glad that he was there to witness the scene firsthand. It was time for him to see for himself how Sheri was allowed to brutalize these two babies while his mother looked the other way. To Sheri's credit, she was a fast learner. After one swat and one time-out, she never bit anyone else that I ever heard of. As for Frances and Margaret, they were never going to change.

One rainy Saturday morning, Jack stopped by to ask Jimmy to help him with a car problem he was having. As they walked toward the door to leave, I asked Jimmy when he would be back. He didn't answer me. While he was gone, I decided to venture out with little Jimmy, drive downtown, and try to learn my way around. I found a place to park and a five- and ten-cent store to shop around in. As I entered the store, the first thing I saw was a lunch counter, actually two lunch counters. I sat little Jimmy on a swivel stool at a counter, and he had fun turning back and forth on the stool. We were the only ones at the counter, and we were getting stares from the waitress, but no one waited on us. I looked around to see if there was something wrong. I noticed that the other counter was busier, and everyone seemed to be getting served. After we moved over to the other counter, I realized that one counter was for blacks, and one was for whites. I was not used to any of this, but I was learning. I then noticed that the bathrooms and water fountains were labeled white and black. I remembered reading about segregation when I was in high school, and I watched on television the reports about the conflict in Little Rock and how blacks were treated. Now I was seeing segregation firsthand. I thought the segregation situation had changed since most of the conflicts were back in the '50s, and this was 1964. Maybe Southern society had changed to some extent, but in downtown Atlanta, segregation was still very much alive.

As the days passed, I was beginning to feel more and more at ease. I had no trouble making friends, and the apartment complex was loaded with young couples, most of them families like us with young children. Several of the women in the complex were pregnant and due around the same time I was. Jimmy worked the 4:00 p.m. to midnight shift, and after he left in the afternoon, I would visit with the neighbors, or they would come to visit me. I stayed busy keeping the apartment spotless, cooking, and taking care of little Jimmy. The summers in Atlanta were hot and humid. Since the sofa opened to a full-size bed, some nights we would open the sofa bed, and all three of us would sleep downstairs where it was cooler.

I missed my family, and thoughts of how I left Bart and Margie behind were tormenting at times. On Friday paydays, Jimmy didn't come straight home from work, and when he did come home, he had been drinking. I didn't make waves about the drinking because I sensed that complaining would just rile his anger and give him the fuel to justify it. When the time got closer for the baby to be born, I asked Jimmy to come home right after work since we didn't have a phone. He did come home early that night, and as I suspected, it was time to go to the hospital. I no sooner was in a room when a nurse came in, gave me an injection, and the next thing I remember was another nurse standing over me telling me that I had a baby boy. Everything was blurry, and I just wanted to go back to sleep. I must have drifted back out of it, and when I woke up again, I was being lifted onto a bed in a ward with three other women who had just given birth. It was September 19, 1964. I had the bed next to the window, and I sat up in bed, trying to stay awake. I remember that I was so groggy that I put sugar on my mashed potatoes, thinking it was salt. Jimmy was there trying to talk to me, but I just wanted to go back to sleep. I asked him if he had seen the baby yet, and he said he had. "How does he look?" I asked.

"He is huge. He weighed eight pounds and five ounces," he said in a sort of bragging tone because, in his family, size mattered. I must have drifted off as he spoke. The next morning, the world looked quite different to me, and I wanted to know all the details and see my new baby. The nurse kept coming in and taking my temperature because she claimed that I had a low-grade fever. Jimmy and I had already decided that if this baby was a boy, he would be named Scott Alva Minor. Scott's middle name was my father's first name and was chosen to honor him. After breakfast, a nurse came around with the babies and handed them to the mothers in the room. I was excited to see my baby for the first time, and I was amazed at the size of him. He was an absolutely beautiful baby; his bald head was perfectly shaped and laced with some light-peach fuzz. He was strong and healthy, and I could tell right away that he looked more like me. He was calm and easy to hold, and I was reluctant to give him up when the nurse came back to get him.

I asked for my tubes to be tied when Scott was born, but the doctors refused, arguing that I was too young. I still feel to this day that it was wrong for them to decide what was right or wrong for me; I was an adult, and it should have been my decision, not theirs. The birth control pill was now the newest, safest, and most effective means of birth control, and when I ended up taking the pill, it gave me a sense of control over my worry about a third pregnancy.

Word of the new baby spread quickly. The buzz through the family was, "Did you hear how much 'Jimmy's' baby weighed?" Big always impressed this family, and size came close to food as a Minor obsession. Jimmy's family came to the hospital to visit me and to see "Jimmy's" baby. Margaret kept saying, "I said I'd have a bigger one than you, but now I am not so sure." The part that amused me the most was the "I said" since another Minor quirk was the belief that saying something would make it so. Now that she had seen Scott's size, she was not so sure that her "saying it" would make her baby bigger than mine after all. All I wanted was a healthy baby, but in the Minor world, boys were more valuable than girls, and big babies were more valuable than little ones. Margaret had enough trouble with my having boys while she had girls, but now I had to outdo her on the size issue as well!

Jimmy had called my family from his mother's house to tell them the news. I was back in the apartment in a few days, and I wasted no time borrowing a camera from a neighbor so I could take pictures of Scott. I wanted my family to see how handsome he was. I was able to call home from time to time from a neighbor's house, but since I had to call collect, I didn't call very often. I remember one time in particular when Bart answered the phone. He told me that he was in a band with two of his friends from school, Bruce Springsteen and George Theiss. Bart said he had bought a new set of drums and was taking lessons. I asked how Daddy was. "He's still a bum," Bart answered. I said nothing, but I felt the sting of his remark. I had never thought of Daddy as a bum; he was all I had to depend on. Maybe things had changed since I left three months ago. The worry of what was really going on at home gnawed at me.

I could sense Jimmy's growing indifference to me. His attitude was becoming less than pleasant. He would pick fights and blame it on how difficult it was for him to live with someone who was on the pill. "Just throw the pills out. You act crazy when you take those things," he would say. He would use the pills as his excuse to stay away from home, go out drinking, or whatever else he did. He was always on edge, antsy, and uncomfortable staying home with us. He still had this warped idea that taking care of babies was not his job. He was annoyed when the babies were crying or needing attention, and he couldn't hear the TV. He never changed a diaper or fed a baby. Our life was supposed to be about him and his needs. The weekends were the most difficult for me with two babies and little else to look forward to. I was grateful for my neighbors, who were kind and friendly. We all had young children and could spend hours talking about how we all coped.

One Saturday soon after Scott was born, Jimmy started picking one of his arguments. He made it plain to me that where he went was none of my business; therefore, I was not to ask any questions about his plans, and he angrily stormed out the door. As evening came, Jimmy had still not showed up. I put the babies to bed, and by 11:00 p.m., I went to bed also. Around 4:00 a.m., I heard a loud knocking and banging on the front door. I was afraid to go to the door, but I slipped on some clothes and walked down the stairway ever so slowly. As I approached the door, I looked through the window and could see that it was Jimmy's old friend Richard and his wife, Bobbie. I opened the door. "Jimmy's in trouble," Bobbie said in a panic. "He's been locked up, and we need some money to get him out."

"I don't have any money," I answered.

"Well, what are we going to do?" Bobbie asked, angered by my answer and a little drunk herself.

"How would I know? I have small children here, including a three-week-old baby. Go see his mother. Maybe she'll help you." I closed and locked the door, went back upstairs, and got back in bed. I thought about the $25 Daddy had sent me when Scott was born and how I had hidden the money in my jacket pocket in the hall closet. I felt that I needed to hang onto whatever money I received from my family; it wasn't much, but it gave me a sense of security. Jimmy handled all the money, and he believed that since he earned the money, it all belonged to him. I was often reminded that none of his money was mine, and if I wanted something, I would have to ask him, and he would decide if my request was valid. I finally went back to sleep, knowing Scott would soon want to be fed. Before 6:00 a.m., I was awakened by the baby's cry. I loved these two babies; their needs were constant, but I did my best to care for them. As we all went down the stairs together, there was still no sign of Jimmy. I knew that eventually I would hear from someone, but for now, I was not going to worry about him.

As the sun was just beginning to shine through the front window, I heard a key turn in the front door lock. Jimmy walked in first, his mother right behind him. One look at him and it was obvious that he had been beaten up. His face was red and swollen, and he had a black eye. They plowed in as if the only thing that mattered was Jimmy. I continued to feed Scott while I waited for some explanation. They acted as if I wasn't there, talking to one another, ignoring me and the children. Frances insisted that Jimmy lie on the sofa, and he listened to her directions as she kept telling him what to do to help his wounds heal. You would have thought she was some kind of a nurse. She kept focusing on Jimmy's wounds, repeating, "I hate what they did to you. I just hate it." She then turned her head toward me and said, "He will probably need something to eat, but not anything too heavy." I ignored her comment, acting as if I didn't hear her. She said nothing else to me, never acknowledged the babies, and just kept doting over Jimmy. I kept waiting for her to leave, but I feared that she might decide to spend the entire day at our apartment. Finally, she stood up and said, "Well, I'll go and let you get some rest. I hope you are feeling better. Let me know if you need anything." I was just glad to hear her say she was leaving.

As soon as the door closed behind her, I thought, *What a joke. He goes out, gets drunk, gets in a fight, and she goes down and bails him out and acts like he's a ten-year-old kid who has come down with the flu.* I am sure that they both saw her actions as nothing more than motherly love, but in reality, there was nothing loving about it. She was an enabler. If she really loved him, she would not have approved of his behavior; she would have allowed him to pay the consequences instead of bailing him out, feeling sorry for him, and making him look like a wimp in front of his wife and children. She clearly gave him the message that he could do whatever he wanted, and she would be there to make sure that he didn't have to suffer any consequences. Thanks to her, he would never learn anything from his mistakes and would never grow up and become a responsible adult.

After she left, I walked over to the sofa and, with my hands on my hips, looked Jimmy straight in the eye and kindly asked, "What happened? You told me you could fight."

"I got jumped by two guys," he explained in a pitiful voice. This incident kept him home for a while; he stopped hanging out at the bars, and our lives improved, as we did more things together as a family. Sometimes on the weekends, we would take the boys to the zoo or to Fun Station where there were rides for the kids. If getting beaten up made such an improvement in his behavior, I believed it needed to happen to him more often.

In hindsight, I can clearly see how similar our two families were. In Jimmy's family, the father abused the mother, and in my family, the mother abused the father. Jimmy and I both grew up in homes where we felt responsible for the happiness and well-being of the abused parent. Both families kept having children to keep the system swinging in the same direction. Also similar in the two families were the two victimized parents, Jimmy's mother and my father. Both were extreme enablers who never sought out solutions that might lead to a better life for themselves and their children. These were not marriages bound by love but by need and by fear, and I was determined not to follow the same pattern. However, the grown siblings from both families were all enmeshed in toxic relationships that had little chance of happiness. The length of a marriage is not the measure of happiness. It is the level of respect, honesty, and trust that you give and receive from each other that binds you, making real love possible.

I was still learning the ropes. This was to be my first Christmas in Atlanta, and Christmas was a big event with the Minor family. Frances called Christmas her "Annual Tree." Little Jimmy was not quite two, and Scott was three months old. Kenneth and Margaret had a new baby girl, born that November, and Jack and Diane were expecting their second baby. Connie had mailed me a box of baby clothes that her boys had outgrown. These were expensive baby clothes that I would have never been able to buy. I had Scott dressed up in a winter-white outfit that got everyone's attention, and his personality was also a hit; he was a happy baby, and everyone who smiled at him got a smile back. The older kids all wanted a turn holding him. Little Jimmy's vocabulary was quite extensive for a two-year-old, and the men especially loved talking to him and asking him questions just so they could hear his answer. I did my best to fit in and be friendly. When I saw the conditions under which Jack and Diane lived in the attic, I was never so glad that I had my own apartment to go home to.

For some unknown reason, Frances seemed more vengeful toward Diane than toward Margaret's husband, Kenneth, or me. When Frances found out that Diane was expecting again, Frances told Jack they would have to move out. It was obvious to me who the favorite children were, and Jack was not among them. Frances claimed that another baby in the house just wasn't going to work for her. I knew Diane was happy when she got that piece of news because Frances's eviction was the only way Diane was ever going to escape living in an unfinished attic in the home of a mother-in-law who hated her. Jack and Diane found an apartment in the same complex Jimmy and I lived in, just a few blocks away.

The months ahead were rocky to say the least as Jimmy's hostility toward me got stronger. He would even complain about how much money I spent on groceries. He gave me a set amount of money that was barely enough for a week's groceries. He was an extremely poor money manager, and yet the checkbook, the car, and the apartment were listed only in his name. He was critical of how I kept house and said that I didn't keep the children quiet enough for him to hear the TV. His moods could change on a dime. He had a system to his madness, which amounted to a system of abuse and reward. For some time, he would have nothing positive to say about me, and he would act cold and indifferent. Then after one of these periods of negativity, he would decide to give me a reward, which was always something he decided I would want. It was never my choice, always his, because he controlled everything. One time, he decided that I could make an appointment to get my hair cut and styled while he watched the kids. I always accepted his offers since I needed the breaks. However, after every reward, the negative behavior would start again. Jimmy didn't abuse the children other than ignoring them. I knew better than to ask him for help with the kids because helping was always going to be his offer and never my request.

That spring, Jimmy suggested that I take a trip to New Jersey to visit my family since they had never seen Scott. I jumped at his offer. Back then, flying was a dress-up event, but I did not have many clothes, let alone a nice dress. My mother wrote me a letter telling me she wanted to buy me a dress for my trip because she was working and could afford it. My mother seemed excited about my visit, and I was excited because I hadn't been home in almost a year. My mother's interest in me was a surprise, and I was kind of elated that she was becoming so attentive to me. Could something have changed? Jimmy made the reservations, and I called to let Daddy know when our plane would arrive at Newark Airport. The closer the time came to leave, the more excited I got. Somehow, I felt that things had changed, and my mother had sobered up, maybe due to her health. Maybe she had had a change of heart about how her life was going, and she had decided to turn things around. All I knew was that I couldn't wait to get back home and see for myself. My mother's communications with me felt good. The unspoken message I got was, "I am glad you are coming. I want to see you and your two babies." I hoped I was reading this right. I needed to be welcomed, to feel some kind of love from my family and some indication that they cared whether I was okay. I wanted to know that I had been missed as much as I had missed them.

The dress came, and I couldn't wait to open it. I tore off the wrappings like a kid. It was a pink-and-white dress in a checked flannel type of fabric. I loved it! I ran upstairs and tried it on. It was perfect! This all added to my anticipation. On the other hand, I wondered why Jimmy had all of a sudden suggested such an expensive reward. Was he really sorry for the disrespectful way he treated me? Maybe he was sorry for calling me a whore in front of the kids, and this was his way of saying he was sorry without actually saying it. Or did he just want the freedom to patronize the bar scene, with me and the kids safely out of the way? It was probably the latter. Whatever the reason, it didn't matter to me; we were going, and I was happy about it.

I was all packed and ready to go the night before our flight. I didn't want to forget anything, and getting out the door in the morning with luggage, diaper bag, and babies was an ordeal. However, in my new dress, I felt like a real person again for the first time since Scott was born. The constant demands of two babies had left little time for me to focus on myself. After we got to the airport and it was time to board, the three of us got situated with Scott on my lap and Jimmy in the seat next to me. Since this was a breakfast flight, I had to balance Scott with the tray table, and he was difficult to hold. I tried to eat while keeping Scott busy with a piece of toast. After I had a few bites, the whole tray turned over, and all the remaining food went all over my dress and on the floor. The stewardess tried to help me to clean up with wet towels, even offering to hold Scott. Of course, he wasn't going for that arrangement and let us both know that he wasn't happy. This was the world of babies; no one was to blame, and no one needed to fix it.

As the plane landed, I could see that it was still winter in New Jersey. I loved the familiar scene of dirty snow piled up everywhere, and I looked forward to watching little Jimmy play in the snow. I was glad to see Daddy as we exited the plane. It was an hour and a half ride from the airport to Freehold. When we pulled up in front of the duplex, I stepped out of the car and glanced at the familiar scene of

Center Street; the cold gray air smelled no different than when I had left. However, I realized how different my life was now as I juggled Scott on one arm and the diaper bag in the other. Daddy took charge of little Jimmy, and they were buddies again. I was sure my mother was waiting inside the duplex, anxious to see us, especially the new baby. However, soon my anticipation turned into disappointment; when I turned the corner into the dining room, my mother stood there, drunk and ranting the same story she had been ranting about when I left. Her glassy eyes wouldn't look at me. I broke down and cried because I had once again allowed myself to be sucked into hopeful expectations that everything would be different this time.

Connie came to see us, and I was glad to see her and her children. She took Scott from me and made a big fuss over him and little Jimmy. Daddy couldn't understand why I was crying. He kept asking Connie, "What are we going to do about Charlene?"

"Just forget about it. She'll get over it." It wasn't something you could explain to him because he still couldn't see anything wrong with the picture. As the house filled up with people and babies, my mother staggered up to her bedroom to "get some rest."

When Bart and Margie came in from school, I was thrilled to see them. Bart was tall and handsome. He told me about his band, which practiced in the living room a few days a week after school. "Where do you find room in the living room to set up a band?" I inquired.

"Oh, we just move all the furniture over to one side, and we have plenty of room." He had nicknamed my mother "the Big E." "If 'the Big E' becomes a problem, I call her down to the basement, run upstairs, and lock the door behind me. I just let her stay down there until we are done practicing. We're pretty good. You'll get to hear us while you're here." Bart showed me his new drum set, and it was first-class. He was very proud of his involvement with the group, and I was happy for him that he had found something to take the edge off his bad home environment. The second afternoon that I was there, Bart's friends came in and put their band equipment together just as Bart said they would. All the furniture was pushed to one side of the room, and the practice began. I stayed out of their way and kept little Jimmy busy so he would not be in their way. Some of the kids in the neighborhood positioned wooden crates under the front windows and listened to the practice. I could hear the band from the kitchen while I started supper. Bart and his friends named their group the Castiles.

Bart also took care of Margie now. He cooked dinner every night and would be there to see that she had what she needed. Bart was a delightful young man, coping as I had before him with the never-ending, intolerable situation. Margie was eleven now, and she loved the babies. I was suddenly glad that I was there to give Bart a break and spend time with him and Margie. I cooked the meals for the week and kept up with the wash. Daddy let me use his car each day so I could go to Connie's apartment and also visit a few girl-friends I had not seen in a while. This gave me a place to go during the day, and little Jimmy loved going since he would have other kids to play with. It was tempting to pretend that I had never left Center Street, and being around my family felt better each day. In my heart, I wished I had never left because I loved my family, and I knew they loved me. However, I also felt in a strange way disconnected from my previous life. Jimmy Minor and his abusive attitude had created a very different atmosphere for me. I felt cold and uncomfortable in my own apartment, but it was my home now, and life with Jimmy and the babies was my new reality. It was a good week away from reality for me, and it was over way too fast.

Since Jimmy and I had been in our apartment for six months now, we were eligible to get our own phone. I listened as Jimmy told his mother about it one day while we were visiting the Minors. "Now don't get your phone number listed," she insisted.

"Why not?" I asked, not understanding why it mattered.

"Because it keeps it more private," Jimmy answered, agreeing with his mother. As soon as Jimmy left the room, I asked his mother to explain the advantage of an unlisted number.

"Bill collectors," she answered. "You don't want bill collectors calling and bothering you." I said nothing; I was now getting the drift of it. If you didn't pay your bills, you wouldn't want anyone calling and suggesting that you pay up. Since Jimmy was the "money manager," having an unlisted phone number would be helpful to him in case he decided not to pay the bills. I wasn't used to this type of thinking because I would never think of not paying bills. So far, we had good credit and had paid what we owed on time. But the Minors were always ready to rip someone off, and once again, I noted a lack of character in their skewed ideas. The mother dictated the family rules, and they all agreed with her. I balked at this unlisted number idea, arguing that it wasn't necessary, but of course, I lost the battle. Anyway, it was a relief for me to have a phone in case of emergency since I was home alone with small children much of the time. I could also call home when I wanted to now and not have to bother the neighbors.

In the weeks ahead, I could sense Jimmy's attitude toward me becoming even more hostile, and lying became a regular occurrence with him. He spent more time at his mother's than he did with us, and Saturday was his day to do as he pleased while I stayed home with the babies. Only his wants, his needs, and his well-being were important. I was merely there to take care of the house and the children and to uphold his twisted image as the perfect husband and father. I could feel my role of wife and mother becoming more and more of a commodity and a convenience to him. I was supposed to be the quiet and obedient house cleaner and childminder, and it was his mother who held the real place of importance in his life.

Spring was especially delightful in Atlanta, and I could smell the freshness in the air. The apartment complex was brimming with blooming azaleas. I would have loved to pack up the kids on Saturdays and take them to Grant Park or anywhere they could swing and play, but there was only one car, and Jimmy was in charge. One Saturday, Jimmy had left early in the morning, and by late afternoon, I had not heard from him, but this long absence was not unusual. That afternoon, Diane walked up to my apartment with her babies in a stroller. She was looking for Jack and thought maybe he was with Jimmy. I invited her in, and after talking awhile, we came to the conclusion that Jimmy and Jack were most likely together. We spent the rest of the day together, and little Jimmy loved having Cindy to play with. Diane's new baby, Nancy, was two months old, and Scott was eight months old. I got out my camera, and we finished up the film, taking pictures of the babies playing and having fun.

As the sun started going down, Diane called "the house" to see if Frances knew where Jimmy and Jack were. Margaret answered the phone. She said she had no clue where Jimmy and Jack were, but Frances and James were on vacation and wouldn't be back until the following day. Diane suggested that we call the police station to see if maybe our husbands had been in an accident or picked up for some other reason. When we made that call, we learned that our husbands had indeed been picked up and were both in jail. We called Margaret back to let her know. Diane and I laughed about what Frances would think about her babies being in jail when she was not there to bail them out.

Diane shared with me some events that had occurred through the years when she lived at "the house" with Frances and James. She told me about one recent night while I was still in New Jersey, and Frances and James were on a binge and making plans to go out for the evening. Frances kept inviting Jimmy to join them; he was refusing to go with them, but Frances kept egging him on to come. "Come and join us. Don't worry about Charlene. She will never know." After more of her coaxing, Jimmy gave in to her request. Around three the next morning, they arrived back home. They had all been drinking and were talking loudly. Diane awoke when they came in, and she went downstairs to use the bathroom. Just as she came into the dining room, she met up with Jimmy and his "date" on their way out. Jimmy was startled to see her. Diane looked Jimmy in the eye but said nothing. Later that day, Jimmy confronted Diane with, "I don't expect you to tell Charlene what you saw last night. Do you hear me?" She couldn't remember what her response was. Diane went on to tell me that when I left that Christmas to go home, Frances told everyone how glad she was that I was finally gone because she had to keep an eye on James and worried constantly that I might be having an affair with him. Over that one, Diane and I both laughed until we couldn't laugh anymore. However, the story about Jimmy and other women worried me. Once again, I wondered what had I gotten myself into and how I was ever going to get out of this mess.

IDENTIFYING THE ENEMY

I had two innocent babies who deserved better than this. I didn't want to believe what Diane was telling me, but I knew it was true. I kept my promise not to let Jimmy know she had told me, but I would think of Diane's story when an issue came up, and I needed to validate my feelings of disgust for both Jimmy and his mother. Diane was going through the same pain and punishment from the family that I was, and we had only each other to share with. I still hoped that in time, things would change, that either life would get better for me, or I would find a way out. Since it was getting late that Saturday, Diane decided to pack up her babies and walk home. After she left, I thought about the situation I was in. Jimmy Minor had so far proved to be of little value as a husband and father. The only thing positive I had accomplished by coming to Atlanta was moving to my little apartment, which was a safe and a peaceful environment for my children.

Late the next morning, Jimmy and Jack wandered in. Jimmy had little to say, but Jack kept complaining about his night in jail and how horrible it was. I did not respond to any of his comments. When Jack left, I expected Jimmy to talk about the ordeal, but when he continued to say nothing, I asked him about it. I was quickly told that where he went and what he did were none of my business. If I questioned his authority, he claimed that "I was pushing my luck." I never understood what "luck" he was referring to. The foundation of our marriage had deep cracks in it. At this point, amends could have been made, but the chances of that happening were slim because Jimmy never showed any remorse for what he did. "I'm sorry" was not part of his vocabulary. His mother saw to it that he paid no consequences, and instead of giving him sound advice, she applauded his bad behavior. It became more and more apparent as time went on that Jimmy believed that men had rights and privileges that women did not have. He believed that women should be subservient and were under the man's authority, a possession rather than a partner. My hope was that in time, he would mature, grow out of his childish behavior and skewed beliefs, sever the ties to his mother, and become a responsible husband and father. The chances of this happening were slim, but for now, I had few choices, small children who depended on me, and no better place to go. Jimmy continued to complain about my birth control pills, but I ignored his remarks and became more determined not to risk another pregnancy. He knew that it was only because of the babies that I was still with him. He also knew that more babies meant that he could continue to control me. I wasn't going for it; I had already had enough of him and his warped family.

The year was 1964. The Beatles were hot, and Lyndon Johnson was president. President Johnson signed the Civil Rights Act of 1964, which prohibited discrimination based on race, color, religion, or national origin. It also provided the federal government with the power to enforce desegregation. This meant there would be no more separate eating counters in restaurants and no more separate water fountains or bathrooms. The Civil Rights Act was a huge victory for black Americans, especially in the South where there was strong resistance to change.

Back in New Jersey, things were not good. My mother's drinking was getting worse. The duplex was a mess, with no meals cooked by a parent, no clothes washed, and the filth piling up. Daddy stopped coming home after work; he ate at the Freehold Diner most nights and hung out with his buddies from Gus's. Tex was having trouble getting gigs for the Castiles, and all the band members but Bruce were losing interest. Bart took an after-school job at the Higgins Funeral Home just a block away on Center Street. The boys still hung out together, but the band was gone. Bart continued to look after Margie. He would come home from work and cook dinner for the two of them. Bart was an exceptional young man who showed far more wisdom, decency, and concern for others than either of his parents.

Whenever I called home, the bad news from Center Street caused me much grief, and I felt guilty for having left my family. When I took a look back at how I struggled with my decision to leave, I became more convinced than ever that I had made a poor choice. Taking care of two babies and tolerating the abuse of Jimmy Minor was making Center Street look more and more like an oasis for me, and I was needed there.

One afternoon that winter, I was surprised by a visit from none other than Frances. Jimmy had already left for work. Frances never came to our apartment except for the times she bailed Jimmy out of jail, and it was unusual for her to just stop by. She explained that she had been down to "Jack's apartment," and she had walked up to my apartment to wait for her ride. She explained that Jack had the flu, and Diane wouldn't take care of him, so she had to go down and "see about him." This was the story as she told it to me.

"I walked upstairs, and there was poor Jack, in bed with a fever. I put a cold washcloth on his head and asked him what his symptoms were. From what he told me, I was sure he had the flu. I got him out of bed, took him into the bathroom, washed his hands and face, and gave him two aspirin. After I put him back to bed, I went downstairs and fixed him something to eat. He was feeling much better when I left." This was just too outrageous, and it was all I could do to keep from smiling as the words rolled out of her mouth. Was Jack not a grown man with a family? The seriousness on her face as she told me was almost unbelievable. She spoke as if she were talking about a five-year-old who needed a mommy. That was how she succeeded in making useless wimps out of all three of her boys.

Jimmy was first in line to get his taxes done as soon as his W-2 arrived. His motivation was the refund. Paying someone to do your taxes was new to me; Daddy always did the taxes. Jimmy and I were both delighted when we found out our refund would be $500. That doesn't sound like much in today's world, but back then, it was enough for a down payment on a house. We started looking at houses for sale. The residential neighborhoods in Atlanta were still segregated, and Jimmy's aunt told him about a repossession across the street from her in a white subdivision called Rebel Forest. We went over to take a look. This house was an FHA repossession, and it had been taken back by the government, completely remodeled and was ready to be resold. It looked as good as new. It had newly refinished hardwood floors, fresh paint, and it showed well. The floor plan was exactly the same as that of Margaret and Kenneth's house. The worst part of the property was the backyard, which had a few feet of level ground and then a hill that went straight up and flattened out sort of like a mesa. The price was good, and we could afford to buy it. So far, our bills had been paid on time, and we had good credit. We both wanted this house, but since I had made so many friends at the apartment complex, I wasn't as excited about leaving as Jimmy was.

I hoped this would be a turning point for us, and things did seem to be better for a while. One Saturday, Jimmy suggested that we all go to Stone Mountain Park, and we had a wonderful day. We rode the train that went around the mountain, and little Jimmy got to ride a pony. We took pictures and had a great time. Scott was not old enough to enjoy much of it, but he did enjoy having me carrying him around all day.

One day, Daddy called to tell me that Bart had joined the Marines and would soon be leaving for boot camp at Camp Lejeune, North Carolina. This news was troubling to me because the Vietnam War was still raging. I questioned why Daddy didn't try to guide Bart in another direction, but Daddy never really guided us in anything. He didn't care what decisions we made as long as it didn't involve him having to go to church or give up drinking. Daddy was smart about a lot of things, but he lacked wisdom about life and how to live it.

Since we were now homeowners, Jimmy applied for a Sears credit card. Once he was approved, Jimmy bought our first lawn mower. By the time the lawn mower was out of the box and put together, it was loaded into the car and taken to his mother's house to cut her grass. This annoyed me, but I dared not to mention it. Weeks later, our grass was still in need of cutting, our lawn mower was still at "Mother's," and our grass had to wait until she decided to return it. His parents were doing better financially, now that James had a loan shark business that he ran at the Chevrolet plant. He loaned money to his coworkers, charging 10 percent interest, in an illegal, under-the-table type of operation. Jimmy now spent more time at "the house." His primary relationship was with his mother, and Jimmy felt about me the way his mother felt about the black lady who ironed for her. I was given a small amount of money each payday to buy the groceries. I had to make that money stretch for the week because if I complained about needing more, Jimmy would ask for the receipts so he could check that I was not spending any of the money on what he considered to be nonessentials.

Daddy called to ask if Margie could stay with us for a while because Bart had left for boot camp, and that left Margie home alone. Jimmy agreed to let her come. Margie's presence with us was a big help to me. For one thing, I would now have some company and some help with the babies. Also, Jimmy's behavior and attitude toward me improved because he was careful not to let Margie see the other side of him. The extra money Daddy sent was also helpful. Margie started school that year in the eighth grade. She made new friends at school and would sometimes spend the night with a girlfriend. The mother of one of her friends tried to encourage me to visit the church she went to. I listened to what she had to say but felt that the fight I would have to have with Jimmy was not going to be worth it. I had no power, no authority, and was afraid to stick up for myself. I encouraged Margie's new friendships, and for the most part, she adjusted as well as could be expected. I knew that she missed Daddy and Bart, and in her short life, she had already lived through a tremendous amount of trauma.

In June that same year, Jimmy's sister Teresa was going to marry her boyfriend, Tommy. This was a big deal in the Minor household, and they were planning a big Catholic wedding. According to Jimmy, because his parents now had money from his dad's "business," the Minors were now a family of great prestige and importance. I silently laughed to myself when Jimmy shared with me that his parents were personal friends of Bert Parks, emcee for the Miss America pageant. When I was alone, I would chuckle at Jimmy's attempts to convince me that these lowbrows were better than I knew they were. In the world of the Minor family, success was not linked to talent or character but to how much money you had, regardless of how it was acquired. Your level of importance was measured by whether you drove a Cadillac or a Ford. It was all about exploiting what they "had" as opposed to who they really were.

With the wedding day approaching, Jimmy came home with a new outfit for me to wear. It was never okay for me to suggest that I pick out my own dress. I was supposed to wear what Jimmy decided on, and if I didn't like it, I was an ungrateful bitch who didn't appreciate anything he did for me. He often told me that I didn't know how lucky I was, that he couldn't understand my ingratitude after all he had done for me, including rescuing me from Center Street. I knew he shared with his mother all his dissatisfaction with me, and she fed his negative attitude, which then made him even more hostile toward me. If we had an argument, she knew all about it. In her opinion, I was a "Yankee" and just not right for her Southern boy. She knew by now that I didn't agree with her Southern way of thinking. Her prejudice was deeply rooted not only against blacks but against anyone who was not part of her network. Anyone who questioned her ways or asked "why" was a threat to her. One thing that I began to put together was why this family had no friends, and their only interactions were with each other. I never knew of one friend outside of family that Frances ever had. The only nonfamily friend I knew that Jimmy had was Richard, one of his bar buddies.

Christmas was only a few months away, and the "Annual Tree" at the Minor house had become a much bigger and more elaborate event. This was our first Christmas in our new house, and Jimmy went all out with elaborate decorations and gifts. It was only because of the extra money Daddy sent that we were able to buy all that we did. Jimmy also had the Sears charge card, which quickly filled up with charges and interest. I was badly in need of some new clothes and shoes but did not dare express this to Jimmy because I was going to have exactly what he wanted me to have and nothing more. Expressing what I wanted was a sure way of not getting it. That Christmas, I had trouble hiding my disappointment when I opened my gift. Jimmy was big on surprises, and he had gone to a lot of trouble, wrapping the gift in several boxes so I wouldn't suspect that it was a piece of jewelry. When I finally got to the smallest box, there it was, just what I needed, a dinner ring. It was an oval pinkie ring made of sterling silver filigree with two blue stones. *Where would I go wearing a dinner ring?* I thought. It wasn't that it wasn't nice or that I didn't like it but that it wasn't practical. I needed clothes, shoes, underwear, a bathrobe, and slippers. Jimmy Minor lacked common sense, but I did understand why he bought me the ring. His life was all about his struggle for importance and his need to show the world that he was as significant as his mother insisted he was. Giving his wife a dinner ring and having her wear it made him feel important. Jimmy was furious when he realized that I wasn't thrilled with the ring, and I was berated for my lack of class. I soon found out that his dad also sold jewelry on the side, so that was another reason I got this useless gift.

Chapter 11

Spousal Abuse Continues and a New Baby

The New Year was 1966, and at our house, the battle raged on about the birth control pills. I wanted to get a job, but I had no transportation, and there was no way Jimmy would help me overcome that barrier. Day care centers were becoming more popular as many mothers were starting to enter the workforce. I called about a few jobs I saw advertised in the paper and mentioned them to Jimmy, but he became angry if I even brought up the subject. I knew he was threatened by the fact that a job would supply me with my own money, more choices and exposure to other people, and eventually a way out. Besides, the wives of important men don't work.

January 8 was little Jimmy's third birthday, and it was the coldest day in Atlanta so far that year. I had a party for little Jimmy. I bought a cake with blue-and-white icing and cowboys, Indians, and horses on top, and I invited some of his little friends from the Wellswood Apartments that he hadn't seen since we moved. His dad made sure he was not around for the event because anything related to children just wasn't his job.

This year when we received our income tax refund, Jimmy decided that we could buy a new living room suite and tables to go with it. This purchase was meant to show me that I didn't need a job. I would rather open a savings account and hold on to that money, but I didn't dare express my ideas. After all, everything was Jimmy's. He told me that the only reason the house had my name on the mortgage was because the law required it. He also told me that if I ever decided to seek a divorce, all he would have to do was transfer the mortgage into his dad's name, and that would prevent me from having any claim on the house. I felt more and more fearful of Jimmy's threats.

Frances was now reaping the rewards of James's loan sharking. She had her hair bleached blond and drove a Cadillac. I was becoming more and more resentful about her constant meddling in our lives. In reality, she was Jimmy's primary partner. I watched out the front window one day as she pulled up in front of our house. When Jimmy walked out to the car, opened the driver-side car door, and got in, Frances slipped out of the driver's seat and slid toward the middle. I watched as he drove away with her sitting right next to him, the two of them looking as if they were on a date. By law, he and I were husband and wife, but really, his mother was his psychological wife. He was the faithful spouse she never had, and I was the "other woman." I believed he had played this supportive role for his mother since childhood. I remember Frances telling me how James would go out womanizing, and Jimmy would stay up with her into the wee hours so she wouldn't be left alone. I felt that I was in the way of their relationship, but I would have been glad to give him back to her. Every time I began thinking about how to get out of this threesome, I would come to the conclusion that I needed a job and a way to earn my own money. I also needed to stay on the birth control pills; I was terrified of another pregnancy because I knew that Jimmy needed babies to keep me captive, and I wanted out.

Back in New Jersey, a car sideswiped my mother as she walked to the bus station one morning on her way to work. My mother was knocked down but was virtually unhurt. However, my mother seldom missed an opportunity, and she insisted she was hurt and needed an ambulance. At the hospital, it was decided that she had a few bumps and bruises but was not in need of hospital care. My mother wasted no time suing the insurance company for damages, and she was awarded a settlement of around $750. Of course, she was not going to share this money with anyone. She called to tell me about her "good news" and said she wanted to get a bus ticket to Atlanta and come down for a visit. The thought of her coming down put me on high alert. What if she came and started drinking? I crossed the conversation off as just talk, and I doubted she would really come. However, a few weeks later, the phone rang in the middle of the night, and it was my mother calling from the downtown Atlanta Greyhound Station. Jimmy got up and drove to the bus station to get her. Even though she sounded okay on the phone, I worried about what condition she might be in. It was barely daylight when Jimmy's car pulled up the driveway. I watched her get out of the car and noticed her disheveled clothes as she came through the front door. She appeared to have just come off a binge; at least I hoped that was the case because that meant it would be more likely she would not be needing a drink for the next few days. My mother's constant chain-smoking annoyed me, and I barely slept while she was there for fear that she would smoke in bed after we were asleep. She did stay sober the few days she was in Atlanta, but just her being in the same house with me was worrisome. I sighed with relief when on the fourth day she told me that she needed to be on her way. She mentioned buying a bus ticket to New York. "Why are you going to New York?" I asked.

"Oh, I did my nurses' training at the Mary Fletcher Hospital in New York, and I think I have a pretty good chance of getting a good job there." I knew she was not going to fare any better there than in Freehold. I tried to convince her to go back to Freehold, but she wasn't going for it. I didn't argue with her; I was just glad she was leaving. I knew a binge was about to happen, and she had the money to support it. I felt relieved the day she left. Spending those few days together, I realized that I didn't know this woman. We found little to talk about, and she had no interest in my life or how I was coping with two babies. I went to extra trouble to cook nice meals, thinking she would appreciate my efforts. Although she seemed to enjoy the meals, she never expressed any gratitude. All the while, I was walking on eggshells in case she might change her mind about leaving and decide to stay longer. The morning she left, I smiled as I watched the car back down the driveway to take her to the bus station. I felt free of the anxiety that loomed whenever she was present.

It was well over a month later that Connie called. "Is Mommy still at your house?"

Sort of shocked at her question, I answered, "No, she left over a month ago. She bought a bus ticket to New York City. Her plan was to go the Mary Fletcher Hospital with hopes of getting a job."

"Well, we don't know where she is. No one has heard from her. We thought maybe she was still at your house."

"Oh no, I tried to convince her to go back to Freehold, but she insisted on New York. I'm not going to worry about it. She'll show up somewhere eventually." I was always so relieved when my mother was gone that I never worried about where she was or what trouble she may have gotten herself into. I had a long time ago detached from her. The not knowing was like a resting place until her face once again emerged, as it always did. For Connie, it was different; she felt she needed to stay connected to our mother.

Less than a week later, Connie called again. She had received a call from the YWCA in New York City saying that her mother was there and needed someone to come get her. She was coming off a month-long drinking binge and had come to the Y from the Bowery section of the city. The Bowery was a slum area of New York City where the drunks slept on the street with newspapers over their heads. Connie agreed to pick up my mother, and she asked Daddy for the $30 she needed to get there and back. Daddy refused, saying he was unwilling to spend the money. He said, "Just leave it alone. Don't worry about it. She will find her way back home, eventually." That was my attitude also, and I would never have been willing to travel to New York City to bring her home. For whatever reason, Connie felt different, and she begged Daddy for the money until he finally gave in, as he always did in the face of Connie's persistence.

Connie found a babysitter for her children and boarded a bus to New York City, carrying a change of clothes for her mother as the lady had instructed her. Connie was a young girl in her early twenties who had not traveled much, and all she had was an address to her destination, a YWCA in a slum area of New York City. Soon Connie found herself walking alone through a very rough neighborhood. Connie was always much braver than I was, and she was never scared of much, but she admitted that she was terrified of this walk of six or so blocks to the Y. Once she reached her destination, the matron ushered Connie down a long flight of steps to the basement. There the rancid smell of filth was sickening. The matron opened one of the many doors, stepped back, and let Connie walk in ahead of her. Connie's first view of our mother was even more nauseating; she was lying on a filthy mattress on the concrete floor of a very small room with cement block walls and no windows. She had been wearing the same clothes for weeks, and her dress was stained with piss and dried vomit. The matron pointed Connie to the bathroom and offered the use of a shower to clean her mother up before putting her in clean clothes. By the time Connie arrived home with our mother, it was dark out. I admired Connie for making this effort, although I didn't believe that anything that was done or not done for our mother would make any difference. After all, she was an addict, and change was never going to depend on any rescue effort mounted by others. Rescuing my mother was never going to help because it just kept her from paying the consequences for the misery she created for herself and others.

A few weeks later, there was another drunken rampage and another fire at the duplex on Center Street. This time, my mother burned her legs pretty badly and had to be hospitalized. Connie and Phil were now settled in a new house in Jackson, a town near Freehold. Connie suggested that Daddy move in with her family since they now had extra space. Connie and Phil agreed that my mother could come also, but if she started drinking, she would be out. The advantage to this move for Daddy was that he would no longer be the legal head of the household. Previously, as long as Daddy maintained a residence and was married, my mother had as much right to live there as he did. Living in a home where Phil was the head of household would change all that. Under this arrangement, if the police were called, Phil did not have to allow my mother to live there. Daddy would now have choices that he never had before. After thirty years of working, Daddy didn't have many possessions to pack. A few cardboard boxes of clothing and a few pieces of furniture were all that were salvaged. Even the old dining room suite was left behind.

Connie explained the new living arrangements to my mother. She was not pleased, but that was the way it was. Connie said that at first, the arrangement worked out fine, and our mother managed to stay sober for almost three months, a record for her. The day she started drinking, her raving was soon in high gear. When Connie had no luck calming our mother down, the police were called. Connie refused to have the same old scenario repeated in her home, around her children. My mother was arrested and taken to jail.

I am sure that Daddy felt a new sense of freedom. He called me one afternoon to tell me that he had quit his job at 3-M. I couldn't believe it! He had applied for his retirement check in a lump sum, and he wanted to come to Atlanta and buy a small business of some kind, like a corner store or a Laundromat. He said he was tired of punching a time clock, but it was unlike him to take such a risk. He came the following week, and his check came two weeks later, for all of $1,500. He searched the paper for businesses for sale, but after less than a month, he realized that the small amount of money he had was not going to buy much. He decided to go back to New Jersey and see if 3-M would give him his old job back. He was welcomed back, but not on the premium day shift that he had before; he would have to work the four-to-twelve shift. Not long afterward, he bought Margie a plane ticket to come home; now they would both be living with Connie and Phil. Margie was excited to be going back home, but she was tired of being shifted around. She really had no home to speak of but had been living in her sisters' homes.

That spring, when Bart was almost finished with boot camp, his platoon was given the weekend off before graduation. He called to tell me that he was hitchhiking down for the weekend, and I was thrilled that he was coming. We spent the next day getting caught up on all the latest news. We cooked hamburgers outside on the grill and enjoyed our time together. We talked for hours about our family problems and how we had survived in spite of them. We laughed at things that were not funny when they happened, but now that time had done some healing, we enjoyed the humor that we couldn't see before. While Bart and I were having a wonderful time together, I could sense Jimmy's anger that I was actually laughing and happy. That evening, Bart suggested that we find a good movie, but Jimmy rejected the idea and said to count him out. It was not possible for Bart and me to take the kids to the movie, so I asked Jimmy if I could leave them with him. He flatly refused: "When are you going to understand that I am not your babysitter?" He spoke with his eyes glued to the TV, without ever looking up at me. When I told Bart, he knew I was having serious problems. My real fear was that Bart would not feel welcomed and would not want to come back to visit again. The next morning, Bart had to leave early since he had to hitchhike, and he was hoping to get a ride straight through. I was sad to see him leave, and I wished he hadn't joined the service. Jimmy's rudeness to me and even to Bart made me feel more and more trapped by this marriage. I realized that I had given up all my rights to make my own decisions or even to be treated with respect. All I could think about was how to get out of the marriage, but with no home to go back to, I could see little hope of my situation changing.

A month after Margie left, Jimmy was laid off from his job at Fisher Body. This gave him lots of extra time, and on the weekends, he was back into the bar scene. He hooked up with his old friend Richard, who had just started a job with Aetna Insurance Company as a sales rep. Since the company was hiring, Jimmy applied, using Richard as a reference. The training was free. and if you did your homework and stuck it out long enough to pass the test, you could eventually become a licensed agent. This job had endless possibilities for advancement, and Jimmy had no trouble getting hired. One afternoon, he brought home a gun and showed it to me. I was terrified as he stood there with a gun in his hand, but he insisted that he needed the gun for the type of work he was doing, which included collecting large sums of money. My fear concerned the combination of the gun with Jimmy's temper, and he had never needed a reason to hate me. However, this job was short-lived, and I never saw the gun again. Neither he nor Richard had the integrity or the wherewithal to stick it out and learn the business, so it was back to unemployment.

Jimmy's real desire was to be a policeman, and I could see why. He liked being in charge, bossing others around, and acting on his and his mother's grandiose belief that he was a superior human being. He liked to brag about the sharpshooter medal he earned in the service. A uniform and a gun would put him in the position he felt he was most qualified for and would also provide good opportunities for womanizing. He was already convinced that he was above the law. He applied a second time at the police academy but was again turned down because of his arrest record. Jimmy filed for unemployment compensation, which paid the rent and bought a few groceries. Of course, he blamed the shortage of money on me. He insisted that I get off the birth control pills because we could no longer afford them. The birth control pills were relatively cheap, but I was barely scraping by with the groceries. At my next appointment, I asked the doctor if he would give me a prescription for a diaphragm, and the following month, instead of getting my birth control pills, I had my prescription filled for the diaphragm.

Jimmy liked collecting the unemployment checks. He now spent most of his time at his mother's, and he only half-heartedly sought out employment. Not having any real skills made it more difficult for him to find employment. I found it difficult to make friends in this Rebel Forest neighborhood. I later found out that Rebel Forest was notorious for being a neighborhood of white trash, repossessions, and renters. Our next-door neighbors used their backyard as a garbage dump. I became extremely lonely staying at home for long periods with two babies. Some days, in desperation, I would take the boys for a walk to a nearby 7-Eleven. The girl that worked there was always very friendly to me, and she and I would make small talk between customers. I never had any money to buy anything, but I needed a place to hang out and someone to talk to. Our conversations were a way for me to connect with another adult human being. I was drowning in loneliness. Jimmy came and went as he pleased, and even when he was home, he would go for days without speaking to me. His silence was a form of mind control. He tried to convince me that I was mentally off-balance, and he often told me that it wouldn't be hard for him to convince a judge to have the kids taken away from me. This usually followed an argument about why he needed to spend so much time with his mother. I knew this was not a marriage but a threesome, and I was the one in the way.

Jimmy ran into the owner of a body shop, and the owner worked out a deal with Jimmy whereby he would train Jimmy to do bodywork if Jimmy would work for one dollar an hour. Of course, he would be paid in cash off the books, and this way, he could continue to collect his unemployment. His dollar an hour didn't amount to much, but it was considered to be, like the rest of what we had, his money.

My name was never put on the checking account. Unfortunately, Jimmy was not qualified to handle a checking account, and after moving around from bank to bank and bouncing too many checks at each one, Jimmy's latest bank closed his checking account and refused to allow him to open another one. Now Jimmy had a proven track record of poor money management. Although I was much better at handling money, Jimmy was not going to allow me to have access to any of "his" money. He would pay the utility bills only when the technicians came to turn off the power. If he wasn't home when they came, it would cost an extra fee to have the power turned back on. Sears began calling about the charge account Jimmy opened to buy the lawn mower, which was now permanently parked in his mother's garage. Sears would insist that I give them a date when they would receive their money, and when I told Jimmy about the calls, he instructed me to just hang up on them. He would complain that Sears had gotten access to our unlisted phone number and threatened to have it changed again. We were losing our good credit standing, but Jimmy argued that we didn't need good credit since we already had a mortgage, and that was credit enough. I was miserably unhappy. I wanted out, and I looked forward to the coming years when both of my children would be in school. I wanted a job, my own income, friends, and a life that mattered.

Because of the constant news stories about crime in the Atlanta area, being home alone with the boys at night had become frightening. One Saturday night around 3:00 a.m., I awoke to the sound of the window in the spare bedroom being pushed open. Terrified, I froze in bed, afraid to move. I heard someone climb through the window and slam it shut, and then I heard footsteps coming toward the bedroom door. Before he turned the corner into our bedroom, I realized that it was Jimmy coming in from his night out. He must have unlocked the window before he left that night, without my knowing it. Jimmy reeked of liquor. He closed the bedroom door behind him, took off all his clothes, and got into bed. Then he started trying to have sex with me; I rejected his advances, but he kept on. The sloppiness of his voice and the smell of him disgusted me. I tried reasoning with him, asking if I could go to the bathroom, but he just mumbled as he held me down. I told him to stop, and the more I fought to get away, the angrier he became. His voice got louder, and I feared he would wake the boys. I just wanted him to leave me alone, and I hoped that if I got away to the bathroom, he would be asleep by the time I got back into bed. However, he kept fighting me until I became exhausted and finally gave up. When it was over, I lay there, feeling overwhelming hatred for Jimmy as he turned over and started snoring. Once the snoring became louder, I slipped out of bed and tiptoed to the bathroom. I sat on the toilet and quietly cried for a long time.

I now felt even more trapped, and I was desperate for a way out. I feared what else Jimmy might do to me. It was years later, thinking back on this night, that I realized the truth, that I had been raped. I continued to suffer mentally from the effects of this incident, but I did not know enough to connect my anguish to the night of terror during which I fought and struggled with Jimmy and lost the battle. I couldn't put words to my feelings after that, but I felt helpless and childlike, like a person without choices or the ability to fight back. My childhood made familiar to me these feelings of intense instability, injustice, betrayal, and the need for rescue. That night changed me, leaving me extremely fearful, and set apart from who I really was. I was always on guard, making sure that my true feelings didn't slip out. If I was someone else, I couldn't feel what I felt or express the rage that I wanted again to scream out to the world to anyone who would listen. But there was no one to listen as there had been no one in my childhood. Even if there were someone I could trust, this was

1966, and there was no such thing as a husband raping his wife. I have since heard of many abusive marriages in which the husband repeatedly begged the wife for forgiveness after violent incidents, but this never happened to me. Jimmy Minor never once expressed remorse for the crimes he committed. He was convinced that anything he did to me was his right as a husband. I was nothing more to him than a piece of property, and if I had only done this or that differently, he wouldn't have had to do what he did. In other words, his actions were always my fault.

The next morning, I awakened to the sound of the TV and a little voice from the next bedroom. "Momma, I'm up," called Scott from his crib. He was just barely two and a delightfully precious child.

"Okay, Mommy's coming," I answered as I climbed out of bed, my eyes still swollen from crying. I wondered how I was going to get through the day, but I knew I had to get up, smile at my children, and act as if everything was all right. I was always on edge after this. I was gripped with fear whenever I allowed myself to think about how I had no power, no money, and no real friends. I now had an additional worry—I had not been allowed to use my diaphragm the night before. I mentally dismissed any thought that I could have gotten pregnant. *No! It didn't happen, didn't happen, didn't happen.*

Jimmy made little conversation with me for the rest of the week, but this was not unusual. What was unusual was Jimmy coming home the following week and acting as if he were a different person. He started talking up a storm about how he wanted to fly up to New Jersey and see if he could get a job. "So you are suggesting that we move to New Jersey?" I confirmed.

"Yeah, I will call Connie and see if I can stay at her house while I search for a job." Remember, there was always a reward that followed the abuse, and this was the reward. I could hardly believe the words coming out of his mouth.

Why, I thought, *would he want to do this? Was he really going to leave his mother?* She would be furious when she found out about his plan. "Is this some kind of a joke?" I asked. Without answering, he picked up the phone and called Connie. Once he had her okay, he called the airlines and made a reservation. We were buddies now, with all the connections in place. I was afraid to jump for joy because he could turn from Dr. Jekyll to Mr. Hyde at any moment from seeing me so happy. "What made you decide to do this?" I asked.

"I just figured this was a good time to make a move, and I know you would be happier living near your family." He was trying to convince me that he cared about my well-being, when I knew he didn't. But how could I not be happy about the prospect of moving to a place where I had some support and people who cared about me?

Jimmy wanted me to sit down with him so we could plan the move together. This all felt too strange since I was never part of any other planning he did. Any plans he made were with his mother, not me. While he was gone, I was supposed to put an ad in the paper to sell the house. By the end of the week, he was on a plane to New Jersey, and the ad was in the paper. He would call every few days to tell me the different places that he had applied for a job and how he was just waiting for a response. The house sold the first week the ad ran. However, at the end of the second week, Jimmy was on his way back to Atlanta without a job. Although I was disappointed, I was not surprised. All along, I had a hard time believing this change would really happen. I believed Jimmy's actions were nothing more than his way of distracting my attention from the night of terror, but that night was still clearly in my thoughts. My next fear was my late period. After I was two weeks late, I knew, and I was terrified that I had lost any hope of getting out. In hindsight, I knew this pregnancy had been Jimmy's plan all along and that he never intended to get a job in New Jersey.

Devastated that freedom from my marriage was now even further off in the future, I found that I could no longer think clearly. Fear is a powerful emotion which can show up without warning. It can dominate our thoughts and does not depart quickly. An abusive partner will work to distort your perception of reality. It becomes so hard to distinguish between right and wrong that you doubt your judgment and can't make right decisions for yourself. My mind was becoming warped by the mental abuse as I became more and more paralyzed by fear.

The Minor family was a system already in place when I became part of it. The family amounted to a network that perceived anyone outside of their group to be not only of lower value than them but a threat to them. The mother held the rank of queen, and she was worshipped and held in highest esteem. She ruled the network comprised of her children, who were all people of perfection. Since spouses were of much lower value, any problems in the marriages were due to the imperfections of the spouses, and any mistreatment of the flawed spouses was applauded and approved by the queen. When Jimmy returned from New Jersey, his mother's hooks in his life were stronger than before he left. To me, Jimmy was no more than a coward, still sucking on his mother's breasts.

One Sunday, Jimmy borrowed his mother's vacuum cleaner to clean out our heater. On Monday morning, the vacuum cleaner still sat in the corner of our bedroom as Jimmy left for work, where he and the car would be all day. Late that morning, Frances called to question me about the vacuum cleaner, very angry that it hadn't been returned. "It's here. You can come and get it," I offered as she huffed and puffed into the phone. I knew she was annoyed by my answer, but not having a car, it was the best I could do.

"You don't seem to understand," she blurted out. "We can't do any work here without it."

My next offer was, "I can set it on the front steps for you."

"Oh, no! I don't have time to come and get it." She rattled on, her voice getting louder and angrier as she spoke.

I finally had listened to enough, so I blasted back. "You know what? I didn't borrow your vacuum cleaner, and I am not responsible for returning it. Jimmy has already left for work with the car, and he will be gone all day. I will have him call you when he gets here."

"Oh, no, that is not going to work. We need it returned today!" she yelled into the phone.

I had finally had enough and started to unload on her, letting her know exactly what I thought. "You're nothing but a meddling old bitch. All you do is meddle in your kids' affairs. It would help if you would get a life instead of spending all your time gossiping, with your hateful opinions of why no one is good enough for your perfect children."

"You just wait," she ranted on. "I'll be over there to face you before this day is over."

"You don't have guts enough to face me," I said, and I hung up. I was shaken, but I felt better. I had blown my stack. So far, no one had ever confronted her or had the guts to tell her what they really thought. News about our conversation traveled fast, and all the kids gathered at her house that day to console the queen. I felt justified about standing up for myself, but when Jimmy found out what had happened, he ranted and raved for days, threatening me that I would pay dearly for what I had done. I wondered just what he could do to me that he had not already done, and my answer was, "Not much." I didn't care anymore. If Jimmy wanted a relationship with his mother more than with me, why didn't he just leave us and go back home where he belonged? Oh no, he wanted to have it all. He wanted his life to look acceptable to the world while he hid the way his life really was. Keeping me pregnant was his way of staying in control of me. Alone in the world with two small children and another on the way, I could not think clearly. I was going down deeper into the pits of despair and depression.

Christmas was less than a month away, and I took Jimmy and Scott to see Santa one day at a local store. Jimmy was almost four, and Scott was two, and they were all excited about going to see Santa. However, once I laid eyes on the Santa, I wished I had not come. This Santa was poorly dressed and unrealistic-looking with a cheap beard almost falling off his face. I knew he would not fool little Jimmy. They both walked up to Santa, slowly examining his costume with apprehension, trying to decide if getting too close was safe. We had already read a story about Santa, and they believed it was true. Now I felt like a liar. As we left, little Jimmy said, "I could tell that Santa wasn't real, Mom."

"You are right. The real one is at the North Pole." I hated lying to little Jimmy, and I hated this whole Santa Claus thing because it was about lies and deceit. I promised myself that if it came up again,

I would tell the truth because lying to my children should not be a requirement for being a good mother.

As I have said, in the Minor family, Christmas was a big deal. After all, Christmas was a very Catholic holiday, and the Minors claimed to be very Catholic. Everything about Christmas had to be done in a certain way. The tree had to be decorated just right, and lights had to be strung all over the front of the house. The whole month of December was consumed with preparing for this one-day event. When Jimmy told me that I was not invited to the "Annual Tree" that year, I was elated. I hoped that Frances might have some compassion for Diane now that the focus of her hatred was directed at me. In addition, I smiled to myself, wondering how Jimmy would handle taking Jimmy and Scott to the event by himself. He had never taken the two of them anywhere without me. I knew that Frances would be no help with the boys because she paid no attention to them, and they hardly knew her. I was loving every minute of my punishment. I was going to get a breather, a few hours to myself, while Jimmy "babysat." Last year, I had received a dinner ring for Christmas. This year, I was getting something of much more value—a much-needed few hours alone to get my thoughts together. What Frances saw as a way of punishing me was the best gift I received that Christmas.

Since our house had been sold, we had to be out by January. Jimmy rented an apartment at Fisher Homes, a nearby apartment complex. I did not see the apartment until the day we moved in. He was in charge, and I was just coming along to babysit, keep the place clean, and do the laundry and grocery shopping. In a way, I was glad to be moving out of Rebel Forest. I was not leaving any friends there, and I never had a sense of safety in that neighborhood. It was also a relief to be rid of Jimmy's aunt, who lived directly across the street from us. Anywhere away from his family was going to be better for me.

Fisher Homes was full of young families and lots of children. Our apartment was on the ground floor in a cul-de-sac. The walls were painted cement block, and the floors were tile over cold hard concrete. The kitchen was very small with barely enough room to work in, but I didn't complain; I had lived in worse places, and comparatively, this was not that bad. I asked Jimmy if he would buy a rug for the living room floor so the boys would have a warmer place to play. He said no, informing me that I wanted the rug because I was too lazy to keep the floors clean.

I made friends easily, and Jimmy and Scott did also. They loved having lots of other kids to play with. The first person I met there was Virginia, who lived in the building next to ours. She was somehow related to Jimmy, a cousin of some sort. Sandra was another one of my neighbors, and Sandra and I became friends. She had gone to high school with Jimmy's sister Teresa. It seemed as if everyone was somehow related to or knew the Minor clan. I wasn't sure whether this was good or bad, but it was just the way it was.

Not long after we moved, a notice came from the Doraville Plant saying that Jimmy could return to work. Knowing that if he didn't go he would lose his unemployment, Jimmy complied. This was good news since it meant that we again had health insurance to cover the cost of this pregnancy. On the weekends, Jimmy hung out at the bars and continued his womanizing. His justification now was how difficult it was for him to live with me since I was pregnant, which was equal to being on the pill. He didn't try to hide his behavior. After Jimmy's night out, I would find his shirt in the hamper smelling like cheap perfume with lipstick smeared on the collar. In his pants pockets, I would find his wedding ring and napkins scribbled with girls' names and phone numbers. His Saturday night escapades became routine, and each time he left, I would hope that this would be the night he would meet someone else. Sometimes I would fantasize about him telling me that he wanted a divorce. I would plan out how I wouldn't react at all to the news, figuring that if I appeared as happy as I really was, he would change his mind. These fantasies gave me some momentary relief, and sometimes I dared to hope that this could really happen. I wanted him to have someone else, someone who didn't make him as miserable as I supposedly made him and maybe even someone who had no problem with his disordered way of thinking and his warped relationship with his mother. I had come to realize that a real man was more than blue eyes and muscles.

A real man was someone who valued his wife and children, treated them with respect, and wanted to be part of raising a family. There is absolutely nothing more terrifying than a sinful man in a position of power, but I still had some hope that there was some woman out there who would want Jimmy.

The year was 1967, and Lyndon Johnson was president. The Vietnam War was raging, and America was in the throes of a nervous breakdown over the war. Bart's safety was a constant worry to me. Lucy Johnson, the president's daughter, was expecting her first child exactly one month before my baby was due, and news of her pregnancy was constantly in the headlines. Lucy and I were both the same age, but I could hardly fathom what a day in her life was like compared to mine. The freedom battle for the blacks was still a hot item. They had won a great victory when the Supreme Court ruled that prohibiting interracial marriage was unconstitutional. I found comfort in knowing that all such civil rights events were infuriating to Frances.

Jimmy suggested that I take the boys and fly up to New Jersey for a week, and I always took advantage of his offers. I was glad I could go since Bart had been deployed to Vietnam, and I would be able to see him before he left. It was a terrible farewell. Bart didn't want to go, and we didn't want him to go. He was to fly to Camp Pendleton, California, for special training before going on to Vietnam. It was terribly painful for all of us as we saw Bart off at the bus station on his way to the airport. He was a wonderfully kind young man, with a gift for loving others in spite of the pain in his own life. He was eighteen years old, and his life was just beginning. He had not been dealt a good hand with this deployment to Vietnam because he had already fought a war at home.

Connie's house was filled with the busyness of small children, and the house was even busier now that Daddy and Margie lived there. I wanted to tell Daddy about Jimmy's behavior toward me, but I felt as if he had enough to worry about. I also had no idea what he could do to help me. I know now that I should have told him anyway. However, moving in with Connie was not, nor would it ever be, an option for me. Her house was already too crowded, and it just wouldn't have worked.

My mother was in some sort of halfway housing situation, and Connie took me there to see her. I vaguely remember the details of where the house was and what it looked like. Connie and I drove down a long driveway, and when she pulled into a parking place in front of a chain-link fence, I could see my mother walking toward us. I watched the rhythm of her gait as she came closer, her face sober and smiling, and a new perm in her hair. She looked well. She smiled at me as if I were the only one there. "Hi, Char." Her face shone with sobriety and love. I will always remember the look on her face that day, and I can still see it. I sensed the love in her face for the first time in decades. It was a special moment for me. Who we are is trapped inside of us unless we have the courage to share it. I wanted to tell her that I loved her. I could see the pitiful sadness and regret in her eyes over the darkness of her life and the years of abusing her family, and now she stood there struggling to connect with me. The tide had turned. When I no longer needed her, she needed me.

"Hi," I answered. She spoke a few words to Connie but kept looking at me. We struggled to keep the small talk going. I was glad to see her looking so well, and I wanted her to stay sober, but I held out little hope for that.

As the following Saturday approached, I became more and more fearful of going back to Atlanta. I tried to put it out of my mind, but the return was constantly in my thoughts. The fear became more of a reality as the plane started its descent. I was wishing I had another place to go or even that our absence would help Jimmy's attitude toward me. As we walked off the ramp, the boys ran ahead when they saw Jimmy waiting for us. Back at the apartment, the first thing I noticed was that Jimmy had bought a rug for the living room floor. I never mentioned it, but I thought that was generous of him. The boys were glad to be back home, and they could hardly wait to get outside and see their friends. However, my week away did nothing to deter Jimmy's hostility toward me, and I was sure that in my absence, his hatred was fueled by the queen.

When I went to the grocery store, I always had to take the boys with me since "he was not a babysitter." I remember Jimmy standing in the kitchen with his arms folded, a hateful smirk on his face as he watched me lug in bags of groceries, making several trips back and forth from the car to the house with bags and children while hugely pregnant. I pretended I didn't notice him standing there. He would go for days without speaking to me, and if he did speak, it was to call me an ugly whore. If I started crying, his badgering would become more severe, and he would keep it up until I finally had to go into the bedroom, close the door, and break down in tears. When I came out, he would tell me that he knew I was crying, and that was proof that I was mentally deranged. He assured me that he would have no trouble proving my insanity in court. When he complained that I slept too close to his side of the bed, he said I had two choices—either stay on my side of the bed or sleep on the sofa. He felt this was only fair so he could get a decent night's sleep. After all, he had to go to work, and I didn't. The abuse was even worse on the weekends when Jimmy did not have to go to work, and he spent his days alternating between being drunk and hungover. Sometimes he would just look at me and say, "Do you put out? Just look at yourself. Admit it. You are an ugly whore. Why can't you just admit it?" Not answering him seemed to give me some power, but when he got no response from me, he would laugh as he walked out the door for his Saturday night fix. Sunday morning he would spend belittling me, starting with how ugly I was and continuing with how lucky I was that he had rescued me from Center Street even though he knew I was no more than a filthy whore. He would go into how much I owed him even though he knew that I would never have any way to repay him. I was always glad when Jimmy left for work because that gave me some reprieve from his abuse.

One Sunday afternoon, there was a rap at the back door. It was an old friend of Jimmy's whom he introduced to me as Rabbit. I decided that Rabbit's name and face were a perfect match, and I wondered how this man knew where we lived. Rabbit kept looking at me and trying to make conversation with me, but I kept watching TV, doing my best to ignore him without being rude. This man was clearly mentally challenged, and I feared that he could come back when Jimmy wasn't home. I had a bad feeling about him. After Rabbit left, Jimmy lit into me about how I treated his friends. He threatened that if my attitude didn't change, I would be sorry. I feared Jimmy's threats because whenever he became enraged, I feared he would kill me. I sometimes thought that dying would be better for me than living the brutal life I was trapped in, but the big question in my mind was always what would happen to my children if I was suddenly gone.

I became extremely fearful, always on edge. I looked forward to my doctor visits because my doctor was gentle, and his voice was kind and loving. The doctor would always ask me how I was doing, and sometimes he would take some blood since I had the Rh factor, and this baby was at risk of being a blue baby. I asked the doctor about tying my tubes after the baby was born, but he said he could not do that because I was still too young. I wanted to tell him what was really going on at home in hopes that he would change his mind. However, Jimmy had me convinced that if I ever did tell anyone about my situation, no one would believe me, and my story would be proof of my insanity. He held me hostage with his threats that he would take away my children. I also knew that Jimmy had all the family support he needed to follow through on this threat. His family would always side with Jimmy and sympathize with his "situation" of being burdened by a crazy wife. They would help him to gain custody of the children, and they would take my place in raising the children. What I did to avoid being deemed unstable was to stay silent about the abuse and find a way to just "file it away." The abuse did not go away, but I knew I needed to endure for the sake of my children. I was clearly on the verge of a breakdown and just barely hanging on.

When my dad called, Jimmy made sure to sit next to me just in case I was thinking about telling the truth about what was really going on. My need to file my feelings away meant that I also started to become disconnected from my children, even though I still loved them. Just as I could not allow myself to feel the true extent of the pain I was in, I could not allow myself to feel the full extent of any emotion. I practiced being numb and reacting to nothing.

Late one night after we had gone to bed, the phone rang. Jimmy didn't move, so I got up and answered it. It was the queen mother. "Could I speak to Jimmy?" she asked.

"Hold on," I said. I laid the phone down on the end table and walked back to the bedroom. I got back in bed, nudged Jimmy, and told him that his mother was on the phone. He answered me but didn't get up. I nudged him and told him again. He answered again, and I went back to sleep. When we got up the next morning, the phone was still off the hook on the end table where I had left it. This incident was all that was needed to fuel Jimmy's anger, and he stared at me with vengeance in his eyes as he dialed his mother's number. I left the room to get away from him. After Jimmy ended the call to his mother, he sat on the sofa and told little Jimmy and Scott that his cousin Sammy, Dorothy's six-year-old son, had been killed. Sammy had been riding his bike and was hit by a car on one of the streets in the back of his house. Jimmy tried to impress on the boys the danger of going into the street. He then took a shower, got dressed, and left without speaking to me.

I had a strong feeling that this tragedy would somehow become my fault. The following night, Jimmy did not come home all night. The next morning when he did come in, I was sitting on the sofa. "Well, where have you been?" I said. He welled up a mouth full of saliva and spewed it at me, hitting me right between the eyes. I started shaking. I said nothing, got up, went into the bathroom, locked the door, and washed my face several times. I felt that Jimmy had gone too far this time. I felt dirty and degraded, and I was afraid I was losing my ability to keep trying. However, I had to pull myself together because I had two children who depended on me. I knew that to avoid losing my sanity, I had to leave. I had to figure out a plan; there had to be someone who could help me. Not only was I being destroyed, but living in this hateful environment was affecting my children as well. My due date was only about six weeks away. I kept going back into the bathroom and washing my face, hoping the tears would soon stop. I looked in the mirror and promised myself that I would get Jimmy Minor out of my life. Whether it took a short time or many years, I promised myself that I was no longer in this relationship for the long haul. Repeating this over and over gave me hope for a better day and a better life. I knew it would take a while, but I also knew that I would not give up until I was rid of him. When I came out, he had gone to bed with the bedroom door closed. I couldn't relax knowing he was in the house; I kept having shaking spells, but washing my face somehow calmed me down.

As I thought about how to leave Jimmy, I knew that I could just walk out the door, but I would have to leave alone. Then what would happen to my children? They would most likely be farmed out by Jimmy's mother. She didn't want them; she didn't even know them. Jimmy told me many times that if I ever thought about leaving, I had better know about the Georgia laws on abandonment. He said abandonment would be a sure way to lose my children forever and never see them again. I had no idea whether his threats were the truth or not, but in those days, there were no shelters for women in abusive situations, so I had nowhere to go even for advice. As I tried to reason it out in my mind, I realized that leaving was not an option, so my feelings of helplessness became overwhelming. I also spent a great deal of time blaming myself for getting myself into this marriage and then staying in it. I remembered from long ago the cowardice Jimmy exhibited when he picked fights with weaker men in bars. Why didn't I pick up on this? I also knew that I had made a wrong choice by leaving New Jersey because had I stayed, Jimmy would not have had this opportunity to trap me. All the telltale signs of his disordered thinking were there from the start, but I did not take them seriously. Jimmy's abusive personality increased with his drinking episodes, and it was difficult to predict what would set him off. My secondary problem was Jimmy's mother, who not only enjoyed his tales of abuse but also fed and applauded his behavior.

Sammy's funeral was the following day, and I was glad when nothing was mentioned about my going. My neighbor Virginia, Jimmy's cousin, stopped by when it was over and asked why I hadn't attended. I told her that I wasn't invited, and I also shared some information about the abuse that I was dealing with. I told her that

I wanted to stay as far away from Jimmy's family as I could, and in a limited way, I asked for her help. "It won't be too long before I go to the hospital to have this baby. I don't know who Jimmy will get to watch the boys, so I will be worried about Jimmy and Scott. Please keep your eyes open as to what is going on over here while I am gone." She promised that she would.

A month before my due date, I decided to get a bag together to take to the hospital. I had two gowns that I had been saving to take with me. I got them out, washed, ironed, and neatly folded them. I put them in my small suitcase with an outfit for the new baby to come home in. Jimmy put the crib together and set it up in our bedroom. It was in good shape, and all that was needed was a new mattress.

Despite all my plans for the new baby, I was tormented with feelings of sadness, despair, and hopelessness. I went into my bedroom one evening after the boys were in bed and got down on my knees and prayed, crying out to God for some relief. My prayer was an effort of last resort. "I do not want to live in this hateful environment any longer. I want my children taken care of, but I cannot live like this anymore. Please find a way out for me. I cannot go on. Please do not let my life continue like it is. You have given me beautiful healthy children, and they deserve a better life than I can offer them. I cannot take care of them if I continue to be abused. Please help me." I felt an overwhelming sense of relief after I prayed.

The next day, a lady came to my door. She spoke with an English accent as she told me that she came from Antioch Baptist Church, and she was giving out literature to encourage people to come to church. Jimmy had already left for work, so I felt free to invite her in. She talked about the church and the programs that they offered. This church was located right across the street from the Chevrolet plant, so I knew that area and how to get there. I knew nothing about the Baptist church, but her invitation was warm and friendly, and I welcomed any help or support that I could find. That Sunday morning, I slipped out of bed quietly and got dressed in the bathroom while Jimmy continued to sleep off his Saturday night out. I fixed the boys a bowl of cereal and hurried things along to get out the door before Jimmy awoke. I feared that he might stop us if he knew where we were going. The boys were excited because they were going to Sunday school. The English lady was waiting for me as I entered the front door of the church, and I was glad to see her. She ushered the boys into a classroom where there were other kids and lots of toys to keep them occupied. She then led me into the sanctuary, introduced me to a few people, and left. One of the men sat down next to me with his Bible in his hand. He asked me a few questions about where I had gone to church before and if I knew Christ as my personal savior. I had no clue as to what he was talking about. "I'm not sure I understand," I said.

He opened his Bible to John 3:16 and held the Bible down so I could see the words as his finger moved along with each word that he read: "For God so loved the world, that he gave his only begotten son, that whosoever believeth in him should not perish but have everlasting life." I felt more relaxed than I had in months as I watched his finger move across each word. The man continued to speak about the scripture. However, what his scripture offered me did not interest me because I wasn't interested in everlasting life; I was interested in my life as it was now. I was in desperate need of help, and I wanted to know what God could do for me today, right now. The man did not ask me any questions about why I was there, and if he had asked, it would have been much too difficult for me to explain. I was still paralyzed by the fear that Jimmy would find out we had been to church. Even though it had taken some courage on my part, I knew that I had stepped out in a right direction. When I left church that morning, I felt lifted and felt stronger, with a feeling of peace that God was with me and that I was going to survive.

It was Fourth of July weekend. Scott was not quite three, and he loved to go outside and play with the other kids. I had temporarily lost sight of him, and I walked out front to check on him. Some of the neighbors were gathered in front of one of the apartments, so I stopped to visit as I walked past them. While standing there, I could feel water leaking, and I walked back to my apartment. As the day wore on, I noticed that the water would leak every twenty minutes or so. I wasn't sure what was happening, but the water continued leaking in the same pattern all night, so first thing that morning, I called the doctor. When the doctor learned that this leaking pattern had started the afternoon before, he asked why I hadn't called then. "Because it was a holiday," I answered.

"That is a poor excuse. We are always available, and you should have called yesterday. You need to come to my office now. Do not wait. You don't need an appointment. Come right now!"

Jimmy was still home, and he stayed with the kids while I drove myself downtown to Georgia Baptist Hospital. When I told the girl at the front desk my name, she led me right in to an examining room, and I was on the table in minutes. After the doctor examined me, he said, "You have a ruptured membrane. This baby will be born within twenty-four hours."

I objected, "He isn't due for three more weeks."

"We cannot stop this from happening. We have no choice. He may be small, but I believe that he is big enough and should be fine." He continued, "When you are dressed, come into my office." He was sitting at his desk when I walked in. "I am going to give you some instructions that you must follow." He looked me straight in the eye. "Who brought you here this morning?"

"I drove myself."

"Where is your husband?"

"He is home with my other two children."

"You are to go straight home, get your hospital bag together, and come immediately back here. You are not to drive yourself. Someone else must bring you." He spoke sternly, and he had a serious look on his face. "Do you understand?" I answered that I did understand, and as I was going out the door, he repeated, "I am expecting to see you in the hospital in no more than an hour and a half." I agreed because I knew he was trying to let me know that this was serious.

I drove straight home and gave Jimmy the news. He called his cousin Virginia and asked her to watch Jimmy and Scott for a few hours while he took me to the hospital. He told her that as soon as he got back, he would make other arrangements. She agreed. Because my bag was all packed, I was ready in a few minutes. "Do you need some gowns?" Jimmy asked.

"No, I have what I need."

Jimmy insisted, "I think we should stop and get you some new gowns for the hospital." I insisted in turn that I was supposed to go straight to the hospital, but Jimmy pulled into the K-Mart parking lot.

"I don't need anything," I repeated.

"We are going to get you some gowns anyhow."

I was thinking to myself, *Why are you all of a sudden worried about what I need?*

"Come on," he urged. "It will just take a minute or two. You can pick out what you want." I knew Jimmy had started to act out a role he thought would please me. The sound of his voice was softer and kinder, but to me, that only sounded all the more untrustworthy. We both got out of the car as I continued to worry about my condition. I knew the doctor would not have wanted me to go shopping, and I didn't want to do it either. I quickly picked out a gown and a duster and waited as Jimmy paid for them, and we were back on our way.

It was a relief when I was finally checked into the hospital. Jimmy left to make arrangements for his sister Teresa to come over and watch the boys. He came back that evening just as the doctor was making his rounds. The doctor told both of us that if I did not go into labor within the next few hours, he would schedule labor to be induced the following morning at 8:00 a.m. He looked straight at Jimmy and said, "You need to be present!"

The following morning, July 6, at 8:00 a.m. sharp, Jimmy arrived. I asked about the boys, and he told me that they were fine and that Teresa had come back over that morning to stay with them. A bed was rolled into the room, and I was lifted onto it. The sides of the bed were lifted up, and I was wheeled out into the hallway. The bed stopped a short way down the hallway where the doctor was waiting. I could hear the doctor asking Jimmy if he wanted to say anything to me before I went into the labor room. Jimmy leaned over the bed and kissed me. He had nothing to say. I wanted to spit in his face because I knew that this was part of his phony performance to save face in front of the doctors. I also knew that he only kissed me because the doctor suggested it and that the doctor could see through his phony behavior. I was wheeled into the labor room, and in a few minutes, there was a nurse standing over me, administering nose drops through a long needle that didn't touch my nose but just allowed the drops to fall. It took quite a few doses before labor eventually started, but once it started, things progressed quickly. After I had dilated far enough, the anesthesiologist was there putting a shot in my arm and telling me to count to ten. The last number I remember was three, then everything went blank.

The next thing I remember was a nurse standing over me, telling me to wake up. She was trying to tell me that Dr. Poole, my pediatrician, was there to see me. "I have just examined your baby, and he appears to be healthy," he said. He went on to give me some instructions about the baby's eyes, but I was still too out of it to understand much of what he was saying. I kept going in and out of consciousness. When I came around again, a nurse was at the side of my bed with a bedpan. She said I had to pee in the bedpan; the jolt of the freezing cold bedpan under my butt helped wake me up.

"Do you know how much my baby weighed?" I asked since this was my concern with the baby coming three weeks early. There was a chalkboard on the wall with information about all the babies who had been born that morning.

"I will find out," she said as she walked toward the wall. As she walked back toward me, she gave me the good news: "Six pounds, eleven ounces."

"When will I get to see him?" I asked.

"You will be going into your room shortly. your husband is waiting there for you."

I was still very foggy, but I could feel the wheels rolling on the gurney as it was being moved. The gurney finally stopped, and I was wheeled into a room containing two beds and lots of windows. Jimmy sat in a chair in the corner, and he stood up as they rolled me in. They let down the sides of the gurney and lifted me onto the bed. "Have you seen the baby yet?" I asked Jimmy.

"Yes, he is very tiny, but he looks good." A nurse came in to give me some instructions about dinner and when the doctor would be in to see me.

She said to Jimmy, "You can go see your baby now. He is in the nursery all cleaned up and dressed."

"Can I see him?" I asked.

"I will bring him in to you tomorrow morning. For now, it's Dads only." Jimmy left to see the new baby, still putting on a show as the perfect husband and father for the doctors and nurses.

"Is it because of the anesthesia that I can't see my baby now?"

"Yes. I will bring him in first thing in the morning." Jimmy came back in to tell me he was on his way home to relieve Teresa, but he would be back in the morning. He was full of conversation, acting as if we were a happy couple who had been looking forward to the birth of our third child. He worked hard at portraying our life together as something it was not.

The next morning, as the sun was coming up, I woke up with a clearer head. I sat up in bed and looked out a window that overlooked a parking lot. I could see people getting in and out of cars, coming in the front door with balloons, gifts, and flowers. I felt safer than I had in a long time, but going home was a worry that I knew I would soon have to face. The nurse came in and helped me into the bathroom. I looked in the mirror; my dark-brown hair fell down to my shoulders in a natural wave. I combed through it and stared into the mirror again. My face looked younger than my age. Even though my body felt very weak, I thought I looked pretty good for all I had been through. I finished brushing my teeth and opened the door. The nurse was still in the room, and I asked again about the baby. She said that after breakfast was over, she would be bringing the babies around. Another girl was moved into the bed next to me, and I introduced myself to her. She said she had had a premature baby girl that morning. I could hear the aides in the hallway as they came around to take our trays. When they came to get my tray, a nurse holding a baby wrapped in a blue receiving blanket followed behind. She carefully handed the bundle to me, saying "Here is your baby. He has just been fed. I will be back later to get him." I looked at the perfect features of my baby's face, examining every detail. He was pink and wrinkly and tiny, but he had a full head of hair. In fact, he was perfect in every way. I held him up close to me, closed my eyes, and thanked God that we had both survived the nine months of terror. I knew at that moment that I loved this child in spite of how he had been conceived. He and I together had survived, and I knew that God had been with us all the way. Today, as I think back to that day, I believe it was nothing short of a miracle that we were both so healthy. I opened the blanket and examined my baby closely, and all my fears were put to rest.

Everything about Mark's birth made it clear to me that God was real and he was with me. When I thought about how easily the baby or I could have died before I ever reached the hospital, I gained new strength that allowed me to go on and not let the satanic forces defeat me. I realized that God was fighting back for me when I had no strength to do it myself. Those days were very deeply etched in my memory, and even today, so many years later, I am grateful that I learned to never underestimate the power of God's presence in our lives.

That afternoon, a neighbor from the apartment complex came up to visit. Her husband worked with Jimmy, and they were my only visitors. Later that day, the doctor came in and told me that the delivery had gone well. The baby was healthy; there were no problems with the baby's blood since he was O positive. All the news was good. The bad news was what would happen after we were home, and Jimmy Minor turned back into who he really was.

We needed a name for this baby, but since Jimmy had barely spoken to me while I was pregnant, we never discussed a name. Jimmy always wanted to saddle the boys with a name that matched one of his family members. Of course, any name was going to be something Jimmy chose. He kept insisting on Michael Anthony after his brother. "No, he needs his own name, not your brother's," I insisted.

"You can name all the girls, and I will name all the boys," he said, thinking this was a clever statement.

"Oh, yeah, that's fair since there will be no more babies." We finally agreed on Mark Anthony. I liked the sound of that.

The photographer came in the next afternoon with the hospital pictures. I agreed to buy one, even though they went to no trouble to make the photos look good. She explained to me that Mark was only one hour old when the picture was taken. The photo included something that looked like old gray sheets unfolded and thrown over a bench, with the baby lying on the bench. I was getting antsy to get out of the hospital because I was feeling a little stronger, and I missed little Jimmy and Scott. I was looking forward to the next morning when I would be on my way, even though my homelife was a continuing worry. I hoped that having a new baby would somehow change Jimmy's nasty attitude toward me because I was too weak to tolerate much more of his abuse.

The next morning, the doctor examined me, and I passed his release test. They brought Mark in for me to dress; I put on his new outfit and marveled at what a perfectly beautiful baby he was. When Jimmy arrived to take us home, we were all dressed and ready. When we got home, little Jimmy and Scott were out front when I walked in the back door, holding Mark. I called to them to let them know I was home. They both came running to the door, and I leaned down and showed them their new brother. They both just looked but said nothing. Finally, Scott asked, "What's wrong with him?"

I answered, "He is a newborn baby. If we take good care of him, he will grow big just like you."

I laid the baby on the sofa and gave both boys a hug. As the days passed, they watched and listened for every whimper from the new baby, and they started to worry if the baby cried for more than two seconds. Then they would run to let me know that I needed to act quickly. I was constantly hearing, "The baby's crying," as if only they could hear him. One day, the boys asked if they could hold the baby, and I told them that I would let them each have a turn. When Mark started to whimper, I took the baby into the bedroom, with both boys following. As I changed Mark's diaper, Scott seemed more interested and stayed for the whole procedure. When I was done, I asked Scott not to touch the baby but just to watch him while I went into the kitchen to heat up a bottle. I soon learned that this was a mistake. As I walked back to the bedroom, there was Scott coming down the hallway with the baby in his arms, Mark's head dropped almost to the floor. I said nothing and calmly took the baby from

Scott with a sigh of relief. The look on my face must have scared Scott, and he started crying, and nothing I said or did was going to console him. Now Mark was screaming for his bottle, and Scott was wailing along with him. When Scott had finally quieted down and Mark was all fed, I carefully placed him on Scott's lap. I kept telling Scott what a good job he was doing and that I could tell how much this baby loved him. All the tears subsided; Scott started smiling, and once again, there was peace.

Unlike the boys, Jimmy showed little interest in the new baby. He never offered to hold or feed him, and I never suggested it. After Mark's bath, I would strap him into his baby seat and place the seat on the kitchen table. I eventually noticed Jimmy talking to Mark, trying to get a smile out of him. That was the first effort on Jimmy's part to acknowledge his new baby.

My neighbors began coming to visit me and see the new baby. One afternoon, my neighbor Sandra came over and told me that while I was in the hospital, she noticed Teresa sitting outside watching Jimmy and Scott. She knew Teresa from high school, so Sandra had walked over to speak to her. According to Sandra, this was how the conversation went: "Teresa Minor, I thought that was you. What are you doing here?"

"Hi. I came over to babysit for my brother, Jimmy. Charlene has gone to the hospital and left him without a babysitter to watch the kids."

"I know Charlene. Has she had the baby yet?"

"Oh, yes, it is another boy. Jimmy is very disgusted and upset about it." Sandra told me that she could clearly feel the hatred and resentment in Teresa's voice.

As Teresa spoke, Sandra kept thinking to herself, *What a stupid thing to say, as if Charlene could decide if the baby was to be a boy or a girl.* Sandra did ask out loud, "Her husband is upset about it?"

Teresa continued, "I feel sorry for Jimmy that he has to put up with her. They had a really nice house, and Charlene sold it out from under him a few months back. Now he is stuck living here." Sandra and I laughed at Teresa's asinine remarks; her ignorance was so ridiculous that we found it amusing.

"Well, unfortunately, she is his sister," I explained. "The rest of the family is no different. They are all at that same low level of intelligence. I cope with their ignorance by staying away from them as much as I possibly can," I said.

"I don't blame you." Sandra agreed.

After Sandra left, I thought more about what she had told me. I knew that Teresa's intent, no matter how ridiculous, was to sympathize with Jimmy, twisting reality around to make it sound as if it was Jimmy who was being victimized. I knew that Teresa's attitude had come directly from the top because her mother's hatred spread to everyone in the family. What I learned from Sandra about current opinions in the Minor family was that my first crime was leaving for the hospital with no one to babysit, leaving Jimmy to "handle it." It appeared that my second crime was that the baby was a boy. Finally, I was to blame for "selling the house out from under Jimmy." Surely, I thought, these crimes I had committed were enough to justify Jimmy seeking a divorce. I had no love for this man, and in all fairness, I would have been truly happy if he had found someone else to put up with him. I didn't tell Jimmy what Sandra had told me because he would have insisted that she was lying and that he "didn't want her in our apartment again." Behind my back, the war against me raged on, and Jimmy's supporters rallied one another to do all they could to condemn, abuse, and destroy me. I knew that after each incident of abuse, Jimmy went to his family, bragging about what he had done to me, and the family applauded. It was too overwhelming for me to figure out how to deal with a tyrant and the family that supported him, so I tried to look the other way for now.

After Mark's birth, I didn't bounce back as quickly as I had with my other two children. I felt weak, and I was struggling to keep going. I had not gained a lot of weight during this pregnancy, and I quickly lost the little I had gained. One day, I had just fed Mark, put him in his crib, and taken out the vacuum cleaner. Jimmy was lying on the sofa with the TV on. The rug had not been vacuumed in weeks, so I ignored Jimmy's TV watching, plugged in the vacuum cleaner, and began to run it over the rug. Jimmy all of a sudden leaped off the sofa, walked over to me, grabbed the vacuum hose out of my hand, and started slamming the metal end of it into my back. He held my arm with one hand and swung the hose with the other. The metal kept slamming into my back. I tried to move away, but he kept pulling on my arm and swinging. He finally let go, and I was able to back away. I staggered into the bathroom, locked the door, and slid to the floor in pain, gagging as I tried to catch my breath. I tried to keep Jimmy from hearing me gasping for breath by running the water as loudly as I could. At least an hour passed before I finally regained my composure. I knew I had to leave. I rounded up the boys, put a few bottles of Mark's formula and some diapers in a bag, and told the boys to get in the car. I picked Mark up as he slept, put him in his baby seat, and loaded our things in the car. The boys kept asking me where we were going. "We're going for a ride," I answered as I tried to hide my tears and the fear in my voice. I knew I had nowhere to go, but I tried to think of someone I knew that I could visit. I drove around the apartment complex as I tried to come up with a plan. My determination to get rid of Jimmy Minor grew stronger. I pulled into an empty parking space, with no cars next to me. As my tears flowed uncontrollably, I again pleaded with God to help me. It was difficult to pray in silence when I wanted to scream at the top of my lungs. Little Jimmy kept asking me what was wrong, but I couldn't answer him. I knew this was all too upsetting to my children. They deserved better, but I lacked the maturity, knowledge, and support to find a way out.

    Today's world is so much different. There would be lots of help for me today, but back then, there was none. I thought about walking up to someone's door and asking if I could use the phone to call Daddy. I wished that I had the guts and boldness that Connie had, but I was too fearful and timid to ask a stranger for help. I realized once again that my only hope of escape was to leave my children behind, but I knew that Jimmy would see to it that I never saw them again. The worry of what might happen to them if I left was greater than the worry of what might happen to me if I stayed. I just could not make myself go without them. I knew I had to pull myself together and march on. I thought about Daddy, who never gave up his struggles to protect his children. I was not going to give up either, not yet. However, I was not going to stay in my marriage any longer than I had to. I knew that my children would not be babies forever. I made myself a promise, and I held out hope that eventually there would be a way out. Hope provided the energy that kept me going. I turned the key in the ignition. Feeling a new sense of determination not to let Jimmy Minor defeat me, I drove back to the apartment.

The situation I was in, having no family nearby, gave Jimmy the power to do what he did. He knew I had nowhere to go and no one to help me. I was also beaten down with the fear of losing my children if I did seek help. A young girl who is away from her family and who must protect her small children is the perfect target for abuse. I would urge all who read this to protect your family members, especially if you do not see them regularly. Make sure you keep in touch and call when you can speak privately. Ask lots of questions. A woman is not likely to volunteer information if she is scared. If you call and she has little to say, most likely she is not in a safe place to talk. There are lots of tyrants out there like Jimmy Minor. You must assure your female relative that you can and will help her if she needs you. One reason that I was reluctant to tell Daddy the truth was that I couldn't see how he could help me. He lived in New Jersey, he lived with Connie, and he still had a job to go to every day. How could he possibly help me? My advice to all young women in my situation is to tell someone, even though it may not make sense to you at the time. I was never encouraged to rely on family; I had been programmed to work things out for myself and not to make a big deal out of anything. The damage this man was doing to me was severe, and I had by now lost my ability to feel the pain I was in. By victimizing me, he was victimizing my children as well because this environment was much too stressful to allow a child to thrive.

The next morning, I woke up with a sharp pain in my chest, and I was having trouble breathing. Sitting or standing upright seemed to ease the pain and the breathing difficulty, but I knew something was wrong, and my condition was too serious to ignore. I called the doctor and was told to come in immediately, so I told Jimmy that I needed to see a doctor as soon as possible. I believe at this point, he was scared as well. I did not trust Jimmy's ability to care for a newborn, so I fed Mark before I left and hoped he would sleep until I returned. I knew this breathing problem was a direct result of the blows to my back the day before, and Jimmy knew it too. The doctor immediately sent me to have a chest X-ray, and the test showed I had pleurisy. The doctor said pleurisy is caused by inflammation to the lining of the lung. He gave me two prescriptions with instructions to notify him if my lungs had not improved substantially in a few days. I was having trouble keeping my focus on what was happening to me because the thought of Jimmy at home with the children terrified me; all I could think of was getting home to see that they were okay. It was not that Jimmy physically abused the boys, but he abused them indirectly through his mistreatment of me. It is not good for children to have their mother on edge and frightened all the time.

I could feel my health failing. I wanted to give up; sometimes I thought I was getting too weak to fight. After a few days of medication for the pleurisy, I began to feel better, but I knew that I was not as well as I should have been. The stress of the constant abuse was taking a huge toll on my health. Today, I would not be able to withstand what I went through then, but a young body seems to fight to survive as it can at no other time in life. Little did I know that years later, I would begin to act out the effects of the abuse. Through the years, I have learned that the memory of the stress never completely goes away, but the healing process began for me the day I became strong enough to tell my story. That is when the fear began to lose its power. Back then, I was able to just practice staying numb, "file it away," and wait until I was in a safer place to open my wounds.

I had been thinking about Jimmy's aunt Dorothy because I had not seen her since she lost Sammy. One day, I decided to stop by her house on my way to the grocery store. As I turned into her driveway, I could see that she was sitting on the sunporch. I wanted to give her my condolences and at the same time let her be the first to see my new baby. Being "first" in this family for anything was a big deal, so I knew that allowing Dorothy to have the first glance would highly annoy Frances. Dorothy saw me pull up and walked out to the car as I rolled down the window on the passenger side. "I was so sorry to hear about the accident. I am especially sorry that I wasn't able to attend the funeral. I wanted you to be the very first one to see my new baby," I said as she looked through the car window at Mark asleep in his baby seat.

"Oh, he is a doll." She also spoke to Jimmy and Scott, who were in the back seat.

"Well, I guess I had better go. I'm on my way to the grocery store."

"Okay, it was good to see you. Your baby is beautiful." As I put the car in reverse, she continued, "I so much appreciated Jimmy coming over and staying with me when the accident first happened. I don't know what I would have done without him." Listening to her words as I slowly rolled the car down her driveway, I thought again how successful Jimmy was at portraying himself as someone he was not. I also thought about how the news of my little visit to Dorothy would spread through the family quickly, and it wasn't long before Jimmy suggested taking Mark to his mother's so she could see him.

One afternoon, Jimmy sat down on the sofa next to me; his presence next to me felt strange. He somberly looked me straight in the eye and asked, "Did you know that I was in the delivery room when Mark was being born? And did you know that you began to talk about me?"

"No, I didn't know that. What did I say?"

"You said that I spit in your face, hung out at the bars, and had sex with other women. You said that I called you an ugly whore and that I planned to take the children away from you. You also said you were going to get a divorce." He spoke in an oddly calm manner, so calm that I became fearful as he spoke. There was an unusual sense of humility in his voice, but knowing him, I feared any change in his demeanor.

"Well, I didn't know I was saying it." His words and his manner shocked me. Because of his absence of anger, I felt as if he was trying to share his pain with me, while letting me know that I was responsible for that pain.

He continued, "I was standing right there in the room, and you kept talking, telling all this to the doctor as he delivered the baby." Now I understood that his reason for telling me what happened was to let me know how I had embarrassed him in front of the doctor, blurting out his dirty secrets as he stood there squirming with no place to hide.

"Well, all I can say is that I didn't know it. I don't remember anything after they put me to sleep." I wanted to assure him that I didn't mean to embarrass him for fear of what my punishment might be. The words he was repeating were definitely mine; I had played these thoughts over in my mind for the past nine months. My subconscious took over under the influence of the anesthesia, which also gave me permission to express the truth about the fear I had been experiencing.

Had Jimmy known the pleasure I would get from his story, I doubt he would ever have told me. As I struggled to keep a straight face, I noticed that Jimmy seemed truly bothered. I believe that he feared that his abusive behavior was catching up with him and that he was particularly worried about my thoughts of divorce. It was true that if I had known of a way out at that time, I would not have hesitated to pursue it, but I had a newborn baby and two other children to take care of. After Jimmy left, I kept going over and over the scenario, drawing a picture in my mind. I could see him standing there, wishing he had some place to run as the medical staff attended to the delivery. This was the baby he wanted no part of until he had to show up to act out his role as the proud new dad. I could imagine the anxiety in his eyes as my words blew the good-dad mask right off his face. I could see his lips getting tight and quivering as he wished his mother would show up to hold his hand and offer him one of her "nerve" pills to ease his pain. My thoughts went back to the night he climbed through the bedroom window, drunk after his night out at the bar, and how he raped me and referred to me as a worthless whore. I thought about how he spat in my face and gave me the silent treatment, and I thought about all the disrespect and mental and physical abuse that went on for the entire nine months. The delivery room was the final showdown, and there he stood, caught in his own trap. I have always wondered exactly what I said in that delivery room because there was probably much more that he was unwilling to tell me. However, I never mentioned the incident again for fear that Jimmy would sense my delight in his suffering.

While the abuse was happening, I was not fully aware of the impact it was having on my life, my well-being, and my health. How we are treated, supported, and loved is as much a part of our health as eating right, exercising, or getting enough rest. I also did not realize the danger I was in. The statistics are frightening. Domestic violence is the leading cause of death among pregnant women. In an abusive domestic relationship, the batterer dominates the woman psychologically as well as physically. He controls the money; he controls the children and threatens to keep them from her. He humiliates her and convinces her that no one would ever believe her claims of abuse if she were to be so foolish as to try to leave. Fear of his threats dominates her world, and despair disables her. We now know that violence without intervention always increases and always gets worse. Most domestic abuse deaths occur among women who are trying to leave the relationship, so the process of leaving must be undertaken with planning and support.

Today, there is a national hotline that helps battered women to take the first steps toward counseling or shelter. It was not until November 1977 that a national plan of action to address domestic violence was established, and it would be many years later before all states would establish shelters. Despite the shelters, there are now almost two thousand domestic homicides each year in the US because abuse is not reported as often as it should be.

Chapter 12

Abuse and Reward

After Jimmy's "confession," the tide turned, and the wind changed direction. I knew something had changed when Jimmy suggested one morning that he wanted to watch the kids so I could go to the beauty salon and get a new hairdo, a perm, highlights, cut—whatever I wanted. Mr. Hyde suddenly turned into Dr. Jekyll. I realized that it was now reward time, which Jimmy always thought justified his abuse. The reward offer implied that Jimmy was going to sacrifice his day to give me something that he was sure I wanted. I knew how his rewards worked; Jimmy was not only justifying the last round of abuse but the next one. In hindsight, I wished I had refused his offers and not been sucked into his game. The rewards allowed Jimmy to stay in control instead of acknowledging his wrong behavior. He assumed that all the dirty things he had done to me would now be forgotten, wiped from the slate of my memory, never to be mentioned again. No apology or acknowledgment from him would ever be necessary since he was offering me the great sacrifice of watching his children for a few hours. I could either take it or leave it. On reward day, Jimmy's nasty demeanor changed, and his voice and attitude were softer, nicer, more relaxed. I knew this kindness was temporary, but nevertheless, I took advantage of it.

One afternoon, Glen Button, Jimmy's uncle and Dorothy's husband, dropped by. Glen had recently received his real estate license, and he saw us as good candidates for a sale. He told us about a house that had just been listed in Decatur. It was an older house, which didn't exactly excite me, but Glen insisted that I should see it and then decide. The price was only $12,500, which meant the payments would be affordably low. We agreed to look at the house, and Glen took us to see it. When Glen pulled up in front of a large two-car detached garage, Jimmy loved that right away. We entered the house through the back door, which led into a small, outdated kitchen. The exposed sinks with little counter space didn't impress me. An archway separated the dining and living rooms. In the living room, the wall-to-wall carpet and the stone fireplace were very impressive. There was also a small sunroom off the living room. There were two bedrooms on the main floor, and a staircase off the second bedroom led up to a huge finished room in the attic. This house also had a basement with washer and dryer connections. I loved the high ceilings, the plush carpet over hardwood floors, and the large windows covered with Venetian blinds. The house was old, warm, and inviting in spite of its faults. Glen was right; it was a lot of house for the money, and we agreed to buy it. It was only two weeks after the contract was signed that we were approved for a loan, and our new address would be 627 Quillian Avenue.

The day we moved in, I immediately knew that I loved this house. I felt that it was a gift that suddenly appeared out of nowhere and that life had improved for me and the boys. In the new house, Jimmy and Scott had their own yard to play in, and they occupied the attic room. We used the second downstairs bedroom as a family room where we could all watch TV together, and the sunroom made the perfect nursery for Mark.

Mark was now seven weeks old. He was gaining weight and becoming an especially beautiful baby; I was always hearing comments from strangers about his good looks. However, as time moved on, I began to have trouble lifting Mark. When my condition became too painful to ignore, I went to the doctor, and the examination revealed a cyst on one of my ovaries. I was given a prescription and another appointment, and I was told that if the prescription did not work, I would be scheduled for surgery. I hoped that surgery would not be necessary because I was in fear of anything that would give Jimmy Minor another way to overpower and take advantage of me.

I looked forward to the letters from Bart that came regularly, and I took pictures of Mark and sent them to Bart. I loved Bart's letters, always written on paper with the Marine Corp logo in the background, because they somehow made me feel connected, as if I were not alone in my pain. I prayed for his safety, which was a daily worry that took the edge off my own pain. Bart and I had already been through our own war while growing old enough to escape the terror of "home." In reality, we had escaped nothing, but we each now experienced terror in another place and time.

I found Quillian Avenue to be a very friendly neighborhood. Just a few weeks after I moved in, I met Janet. She and her husband rented a house in the back of ours, and Janet and I had a lot in common. We were both about the same age, both met our husbands, while the husbands were in the service stationed near our family homes, and both of us were now living away from our families. She had one little boy, Michael, who at three years old was the same age as Scott. Her friendship to me while I lived on Quillian Avenue proved to be invaluable, and there were several other neighbors I was friendly with.

Jimmy's body shop training began to pay off when he was offered a full-time job at an independent body shop. Finally, Jimmy gave me the job of taking care of the checkbook and the privilege of paying the bills. Although he still made demeaning remarks about how "his" money was spent, I welcomed this opportunity because I knew I was more qualified to handle money. Jimmy put only enough money in the account to cover the bare necessities; I did my best to scrimp and save, but there was never any extra. Jimmy did not understand the principles of money management, and there was no way to explain it to him. Our discussions about money always ended up in an argument consisting of him telling me that he knew how women tried to rip men off when they had access to extra money. His inability to work with me to save and do better was a huge stumbling block to our financial success, but Jimmy still believed that the money and anything else we had was his. I did not argue with him, knowing that he was only in my life for the short term. For the most part, Jimmy's attitude toward me had improved, probably because his mother backed away from intruding in our lives. Although she was still a strong and negative influence in his life, I seldom saw her or heard from her.

Sandra and I remained friends even after I moved from the apartment, and one afternoon that fall, she stopped by to visit with her son. The boys were upstairs playing in their room, and Mark was taking his nap. Sandra and I were sitting on the sofa in the family room when the phone rang. I excused myself to get up and answer the phone. It was Connie, and she was crying. "What's the matter?" I asked.

"Bart's been killed in Vietnam."

"Oh, no!" I responded, with tears rolling down my face. Sandra got up and walked toward me. "It was my sister in New Jersey. My brother has been killed in Vietnam." Sandra hugged me and kept repeating how sorry she was. I wanted to be alone; I wanted to break down and scream at the top of my lungs, but I tried to keep my composure because I didn't want to upset my children. Sandra called to her son to come downstairs, saying that they had to get going. After she left, I called Jimmy and told him the news, and by five o'clock, his whole family, his mother, aunts, the whole shebang had filled up the living room. I was devastated that they came because I felt they were intruding. I didn't need them. What did they want anyhow? It must have been their guilt from just a few months before when they were so hateful to me. Was this their way of saying they had changed their tune, and they wanted to make it up to me? Show me how much they loved me?

I wanted to be alone to grieve, to call and talk with Daddy about Bart. I was worried about him and Margie. I went into my bedroom, closed the door, and hoped the Minors would soon leave. When Jimmy finally opened the bedroom door, I said, "Let me know when they have left so I can call my family and talk in private with them." The Minors began to clear out, and I called Daddy. He was as devastated as I was. I asked about my mother, but they hadn't been able to locate her. Bart's remains were to be returned to Freehold, and the funeral would be held in a few days. Bart's death was a tremendous loss to all of us. He was a good man, and he didn't deserve to die at nineteen years old. I would have to go to New Jersey to attend the funeral; Jimmy's mother offered to take care of Jimmy and Scott, and Margaret offered to take Mark. I was at peace with Mark staying with Margaret, but Jimmy and Scott staying with Frances was a worry. However, I was simply too fragile to turn down their offer, and the next day, I was on a plane to New Jersey. As the plane landed and taxied to the terminal, I could see Daddy, still easy to spot as he stood in the crowd in his red jacket.

We all gathered at Connie's house. By the time I arrived, my mother had been located in a jail in a neighboring town. Connie was the official bearer of bad news to our mother. Daddy paid my mother's bail so she could come to the funeral; he said it was the right thing to do. I was glad that two of Daddy's brothers, Virgil and Ferd, came to be with him. I remember Virgil and Ferd sitting at the kitchen table as my mother made nasty remarks to Daddy that were meant to demean him in front of his brothers. I hated this woman as much as ever. She never cared whom she insulted, belittled, or stepped on, even in the midst of a family tragedy. I was also embarrassed by her worn-out housecoat laced with cigarette burns, so loosely pinned together that it exposed her bare flesh. As usual, I wanted Daddy to stand up to her outrageous behavior.

A neighbor offered Connie some foldout cots for us to sleep on, and we set the cots up in the living room. This allowed the beds to be given to Daddy and his brothers. My mother ranted about how the "shit slingers" got the best beds, and she had to sleep on a small cot. We told her to shut up, and if she didn't like it, she could find somewhere else to sleep. When she finally stopped complaining, she unfolded her bed, put her sheet and blanket on it, and went into the bathroom. Connie and I kind of got a kick out of the fact that she was not going to get her way. We laughed about how all through the years, she had demanded the best bed in the house. She never cared where anyone else slept or what they slept on as long as she had the best. When we heard our mother coming back down the hall, we noticed that her cot had slowly moved back into the folded position.

We knew she would pitch a fit when she saw the cot, and we were laughing so hard we could hardly speak. "Oh yeah," she exclaimed. "Look at this bed. How am I going to sleep in it?"

Connie came back with, "Just shut up! Open it back up and go to sleep. We are sick of hearing your complaints." We kept laughing as our mother huffed and puffed, putting the bed back together. Our fun took the edge off what we were going to face the next day. I remember hearing Daddy crying loudly in the night. I knew he was in great pain, and I wished I could help him, but there was nothing I could do. We all loved Bart, and there was no way to ease anyone's grief over his loss. Daddy was grieving for his only son, and I knew he needed to do this in his own way, but it didn't make it any less painful to hear.

The next day was the day of Bart's funeral. His body was laid out at Higgins Funeral Home, where Bart worked as a teen. Mr. Higgins knew Bart well, and he shared with us how Bart's death was a loss for him as well. We were allowed to go to the funeral home and view the body before anyone else arrived. Actually seeing Bart in the coffin was more difficult than any of us had imagined. He was too young to die. He had been so full of life, full of fun, and he had such a great future ahead of him. I didn't understand why life worked the way it did. Why did God allow this to happen? We had already suffered enough in our childhood. Since we had no religious affiliation, the funeral was held at the funeral home. Bart's friends came from all over, but I didn't know many of them. I knew some of the neighbors who still lived on Center Street, and I enjoyed seeing Catherine Kennedy again. Some of the neighbors told us stories about how they would try to get Bart to stay for dinner at their house, but he would insist that he had to go home to cook for his little sister. He faithfully looked after Margie after I left. Bart deserved better than any of us gave him. I thought back to the weekend Bart hitchhiked to Atlanta to visit me. I wanted so much for him to have a good time, but Jimmy made sure it didn't work out that way.

The body was finally loaded onto the hearse, and people on the street stopped, dropping their heads in silence as the hearse made its way through Freehold. It was a military burial, including the playing of taps and the twenty-one gun salute. The flag was folded and handed to Daddy, who was sitting in the front row next to my mother. It was a cold overcast October day, with the wind blowing and the leaves falling abundantly. I looked up at the trees that were filled with light and took comfort in the fact that Bart was safe; the pain and darkness that riddled his short life could no longer harm him.

We all drove back to Connie's house, where neighbors had brought in lots of food. We all sat down and ate together. My dad's brother Ferd asked where my mother would be going now that the funeral was over. He insisted that someone needed to drop her off somewhere because Daddy and his brothers wanted to have a drink, and that was not going to be anything but unpleasant with her in the house. In addition, Phil wasn't going to allow my mother to stay in his house any longer than he had to. Connie suggested that we take her to Marlboro State Hospital; she had been there before, and they were aware of her problem. Connie and I loaded her in the car. I was afraid she would refuse to get out of the car when we arrived, but she didn't, and we all walked in together. Connie explained the situation to the lady at the front desk. In just a few minutes, another lady came to escort my mother away, and Connie and I watched as she walked through the door out of our sight.

When I arrived back home in Atlanta, all seemed well. The boys were as glad to see me as I was to see them. Frances was very friendly, and she assured me that the boys had been no trouble to her. I doubted that was the truth, but I felt that I had "earned" her regard because of my family tragedy. Christmas was quickly approaching, and since I was back in Frances's good graces, I was invited to the Annual Tree. Knowing no graceful way to reject such an honor, I felt it was in the best interest of my children not to make waves. The rules of this mightier-than-thou event were established by Frances. The cousins would all draw names. In addition, every family was expected to buy a gift for Frances, James, Mike, Sherry, and Teresa. Although the unfairness of this system was quite obvious, I said nothing and went along with it. So far, I had never received a gift from any Minor that I could use or that fit me. A typical gift might be a sweater in a child's size 10 instead of an adult size 10 or a child's watch or a wax paper dispenser that was a piece of junk. It was all nonsense in my opinion. Wanting to stay as disconnected from this family as I could, I made it a point to be friendly while keeping my distance. The biggest part of the evening came after everyone had opened their gifts. That was when the time came for the Queen Mother to sit on her throne and open her gifts. It was a sort of competition as to who would be the one to come up with the gift she loved the most. It was almost sickening to watch this woman with rings on each finger of both hands laughing like a kid in a toy store, making little remarks about each gift while her children all shone with pride at her enjoyment. I always felt sad for Jack and Diane, who had little money. When she opened their gift, she would hold it up and repeat what it was with a giggle in her voice that indicated that their gift would not win the prize. It was an event I endured, knowing that I had a whole year before it would come again.

Considering the severity of the abuse I had endured in 1967 and the loss of my only brother, one thing was clear—life would never be the same for me. I had lost an important part of myself, and it would be years before I would find a way to come out from under the dark cloud of hopelessness and fear. Rape and chronic abuse caused serious psychological trauma. The trauma may not show up until years later, but it would show up somewhere along the way. Each abusive act done to me was burned into my memory, each delivering the message that I was worthless and that my feelings and needs didn't matter. Even though Jimmy Minor's attitude toward me had softened somewhat, his verbal abuse continued. I was always on guard, never knowing when the next episode would take place.

When Daddy received Bart's military insurance early in 1968, he decided to split it among us, and he called me to say that Connie, Margie, and I would each receive $1,500. That was a lot of money for someone in my predicament, so I wanted to think this through and make the right decision about how to use it. I called Christine, a friend I knew from way back when I lived in the Wellswood Apartments. She was a teacher, and she and her husband were both older, stable adults. When I told her about the money, she suggested that I use it for something like a college fund for the boys. I agreed with her suggestion and decided to follow her advice, but then I made the mistake of calling Jimmy at work and telling him about the money.

"Why don't you just sit around the house and not worry about doing any work for the rest of the day," he said. His words smelled, and I knew I had made a huge mistake by calling him. I had thought about not telling him and just putting the money in a savings account in my name only. I also weighed the consequences I would suffer if he found out. I never liked secrets, but now I would have to hash it out with him as to how best to use the money, and I was sure we would never agree on what was best. Of course, he considered this "our" money, yet everything else remained "his." When Jimmy got home, I told him that I wanted to put the money into some kind of college savings plan for the boys. Jimmy, however, insisted that we use a thousand dollars to fix up a wrecked MG he had recently bought and intended to fix up. Jimmy said that once we fixed up the MG, he could sell it and more than double the thousand dollars. He did promise that the rest of the money, $500, would go into a college fund. His plan sounded good, but I didn't trust him. While he was badgering me about his plan, his whole persona changed. He became affectionate, with a happy, loving tone to his voice. I had never met this person before, so I knew it was phony and that his motive was no more than using this money to accommodate himself. We went back and forth about the money for the next few days. When the check finally arrived in the mail, it was made out to me only. I told Jimmy that I would think about his plan but that, for now, I wanted to open a savings account and deposit it. He insisted that the money be put in the savings account we already had opened in both our names that now contained only $5. Jimmy also insisted that it would be best if he just made the deposit on his way to work. He agreed to deposit half the money and keep the other half to fix up his MG and "double the money."

"Okay," I said as I verified that he agreed to stick with the plan to fix the MG, and when it was sold, the money would be replaced. The other half was to be deposited into our joint savings account.

The check was no sooner signed and in his hand than I began to feel uncomfortable. I wanted him to give the check back to me, but I knew he wouldn't. I watched him walk out the back door, check in hand. Watching his car as it backed down the driveway, I knew I had left myself open to be victimized, and I worried about it all day. When Jimmy got home that evening, I asked for the deposit slip; he claimed that he didn't have it but that the money was safely deposited. Jimmy made it clear that he didn't like being questioned, and his attitude quickly dissolved back to his old self. I wanted to kick myself for allowing him to fool me again. I was always looking for a sign that he had changed, and I wanted to be able to trust him, but his behavior kept reminding me that was not the way it was.

A few days later, a Volkswagen shell was delivered and deposited in our backyard. It was green, no engine and no wheels, just a shell, and I knew Jimmy had bought it with my money. I started to question him about when the MG would be fixed and sold, but I was again reminded that Jimmy Minor did not like being questioned about anything. I told him that I was going to file for divorce. The next day, I asked a neighbor to take me to the bank, where I planned to withdraw the money that Jimmy said he had deposited in our joint savings account. The banker explained to me that five hundred dollars had been put into a CD in Jimmy's name only. "I am his wife, and this is my money," I replied with tears welling up in my eyes.

"Are you aware that there will be a substantial penalty for early withdrawal?" he asked.

"This was not his money to put into a CD," I explained. "It was mine." I was visibly shaken and my voice quivering, but I was trying not to make a scene.

"Since the money was deposited in his name only, we will need his permission to let you withdraw it." I took the forms, turned, and walked out. I hated myself. How could I let him do this to me? I should have known better. That evening, I got out the papers that were given to me at the bank and confronted Jimmy. "I thought we agreed that you would keep $750 and put the other $750 in our joint savings account," I said. He wouldn't answer me, and the anger boiled inside me. "I have a form that I need you to sign so I can withdraw the rest of my money." He ignored my request, and I knew he had no intention of signing the paper. The Volkswagen shell sat in the back of the yard for the rest of the winter. He did have some new seats made for the MG, but it sat in the garage and was never repaired enough to be driven.

One afternoon in spring of 1968, I was doing some grocery shopping with all three boys in tow. Mark, who was eight months old by now, was sitting in the seat of a grocery cart when I noticed that he was shaking as if he were cold. I knew something was wrong, so I quickly paid for my groceries, got in the car, and went straight home. Once home, I took Mark's temperature, and it was 102 degrees. I called the doctor's office and left a message for the doctor on call to call me back. It was late afternoon. I called Jimmy at work, told him that Mark was sick with a high fever, and asked him to come straight home after work in case the doctor called in a prescription. When I took Mark's temperature again, it was 104 degrees. I tried to stay calm, but I knew I had to somehow get Mark's temperature down. The doctor called back and gave me instructions on how to bring the fever down, and he also called in a prescription. I called Jimmy back and let him know so he could pick up the prescription on his way home, but he told me that it would be a few hours before he could be home. I hung up and called the neighbor across the street since I knew she had a car. I asked if she would pick up the prescription, explaining that I had no money but would reimburse her the following day. She agreed to help me. In the meantime, I kept working on the fever. By the time the neighbor arrived with the prescription, Mark's fever was 105. The neighbor stayed to help me, and I felt better with her there because she was an experienced mother of three children. Between the two of us, we finally got Mark's fever down. While my neighbor and I gave our full attention to Mark, Jimmy and Scott pretty much destroyed the house. They had not had dinner yet and were complaining that they were hungry. It wasn't until around 10:00 p.m. that I could feed the boys and get them to bed. I put Mark in bed with me. I didn't call Jimmy back because I did not need his help anymore. I never heard another word from him that night. Early the next morning, as the light was just starting to filter through my bedroom window, I heard the back door open and the sound of Jimmy Minor's footsteps tiptoeing through the kitchen.

In April of 1968, all the TV stations broke in with the news that Martin Luther King had been shot in Memphis. Frances called, asking for Jimmy; I gave him the phone, and you would have thought they had won the lottery. Jimmy and his mother were both rejoicing, and Jimmy's exultant voice echoed through the house as if his favorite team had scored a touchdown. At this point, it was not clear whether King had died or not. The phone rang every few minutes as he and Frances discussed what they both considered a huge victory, enjoying this moment like no other. Jimmy whooped and hollered when the station confirmed that Martin Luther King had in fact died. I thought back to a year earlier and how they probably rejoiced in the same way about each incident of Jimmy's brutality toward me. I thought about how it could have so easily been me who was murdered, and I felt a moment of paralyzing fear of what the two of them were capable of.

I was very busy in the months ahead. Janet and I were in touch every day. On the days when she had her car, we would pile all the kids into her little Volkswagen and go shopping. I never had much money to spend, but just getting out and going somewhere was a break for all of us. Since I was on my own raising the boys, Janet was a great help to me. She would ride along to help me with doctor appointments or sit with the boys when I had an appointment. Even though Janet and her husband were a nice couple our age, we never were couples friends. That was because of Jimmy's negative attitude toward Janet and her husband, whom he saw as a threat to his plan to keep me isolated. Jimmy complained about my friendship with Janet unless she was going to babysit or help in some way that was also a help to him.

I loved trying new recipes. I enjoyed cooking a nice meal each evening so we could all sit down and eat dinner together. If Jimmy was not home from work, the boys and I would just go ahead without him. Mark would sit in his high chair, and little Jimmy would tell us what he did in school that day. The boys were easy to please when it came to food; they loved to try new things and ate whatever I fixed without complaint. Scott especially loved dessert; his favorite was butterscotch pudding, which he called "scotch pudding." The boys were all extremely bright, delightful children, and I loved them more than they will ever know. I wanted to be a good mother, and I did my best to give my children what I thought they needed. However, because of my childhood, I had little knowledge of normal parenting, nor did I receive any help from my husband. I struggled to cope with my sense of obligation to my children and how that obligation tied me to Jimmy Minor. Because I felt that I had to stay in my marriage to protect my children, they kept me grounded in doing the right thing. I was never unfaithful to Jimmy, but I still dreamed of the day when I would be able to gather up my children and walk away. I didn't know how this would happen, but I believed that it was only a matter of time.

Cooking, keeping the house in order, and watching my children grow gave me a great amount of satisfaction. All these activities fed and nurtured my sense of well-being, even though Jimmy Minor never found any value in anything I did. He never had a kind or complimentary word to say about a meal that I had served or an outfit I made. He never had any trouble eating what I cooked, but nothing I did was ever going to please him. It was the boys who applauded my efforts and gave me the staying power I needed.

One Sunday afternoon during this time, I put a ham in the oven and started to make some fresh applesauce. As Jimmy watched me peel the apples and put them in the pot, he asked, "What are you making?"

"Applesauce," I replied.

"Why are you making applesauce? No one is going to eat that junk."

"Well, you don't have to eat any if you don't want to," I answered.

"You live in the South, and we don't eat boiled apples." I ignored his remarks and just kept working. "When are you going to learn to cook decent meals? We aren't going to eat that kind of junk." I continued to ignore his remarks. As the apples cooked and the windows misted up with steam, the aroma of the ham and the apples was inviting. When the apples were soft, I added some cinnamon and a little sugar, stirring to get the right consistency. The aroma was delightfully stronger now, and the boys kept coming into the kitchen to ask when supper would be ready. I finally had it all together and called them into the dining room. I had dished out the warm applesauce into custard dishes for each plate except Jimmy's. The boys sat down and began eating the applesauce.

"Wow! This is good!" little Jimmy exclaimed.

Then Scott chimed in, "Yeah, I like this, Mom. It's really good!"

"Did you try some applesauce, Daddy?" asked Jimmy.

"No," he answered.

"You need to try it. It's good," little Jimmy insisted.

"Yeah, Daddy, it is good," Scott added as he dug in. I was just gloating with amusement as the conversation continued. I glanced over to see the look on Jimmy's face; our eyes met, and there was a long pause.

He finally but reluctantly said in a low voice, "Well, I guess I was wrong." This was a first for Jimmy Minor. Even though there was no apology, it was his first admission that he could be wrong about anything. I felt acknowledged, validated, and rewarded for my efforts. It was at these times that I was sure that persevering through the pain of Jimmy Minor's wrath, if only for my children's sake, was worth it. I let the chatter between Jimmy and the boys continue as I kept working on fixing the plates, smiling at how these little boys so easily made Jimmy admit he was wrong.

In 1968, the country was all doom and gloom. In June, Bobby Kennedy, only four months into his campaign for president, was gunned down by an assassin's bullet. Many had hoped that Bobby was the person who could turn the country around, but that hope was now squashed. I remember watching on live TV the train that carried Bobby's body back to Washington, DC, for burial. The television audience watched as millions of people stood at the train stations along the route, saying their last goodbyes. We all felt the profound sadness and hopelessness of the times we were living in. Everyone was either marching, chanting, or rioting to protest the war that had taken my brother. Nothing like these protests had ever happened before. As the war raged on year after year, our young men were dropping like flies. I believed more and more that this war had nothing to do with our freedom or our safety and everything to do with the wrong and egotistical decisions of our government leaders.

We signed little Jimmy up to play Little League baseball. Because of his natural athletic ability, Jimmy was chosen to be the pitcher. I enjoyed watching the games, and when they asked for volunteers to coach, Jimmy was their man. He liked being in the spotlight, especially when his kid was the best player. Jimmy's mother used Jimmy's coaching to brag about what an exceptional father he was. Of course, Jimmy still did nothing with the boys at home. If one of the boys tried to get Jimmy to play ball in the backyard, he would answer, "I'm not your playmate. Go outside and play by yourself." When Jimmy refused them, I would offer to play ball instead. Little Jimmy loved to hit the ball; I would pitch, and he would swing, and there was no doubt that he was good.

In the summer of 1968, as Mark turned a year old, I began to feel that I was losing myself. I had been married to Jimmy Minor now for six miserable years, persevering through the worst of his disordered ways. I began to lose hope as I worried that my imprisonment and lack of choices would last forever. I berated myself for ever getting involved with Jimmy in the first place; how young, foolish, and misled I was. At this point, I felt that I had already paid way too much for one wrong decision. I wanted a way out; surely, sooner or later, something better would come my way. My feelings of self-pity and hopelessness that summer were the beginning of my grieving for the loss of my sense of self and for the loss of six years of my life. Only through this mourning process for the past could I contemplate and accept a new beginning.

In the midst of that miserable summer, a lady from a local church came by to encourage me to visit her church and take the boys to Sunday school. Mrs. Mashburn was older and wiser than I was; she was happily married with teenagers. The boys and I started going to Sunday school, but I never felt as if I fit into Mrs. Mashburn's class because my life was so different from the lives of the other girls who had Christian husbands and seemingly normal lives. I was the oddball, and I knew it. However, when Mrs. Mashburn invited me to lunch with her one afternoon, I felt that somehow my life held some importance for her. At lunch, I shared with her that I wanted to divorce Jimmy Minor. She didn't advise me as to what to do or ask me any details; she just listened. She also invited me to bring the boys to her house so we could talk more. She had a beautiful house that overlooked a huge manicured backyard. Her friendship gave me a feeling of support and a safe place to share my feelings. She was a tremendous blessing in my chaotic life.

Also that summer, we drove up to New Jersey to visit my family. It was a miserable, grueling trip because, of course, Jimmy was in charge. We left at night so the boys would sleep most of the way, and there was little stopping to eat or stretch our legs. It was a brutal trip, especially for a one-year-old baby who didn't understand what was going on and why he couldn't get down and play. Jimmy and Scott were also unhappy, imprisoned in the back seat for seventeen hours. We left around 9:00 p.m. on a Friday evening and arrived Saturday afternoon around 2:00 p.m. A long car trip with Jimmy Minor was guaranteed to be a nightmare since he ran the show with no consideration for anyone else's needs.

On Sunday, Connie drove to Keyport and picked up my mother so she could join us for dinner. She was in her late fifties now, but she looked much older. She was bloated, and her skin was blotchy; the burn marks on her arms and neck were much more visible. She was sober but obviously in poor health, and she showed little interest in me or my children. When I asked her about her waitress job, she complained to Daddy that she was too old to be working. He retorted that he was older than she, and he was still working. I could feel the huge distance between them; their happier days of drinking together in the dark and planning for their future were long gone. Since Daddy had moved to Connie's, he felt no further obligation to my mother, even though they were still legally married. I was glad to see Daddy finally detaching and allowing my mother to face her own consequences, thanks to Connie and Phil offering him a way out. When Connie drove my mother back to Keyport the following evening, I knew I would never see her again.

In the fall of 1968, little Jimmy went to school for the first time. Public kindergarten was not offered in Georgia back then, so many parents enrolled their kids in a day-care-type kindergarten that they paid for. I suggested signing little Jimmy up for the kindergarten program, and to my surprise, Jimmy agreed. I loved to watch little Jimmy as the bus pulled up in front, and he turned and waved to me as he stepped onto the bus. He loved going to school, and I knew this was good for him.

Each fall, the Southeastern Fair came to Atlanta. It was a big event that drew crowds from all over, and it was fun for the whole family. Jimmy suggested that we find a babysitter for Mark and take Jimmy and Scott to the fair on September 29 to celebrate my birthday. I was pleased with his suggestion since we seldom went anywhere together as a family. I was grateful that Janet agreed to keep Mark for me, and I promised that we would be back before dark. The day arrived, and the boys and I were all geared up for a fun time. It was a delightfully crisp fall day, and I was as excited as the boys to be going somewhere. The boys rode all the rides, and we all tried some of the games of chance, throwing darts and pitching pennies. We bought balloon animals from a clown and ate hot dogs and cotton candy. We all rooted for Jimmy as he succeeded at a game that tested his strength. As the sun started to fade, I suggested that we get started home so I could pick up Mark before dark. We all piled into the car, with the boys still holding onto their helium balloons.

As we got on the road, instead of driving home, Jimmy started driving in the opposite direction. I asked him where he was going. "What's the hurry?" he asked.

"It's getting late, and I am concerned about Mark. I told Janet I would be home around five." Jimmy ignored me. I was getting annoyed because we were not paying Janet to babysit; she was doing it as a favor because I was her friend. All of a sudden, Jimmy pulled into a McDonald's parking lot. Now I was furious because Jimmy always had a way of ruining a pleasant day, and making Janet angry would certainly ruin my day. I said I would wait in the car because I figured this might help make things go faster.

"What do you want?" Jimmy asked.

"Nothing, I just want to get home."

By the time we were on the road again, it was almost six thirty, and when we pulled into our driveway on Quillian Avenue, it was after seven. I was the first one out of the car and in the back door. As I turned from the kitchen into the dining room, there sat Jimmy's family. When they saw me, they yelled in unison, "Happy birthday!" I was startled, absolutely startled. Wrapped gifts sat on the coffee table, and the dining room table was decorated with a birthday tablecloth, a sheet cake, and dishes of finger foods. I stood there in disbelief, not knowing quite what to say.

I mumbled something about having to get Mark, turned into the hallway, picked up the phone, and dialed Janet's number. When she answered, I apologized for being so late and asked her to meet me at the fence with Mark. I hung up the phone, walked past the party crowd without saying a word, and went out the back door to meet Janet. I quickly explained what was going on, and neither she nor I could believe it. As I walked back into the house, I wondered what motivated the Minors to do this. Were they trying to soothe their feelings of guilt? I noticed Teresa acting as if she were someone other than the person who told my neighbor just over a year ago how I had sold the house out from under Jimmy. Was this party a gesture from the Minor family to say they were sorry without actually saying it? I finally joined the family and began to open the gifts at their insistence, then we all ate cake, talked about our children, and laughed about nothing. As everyone left, I sincerely thanked them. Even though I didn't trust these people or their motives, I went to bed that night with the feeling that in some small way, I mattered.

One of my gifts was a set of casserole dishes, and I used one of those dishes as I prepared a new recipe for dinner the next night. When Jimmy got home, I had dinner ready to put on the table, and I felt contented as we gathered around the table. However, I quickly noticed Jimmy's negative attitude as he glared at me with his usual disapproval and refused to join in any conversation at the table. The message was clear that he was simply not going to allow me to enjoy anything for very long.

A few weeks later, when I came home from the grocery store, Jimmy was sitting in the family room watching his brand-new color television that he had put on a credit card to the tune of $500. He still believed as always that all the money was his, and therefore all the decisions about money were his alone. Color TVs were the latest new technology, and I knew that this purchase was his way of "getting me back" for the party and gifts he thought I had enjoyed too much. What he didn't know was that I didn't care anymore what he did. I did not react to his TV, never mentioned it, and acted as if I didn't notice it was there. I just went about my business as usual. As I think back, I am amused at how a gift of a new casserole dish was all it took to lift up my day, but for Jimmy, it took a five-hundred-dollar TV. He had a strange and unhealthy attachment to things. My greatest fear about his spending priorities was his lack of concern that we had no health or life insurance. Jimmy argued that my wish for insurance was an attempt to squander his money on something that was never going to benefit him. Even though he complained when I took the boys to the dentist or doctor for checkups, I took them anyway. I never bought new clothes for myself or spent money on luxuries like makeup; I made do with what I had. I remember once when a girlfriend bought herself all-new makeup and gave her old supplies to me. I bought my winter coat on sale and made it last through four winters before it wore out. But in Jimmy's mind, I would remain a spendthrift for wanting medical care for our sons.

There were days when I still actively mourned the loss of Bart, who had been gone a year now. One of the popular songs of the day was Joe South's "Don't It Make You Want to Go Home." Hearing this song made my mind wander back to previous years and wish I could, through some miracle, go back and fix my life. If only I could go back to Center Street and start all over. In my fantasy, I would be aware of the danger signals before getting involved with someone as destructive as Jimmy Minor. I would know how to prevent Bart from ever joining the service. I would have been there to make dinner for Bart and Margie instead of wasting my life with Jimmy Minor. How much better life would have been for all of us. I was feeling great remorse for the wrong choices I had made, and my children were the only bright spot in it all.

In spite of Martin Luther King's assassination, his movement lived on. President Lyndon Johnson signed the Civil Rights Act, which prohibited discrimination in the sale or rental of housing. At that time, the neighborhoods in Atlanta were divided between white and black, but this new law would change all that. Frances was livid because she saw these changes as an injustice to her race. She rattled on about how she wanted to sit in her living room window and shoot black people as they walked by. She felt that black people's progress in some way diminished her Southern white superiority. Whenever she spoke about this subject, I could feel her eyes looking straight at me, but I would never look at her because I knew she was looking for some gesture from me that showed my agreement with her. Her remarks became so violent that I feared that she might actually carry out her plan. I never did understand such hatred toward an entire race of people. I eventually attributed the Minors' racial attitudes to their pride, their lack of education, and their lack of compassion for others. I knew what they had done to me when I attempted to stick up for myself. I was still very fearful, and appearing to stay neutral was a way of protecting myself. However, I truly believed as Daddy did; he loved all people and didn't care if they were rich or poor, white or black. He especially admired those who, in spite of their poverty and lack of opportunity, rose above their circumstances and accomplished great things.

Chapter 13

Fighting Back

In the middle of December of 1968, amid the preparations for Christmas, I received an unexpected call from Connie. She was crying as she told me that our mother was dead. Connie had not heard from our mother in two weeks, and as she and Daddy sat at the kitchen table wondering why my mother had not called as she usually did, the phone rang. It was the police, who told them that my mother had been found dead in her room. The police waited as Daddy and Phil drove to Keyport to meet them and identify the body. The police estimated that she had been dead for at least ten days before anyone noticed.

Daddy later called me to let me know there would be a funeral at Higgins Funeral Home and that, if I wanted to come, he would pay my airfare. I decided not to go, mostly because of the difficulty of finding someone to keep my children. When I hung up the phone, all I could think about was the never-ending misery that this woman inflicted on herself and others. I had a feeling of relief that she was gone, and I hoped that Daddy would be able to pick up the pieces and possibly find a better life for himself. For me, the sadness of her life was much more overwhelming than any sadness over her death. The reality was that I never knew this person, and she never knew me. My mother's life was wasted away by the severest case of alcohol addiction I have ever encountered, even to this day. Daddy called when the funeral was over. The only people who had attended were Daddy, Connie, Phil, and Margie.

Just before Christmas, the boys were all excited and wanted all the toys they saw advertised on TV. Jimmy and I went to Sears one weekend, picked out their toys, and put them on layaway. Sears offered free delivery and a special discount if you spent at least $50. The boys and I decorated the tree one Saturday morning. I strung the lights, making sure they all worked, and the boys helped with the ornaments and tinsel. When we were finished, the living room, with its Christmas tree and stone fireplace, looked as pretty as a postcard.

Not long after we were finished decorating, the doorbell rang, and the boys came running to see who it was. I went to the door with all the boys running ahead of me. It was the Sears deliveryman with a huge cardboard box secured with tape and strong string. I told the man just to set the box in the corner next to the front door. "What's in the box?" little Jimmy asked.

"I am not sure. We are going to leave it right there, and I'll look at it later." I knew they had pretty much figured out what the contents of the box were, and they were not going to just let it be.

"Can we open it?" Scott asked.

"No! We don't know who it is for. I'll look at it later. Go on back to your cartoons." I had already figured out how I was going to handle this. After lunch, I would put Mark down for his nap and send the other two out to play, which would give me a few minutes to drag the box down to the basement.

A few minutes later, the doorbell rang again. It was Janet with her dad, who had come to visit her for a few days. I was glad that Janet had brought him by to meet me, and I invited them in. Janet's dad had retired after a career in the Navy, and I was soon to learn that he was used to doing things his way. When Janet asked about the box, I explained the toys to them quietly so that the boys would not hear me. Janet's dad offered to take the box down to the basement for me, and I tried my best to assure him that his help was not necessary. I tried to change the subject, but he was not going to let it go. "It'll just take me a minute." I soon got the message that ignoring him was not going to work. The boys were still in the house watching cartoons, and they didn't miss a trick, so I wanted to handle the box my way. However, Janet's dad just walked over to the box and picked it up, not noticing as he struggled that he had also picked up the cord from the tree lights. When he finally had a good grasp on the box and proceeded toward the basement door, Janet and I could see that he had picked up the cord, and we tried to stop him. He paid no attention, and as he went one step too far, the whole tree toppled over and crashed in the middle of the living room floor. All the new balls I had just bought were in millions of small pieces embedded in the rug. Tinsel was everywhere. The water in the tray under the tree had leaked out and left a huge wet spot on the rug. "Oh no!" he said as he put the box down and ran over to pick up the tree. While Janet and I tried to clean up the mess, Janet's dad continued to struggle to pull the box down to the basement. The crash had brought the boys running into the living room just in time to see Janet's dad going down to the basement with the box.

"What happened to our tree?" little Jimmy asked.

"We had a little accident, but it is going to be okay," I answered. The boys just stood there looking on as Janet and I cleaned up the mess as best we could. I felt a sigh of relief when Janet announced that she and her dad had to get going.

While going on a trip to Mexico, Daddy decided to stop in Atlanta to spend a few days with us. Of course, Jimmy did his best acting as the perfect husband and father. Even though I knew what he was doing, I did appreciate his creating a more relaxed atmosphere during my father's visit. One afternoon, Daddy asked where the liquor store was so he could have an afternoon drink. I had no clue where a liquor store was, and I cringed at the idea that he would be drinking in our house. I never argued with Daddy or expressed my true feelings, but this idea made me very uncomfortable. I told him that I didn't want any drinking while Jimmy was around, and when he brought it up again, I simply told him that as far as I knew, there weren't any liquor stores in the area. Since Daddy was not with us long, I felt that his need for a drink could wait. From the outside, Daddy's drinking looked harmless; he was never drunk, and he did not slur his words or become nasty. He seemed to know his limits and would stop drinking before any signs of impairment became apparent. However, he promoted drinking, and he wanted to be around those who felt the same. I hated liquor, and I hated the smell of it because I knew the damage that it could do. Daddy always said that he never saw a Southerner who could drink, and he was referring to Jimmy, whose ignorance and abusive tendencies escalated when he drank. Since Jimmy did not drink at home but only in bars, so far, there had been no drinking in our home. I didn't care who could or couldn't handle their liquor; I didn't want it in my house around my children.

One evening, Jimmy brought home a miniature poodle puppy. He was so precious, a little beige-colored ball of fur. The boys loved him and begged to keep him, which we did. We named our new dog Cotton. Cotton was smart and easily housebroken, and he had a wonderful temperament with the boys. He was especially tolerant of Mark, who was always pulling on him and trying to pick him up the wrong way. Cotton never growled or showed any sign of aggression toward Mark. Cotton soon won us all over and became part of our family.

The days ahead were filled with the busyness of Little League baseball. Jimmy and Scott both played now. I baked cakes and planned birthday parties. I got a library card, and once every two weeks, I took the boys to the library to pick out books that they wanted me to read to them. I was working with a tight budget and always found it difficult to squeeze out enough money to make ends meet. When I became friends with the girl who worked at the CVS drugstore, we found out that we had a lot in common. We were both from Freehold and graduated the same year. She needed a babysitter for her little girl, Angel; she asked me if I would be interested and offered to pay me $12 a week. Since I was home all day anyway and needed some money of my own, I agreed to do it. Jimmy and Scott were glad to have another child to play with, and Angel fit right in. The extra money allowed me to buy some decent clothes and just to have some money of my own. I kept a set of bowls on the top shelf of the kitchen cabinets, and every week when I got paid, I put a few dollars in the middle bowl to save for a rainy day. I even had enough to buy a new dress for Easter. I loved having my own money, and even though it was not much, it gave me a sense of control and gave me choices that I never had before.

As the year rolled on, the war was still raging, but few supported it; this era was also the beginning of the hippie, love-child revolution. People would drive to downtown Atlanta just to take a look at the sights of young people hanging out on street corners with long hair, beads, headbands that said "flower power," and vests made out of the American flag.

Early one Saturday morning, I awoke to the sound of Jimmy coming in from his night out. He told me that he had been playing poker all night, and he had won a car, a station wagon. Jimmy then handed me the keys and suggested that I drive the station wagon if I needed to go anywhere that day while he slept. As I looked out the kitchen window, I could see the back end of the car sitting in the garage. It looked decent, and Jimmy said it was a running car. After breakfast, I piled the boys in to go grocery shopping. The car started up with no trouble, and I slowly backed down the driveway and proceeded down Quillian Avenue. When we approached McAfee, which was a much busier street, I couldn't stop. I pumped the brake pedal as hard as I could, but this car was not stopping. The brakes were gone, and I was lucky that it was early enough in the day that there was little traffic and nothing was coming the other way. I was able to coast into a driveway and slowly turn around back onto Quillian. It was times like this that I felt like such a fool for trusting anything Jimmy said because he never showed concern for anyone but himself.

So far, most of the healthy relationships I had observed were on television sitcoms. I also remembered the McCues and their respect for one another. They were a team, working together toward a common goal. Each of them seemed to understand that the well-being of the spouse contributed to the ultimate success and well-being of their children. I wanted to be part of that kind of a team, but Jimmy Minor was never going to fill that bill. I knew that if I was ever going to find a better life, then it would have to be with someone else. I also knew that Jimmy was never going to support me or his children if I did find a way out. I still had my little stash in the kitchen cabinet, and that little stash gave me the feeling that I could at any time do what I had threatened so many times. Thoughts of contacting an attorney to begin divorce proceedings increased every time Jimmy became physically violent with me. Whenever I threatened to call the police, Jimmy would believe me and jerk the phone line out of the wall. However, when I threatened that I was going to see an attorney, Jimmy didn't believe me because I had threatened divorce too many times, and he was sure that I had no way to carry out these threats. Now that I had some money, I decided to act. One day when Jimmy left for work, I called a local attorney and asked how much money I would need to file for a divorce. I was told that I would need $25 to start the process. I felt empowered by this news because I had almost that amount saved.

The only time I saw Jimmy's family now was at the Christmas get-togethers. Frances was still a large part of Jimmy's life, but I was for the most part detached from his family. Every now and then, we would drop by to visit Frances; Jimmy told me that she had been diagnosed with some sort of cancer, and he was worried that she would not live very long. It was a Minor family pattern to diagnose their own illnesses, blowing everything out of proportion, and making grandiose assumptions that death was at their doorstep. I knew that this was nothing more than their way of drawing attention to themselves. Everyone seemed to diagnose themselves with some sort of cancer, but no one ever died from cancer, and they all continued to look healthy. One day, when we visited Frances, it was apparent to me that Frances was not sick, but when I remarked to Jimmy that I thought his mother looked well, I knew right away that I had stepped on one of his raw nerves. Jimmy left the house mad, and when he came back, he had been drinking. When he started pushing me around, I ran across the street to a neighbor's house, called the police, and waited outside for them to come. Jimmy drove away. When the officer arrived, I explained to him what had happened and told him that I feared what my husband might do to me when he came home. The officer suggested that I file a complaint against Jimmy, which I did. There was now a warrant out for Jimmy's arrest. I was sure he had run to Mama so she could hear his story and acknowledge how badly he was being treated.

I didn't hear from Jimmy again until the second night. It was about two or three in the morning when the phone rang. It was Jimmy, announcing that I was nothing but an ungrateful f—ing bitch and a sleazy whore, and I was not going to get away with calling the police on him. I hung up and dialed the police station, and they kept me on the line for over an hour in case Jimmy came home. When he didn't make good on his threat, the lady I spoke with told me that she would assign a patrol car in my neighborhood. She told me to call back if I were to hear from Jimmy again. I was too scared to go back to sleep, and I sat on the sofa, trying to figure a way out of this mess. The house seemed so much bigger than it was as I walked from room to room, checking to be sure all the windows and doors were locked. I had the only key to the front door, and at times like this, I would remove Jimmy's key to the back door from where he kept it on a ledge over the door. However, I worried that Jimmy could come through the little window in the basement. I sat up the rest of the night and watched the night turn to day. When the boys got up, I tried to act as if none of this were happening. However, I shared with Janet what was going on, and I called the attorney's office and made an appointment to come in to sign the papers and start the divorce proceedings. Janet drove me to the attorney's office and waited for me in the car with the boys while I went in.

It was my friends who gave me the courage to step out of my pattern and stop Jimmy's abuse. They were there for me, helping me and encouraging me. When I called the police, I broke Jimmy's pattern of abuse; when I didn't back down this time, I sent him a powerful message. The next day, I received a call from a Dekalb County judge. "This is Judge Smith from the Dekalb County Court. Are you Charlene Minor?"

"Yes, I am."

"Your husband is James Minor?"

"Yes, that is correct."

"I have him sitting right here in my office and am calling to ask you if he has bothered you since the complaint you filed against him."

"Yes, sir, he did. He called me two evenings ago and threatened to come here and kill me. I called and talked with the police department. They kept me on the phone for a long time, asking me questions about his threat, but he never came home. I have since filed for a divorce."

"Thank you. That is all I needed to know."

I was still keeping the doors well locked. The doorbell rang later that day. I yelled, "Who is it?"

Jimmy yelled back, "Let me in."

"No, go away," I answered.

He said he wanted to give me money to pay for kindergarten, but I didn't trust him. In fact, I knew he was lying. His anger was apparent as he started turning the knob while pushing and banging on the door. I ignored him, and he finally went away. Janet called and told me that he drove into her driveway and smashed his car into the back of her brother's car that was sitting in her driveway. Now he was attacking Janet because he knew that she was helping me. I hated what he had done to her, but I also knew that anyone helping me would be in his line of fire. I told her to call the police and tell them what he had done, but she never did.

I was counting on my attorney to serve Jimmy the divorce papers and make sure he paid the bills while I waited it out. After several weeks, I became annoyed that Jimmy had not been served, so I asked the lawyer for a refund. By now, Jimmy was on his best behavior and begging to come back, so I did let him come home. The lawyer said he would cancel my divorce proceedings, but if I changed my mind, all I had to do was call, and the divorce would be on. I was relieved in a sense to delay the divorce because I had three small children, no job, and nowhere else to go. Also, just by acting on my threats I had delivered a strong message to Jimmy that there was a limit to my tolerance.

One Saturday afternoon in the summer of 1969, Jimmy came home after having a few drinks, and he seemed in prime shape to start an argument. He insisted that I stop the babysitting because I had enough to do to take care of my own children. However, I knew that it was the extra money he objected to. He knew I liked having my own money and being able to buy new clothes and other "luxuries." It seemed that Jimmy was willing to attack anything that made me happy, so he walked into our bedroom closet, pulled out the new culottes I had just bought, and ripped them up. I said nothing but just let him go ahead and do it. When he couldn't get a reaction from me, he walked out the back door, got in his car, and left.

I felt extreme anger and hatred toward this man. As I walked out to the garage, there sat Jimmy's little MG with its new blue metal flake paint. Jimmy had just painted the car that week. He loved this car, and in Jimmy's sick mind, that car held much greater importance than any of us. I knew that Jimmy's plan to sell the MG and give me back the insurance money he stole from me was just another lie. I was through being harassed, attacked, and demeaned by my husband. I picked up a sledgehammer and smashed the car with all I had, crying louder each time the hammer hit the metal. Finally exhausted and emotionally drained, I walked back into the house and watched for Jimmy to pull back into the driveway. I feared what he would do to me when he saw what I had done to his car. I was beginning to fight back; he had mistreated me for the last time, and he was now going to pay the consequences. I saw Jimmy pull into the garage, and then I could see him looking at the car. As he came closer to the house, I walked into the living room and stood at the front door, ready to run across the street to a neighbor's house to call the police. When Jimmy entered the kitchen, he could see me at the front door; the liquor had worn off, and he was extremely calm. What I had done stunned him. "I saw what you did to my car," he said.

"I saw what you did to my clothes," I answered.

"Okay, now we are even," he mumbled as he walked into the family room and turned on the TV. His response was not what I had expected. This was my first attempt at fighting back. It was not in my nature to do anything violent, and I never planned to do it. It was a reaction to what had been done to me over and over again for the past six years. I knew this was not the end of Jimmy's angry attacks, but it was the beginning of how I would respond to them. I believe now that the change in me was a result of having an attorney who could restart a divorce with a simple phone call; I felt as if I now had choices I didn't know about before. From that point on, I was no longer Jimmy Minor's victim, and he knew it.

Even though our marriage was in trouble, the word *counseling* was never brought up. Jimmy would never have acknowledged any of his abuses, with or without counseling. I had no way to pay for counseling for myself, and even if I had the money, I would not have dared to seek help because Jimmy could have used my "seeing someone" as proof that I was mentally unstable. Even though Jimmy delighted in calling me crazy, I had a clean record, and I was determined that when I had my day in court, Jimmy wouldn't have a leg to stand on if he tried to portray me as an unfit mother.

In August of 1969, the Woodstock Music and Art Fair in Woodstock, New York, drew more than 450,000 people to a pasture in Sullivan County. For four days, the site became a mini-nation in which minds were open, drugs were legal, and love was "free." The music began Friday afternoon and continued until midmorning Monday, August 18. The festival closed the New York State Thruway and created one of the worst traffic jams in US history. It was a gathering of liars, lovers, prophets, and profiteers, who made love, made money, and made history.

One Saturday morning in September, Jimmy was up and gone early, and it was midafternoon when I heard his voice as he came in the back door. I knew he had been drinking, and he walked toward me insisting that we have sex. I tried to ward him off by telling him that I had not taken my pill, but he replied that it was time for us to have another baby. He insisted that as his wife, it was my responsibility to provide him with sex and babies as he pleased. He kept pushing, trying to overpower me physically and get me into bed. I struggled to get away from his advances, and I was finally able to get out the front door. It was daytime, and the boys were all home. I ran across the street to a neighbor's house and called the police. I walked back home without fear, knowing that a police car would be arriving soon. Jimmy quickly figured out what I had done, rounded up the boys, went out in the backyard, and started playing ball with them. It looked odd; I had never seen him playing in the yard with the boys.

A few minutes later, a police car pulled up in the driveway. The officer got out, and I walked toward him. "Is this the Minor residence?" he asked.

"Yes," I answered.

"Are you Charlene?"

"Yes. I called you. As you can see, my husband is here playing ball with the kids. This started when he knew that you were on the way. He has been drinking, and before he came out here, he was attacking me physically and verbally. I am afraid of him."

The officer spoke to Jimmy. "Are you James Minor?"

"Yes, sir, as you can see, I am just out here playing some ball with my children."

"Well, your wife tells me that you were attacking her."

"I never laid a hand on her. For some unknown reason, she likes to call the police on me." The officer noted that things seemed to have calmed down.

I protested, "Yes, they have calmed down while you are here, but as soon as you leave, it will start up again, and I am afraid that he will harm me. He has a record of domestic violence. What can I do about this?"

"You can file a warrant of protection against him."

"How do I do that?" I asked.

"Well, since today is Saturday, you will have to go to a county that is open on Saturdays."

"Can you take me there?"

"No, because it is out of my area."

"Well, I have no way of getting there, and I know that when you leave, I will be in serious danger."

He got in his car and made a call, and when he got back out, he said that he would be able to take me. I quickly picked up Mark, but Jimmy grabbed little Jimmy and Scott by the hand so I wouldn't be able to take them also. I instructed little Jimmy and Scott to come with me, but Jimmy still had a grasp on them. He yelled back, "They're staying with me." I slid into the back seat of the police car, holding on to Mark. As the car rolled down the driveway, I could see the anger on Jimmy's face, and then he started shaking his fist at me.

The officer took me to file a protection warrant, and then he drove me back home. It was dark by now, and there were no lights on in the house. I asked the officer if he would walk in with me to be sure that Jimmy was not inside, waiting for me. He went in first, and I followed. The officer checked all the rooms, and when it appeared safe, he left. With this trauma, I was back to my old routine. I knew where Jimmy took the boys; his mother's house was Jimmy's place of refuge where he could be consoled, pampered, and told how none of this was his fault. When the next day came and went with no word of Jimmy or the boys, I called Mrs. Mashburn. She told me to relax and not worry about where they were; she was sure that the boys were safe. By the next day and still no word, I called Frances in desperation. "I was wondering if Jimmy is staying at your house with little Jimmy and Scott."

"No, I haven't seen them. Jimmy did call me and told me that there was a warrant out for his arrest, and all he could do was hide out in case they found him. You know that if they do find him, they will arrest him, and the boys will be placed in foster care."

"Well, maybe he will learn that he cannot hit me and get away with it anymore."

"I asked him if he hit you, and he assured me that he had not laid a hand on you."

"Well, he is a liar," I sharply replied.

"He doesn't understand why you keep having him arrested for no reason."

"I am not concerned about whatever lies he has told you. I am just concerned about my children," I said as I hung up.

I called Mrs. Mashburn back and told her what Jimmy's mother had told me, and she assured me that the boys would not be put in foster care. She calmed and soothed my fears, and I was so glad that I had someone to talk to who could give me some guidance. She also gave me the name of an attorney she thought might be able to help me, and she suggested that I call him. That evening, I picked up the phone and made the call. This attorney was a personal friend of Mrs. Mashburn's; he was very accommodating and wanted to know what was going on. I tried to explain it all to him, but I became so emotional as I spoke of the terrors I had endured that I broke down in tears and couldn't go on. Even so, this attorney waited patiently until I was able to talk. It was a healing moment for me, and after I hung up, I felt as if I had unloaded a lifetime of grief in that twenty or so minutes.

The following day, Jimmy called and said he was bringing the boys home. It had been four days now, and he probably feared that the school would begin to question why little Jimmy had not been in school. I later found out that Jimmy and the boys had been staying with one of his mother's sisters, which means that Frances had lied about not knowing where they were.

Soon after this episode, Jimmy called one afternoon, sounding as if he were Prince Charming, and asked whether I would go out on a date with him. It was early fall, and he said he wanted to take me to his brother Michael's football game. He explained that the game was being played at the same stadium he played in when he was in high school. Afterward, we would go to Krispy Kreme and have a fresh hot doughnut right off the belt. I had always struggled over wanting to trust Jimmy, even though he had proved to me over and over that he was not trustworthy. Once again, I suspended my disbelief, and I agreed to go out with Jimmy. It was a wonderful "date," and we did exactly as he told me we would. It was hard to believe that this was the same person I had dealt with the week before. Jimmy was on his best behavior, and he went out of his way to cater to me. He kept the conversation going, telling me all about the stadium and explaining who everyone was. This was the first time I had felt any sense of respect from Jimmy, but I strongly suspected that it was all an act designed to ward off the police and the divorce. It was going to take much more than one good evening to heal the damage Jimmy had done to me over the years.

From that point on, Jimmy's attitude toward me did change significantly for the better. One Sunday in November, as the boys and I came in from church, he suggested that we all go to Chaus Woods. He was in high gear, rattling on and on about how he used to play in those woods when he was a boy. He never spoke much about his childhood, but I could tell that these woods had some profound meaning for him. The day was cold and windy, and I bundled the boys up as we left for Chaus Woods. I wasn't sure what this was all about, and I had seldom seen Jimmy in this kind of mood. When we got to Chaus Woods, the area was like a heavily wooded undeveloped playground. It was a Robin Hood type of atmosphere, a kind of boys' heaven where they could get lost in their play world and challenge one another's courage as they tested how high they could climb. Jimmy showed the boys which trees he used to climb and how high he could go. It was fun for a while, but it was getting cold. I felt Jimmy's unusual need that day to bring us together, as if he were trying to say how sorry he was but just couldn't express what he really felt. Did he really think he was going to make everything right in a few hours in the woods? He had gone way too far too many times to think this was going to change my mind about wanting out. Even though he seemed to brush off my threats of divorce, I now believe that it worried him more than I knew. He knew I wanted out, and he knew that I was just biding my time until I found the courage and the means to make my move.

A week or so later, Jimmy told me that he was going to see a doctor about having a vasectomy. He knew that would please me. He wasted no time making the appointment, and I was shocked that he went through with the vasectomy as he promised. The day of his surgery, his mother called to "check on him," and I answered the phone. "I just hate it that he has done such a thing to himself. You know that this is against his religion." Above all else, I enjoyed hearing how annoyed she was, and I felt as if my struggles with her were in some ways over.

In November of 1969, Richard Nixon was elected president. The Vietnam War was still going strong, and the protests were increasing. College campuses all over the country were holding marches and rallies to end the war. We had already lost too many young men like Bart, and there was no end in sight. Government leaders held on to their pride about "winning" in spite of having no legitimate reasons for staying in the war. Richard Nixon's election victory was strongly based on his plan to end the war. I have come to believe that very few if any of our country's recent wars have been based on protecting our freedom, but that was what the government leaders wanted the American people to believe. How many more walls to honor the fallen would be built to support these wrong decisions?

During December of 1969, little Jimmy was a month shy of seven, and Scott was five. Mark was two, and I had just begun to potty train him. Janet had landed a job at Rich's for the Christmas season, so when we went shopping, she would share her discount with me. One afternoon, we stopped to look at Rich's children's department, where baby carriages, cribs, walkers, and potty chairs were all lined up against a wall. I must have taken my eyes off Mark for just a moment when Janet told me to look over at the wall. There sat Mark on one of the potty chairs; he had peed in the potty chair, right through his pants. He kept telling me loudly to "look," proudly showing me what he had done as I quickly picked him up. Trying to keep from laughing, Janet suggested that we get out of there before someone noticed. We quickly left the mall, got in the car, and laughed all the way home.

Jimmy had been doing auto body work for several years, and he was good at what he did. He was now working at the local Volkswagen dealership. The dealerships provided the best jobs in the auto body business because the working conditions were better, and they offered benefits. This Volkswagen dealer gave an impressive Christmas party for the employees each year. That Christmas when Jimmy came home after the party, he began apologizing to me as soon as he walked in the door for having too much to drink. I was taken aback that he was admitting that he had screwed up and that he said he was sorry. It was almost too odd for me to understand, and I didn't know what to think.

I savored a feeling of confidence knowing that I could file for a divorce at any time; all the information I needed was just a phone call away. Jimmy knew that his abusive, irresponsible behavior would no longer be tolerated, and his awareness that I really could leave changed how he treated me. Soon after Janet got her job, I told Jimmy that I wanted to get a part-time job but needed help with the boys. He told me that if I applied for a job working nights or Saturdays, he would take care of the children. I was shocked, but I moved forward and applied at Rich's. I was hired to work in the bakery department two nights a week and every other Saturday. Before I left for my first night of work, Jimmy stepped right up to the plate and promised he would wash the clothes and give the boys a bath. He rattled on and on about how I was going to be treated like a "queen." The strange thing was that when I got back home, the house was spotless, the boys were all in bed, and Jimmy was folding a load of clothes, as promised. His new behavior was so extreme that I had a hard time believing either that it was genuine or that it would last. However, he really did come through for me on this one. It was a strange sight for me to see him on a Saturday coming up the escalator with all three boys in tow. I could hardly believe it was really him. Because change was again in the air, I enjoyed Christmas of 1969 above any others. I was able to buy myself a new outfit to wear to the Christmas get-together, and I was able to buy the boys matching red sweatshirts and jeans. I was extremely proud of my children; they were smart, good-looking, and a joy.

After Christmas, I was laid off from Rich's, and Jimmy was thrilled. He had gone the extra mile to allow me to do something I wanted to do. When the children were younger, he had never fed or changed a baby, held a baby while I fixed a bottle, or taken a kid trick-or-treating, to a school conference, or to a doctor's appointment. Now during the Christmas season of 1969, I felt the benefit of not allowing Jimmy to dominate and abuse me, and I was beginning to feel more at ease with my place in the family. However, I was still on edge, free in many ways and terrified in other ways. I had choices now, which gave me a sense of control over my situation, but each day, I knew very well that this could be the very day that Jimmy turned back into Mr. Hyde.

Winter in Atlanta was a dream compared to winter in New Jersey. Even though some days were cold, short, and overcast, most days were delightfully cool and sunny. One cold overcast day, Mark wanted to go out and play with his cars in his sandbox. He was not quite old enough to go out by himself, so I went outside and sat on the swing as I watched him play. As I sat there, I glanced up at the sky and focused on the clouds. I was entranced as I watched them move across the sky so effortlessly and in harmony. They seemed to be quietly dancing to music I could not hear. As I watched the motion of the clouds, I could feel myself relax, and a sense of calm came over me as never before. I wondered if there was any hope for me to find that same kind of harmony in my life. I wanted so badly to be out of this marriage, and I knew there would be no harmony for me until that happened. The movement in the clouds that day gave me an unspoken sense of hope, and I felt the calm and peace of the moment in some strange way communicating with me.

It was difficult for me to believe that Jimmy's new attitude was going to last, but as the months rolled on, he spent more time at home, and he no longer stayed out all night. As our family became more of a priority to Jimmy, his mother lost some of her control over him. I never thought I would see this day come, and I still had trouble believing that this new Jimmy would last. My plan to get out of the marriage stayed on the back burner during this period. Although it didn't look as if I was going anywhere, I was still thinking through how I could best get out of the marriage without harming my children. Luckily, with Jimmy on his best behavior, I felt relaxed enough to believe that time was on my side.

One afternoon, as I folded clothes, Jimmy sat down on the sofa and began to explain to me that since he was now an experienced auto body mechanic, he could get a job anywhere, and we could live wherever we wanted to. He suggested that we pack up and move to New Jersey. Like the vasectomy, this proposed move was another way to please me and keep me from seeking a divorce. When I asked him what made him think about New Jersey, he said that when he went before the judge this last time, the judge suggested that maybe it would be better if we were to move closer to my family since it seemed that New Jersey was where my roots were. I didn't believe that nonsense for one minute. Our problems had nothing to do with where we lived but were about the terror that my children and I were forced to live through. I was sure that he had approached the judge with his skewed reasoning that my frustration had nothing to do with his abuse, his womanizing, or his allegiance to his mother. He knew the truth, but since he could not face the truth, he decided that the reason I had him arrested so many times for "no real reason" was that I wanted to live near my family. So now he was going to fix the problems in our marriage by moving us all up to New Jersey. In one way, he was not acknowledging that my discontent was based on years of emotional and physical abuse and his inability to be a participating father and husband. However, in another way, he was letting me know that he was now divorcing his mother and allowing me the privilege of stepping up to the role of female head of the family.

Now I had two options. I could stay put and move forward with my plans to divorce Jimmy, or I could go along with his plan and move with him to New Jersey. The true benefit I saw in moving to New Jersey was that I would be closer to my family, and I believed that Daddy would help me if I needed him to. The move would also offer me protection from Jimmy's violent behavior because Jimmy had always acted the role of the good husband around my father. Besides, I seriously doubted that Jimmy Minor was actually going to "leave" his mother and move to New Jersey forever. There had to be something more to it from Jimmy's point of view, but I didn't know what it was. Because I was so sure that Jimmy couldn't possibly stay in New Jersey, the move seemed even more beneficial to me and my children. If he left me, I wouldn't have to leave him. I was also aware that in New Jersey, there was help for single women with children whether the mother was able to obtain child support or not.

As I have looked back on my life and tried to make sense of it, I have seen clearly all the mistakes I have made. One mistake was my constantly being sucked into Jimmy's pattern of punishment and reward, and this latest offer to move to New Jersey felt like another one of Jimmy's rewards. Every time I had accepted a reward in the past, I had set myself up for the next round of abuse. However, it seemed to me that I could turn this New Jersey plan of Jimmy's into something that benefited me. Because I had started to stand up for myself, I had gained some measure of control and diminished Jimmy's power over me. When I started to call the police each time Jimmy threatened or attacked me, I was letting him know that there would be consequences for his behavior. My resistance also meant that he could not hide his abuse anymore because each fine, each police report, and each appearance before a judge was documented on paper, recorded for all to see.

As the weather began to warm up, we began to do things together as a family. One Saturday that spring, we took the boys to the circus. There were also weekends in May of 1970 when we spent the day swimming at Lake Spivey, a sandy beach that offered kids' activities. They had a cowboy village where the men were all dressed up in cowpoke clothes and acted out a gun battle. The boys and I looked forward to going anywhere since family outings had been so few. I especially loved watching the boys have fun. A few times, Jimmy suggested we get a babysitter so he and I could go out to a movie. It seemed strange to me now how quickly I forgot about the fear and abuse when it was less of a threat. Jimmy's new attitude changed the quality of our lives, but it did not change my promise to myself. I was enjoying the now, but I was also looking toward a future free of Jimmy. The fact that I did not go to bed every night fearing for my life did not make this a good marriage.

In the spring of 1970, Daddy and Margie were still living with Connie and Phil in Jackson, New Jersey. Margie was now a teenager, and she was trying to find a way out of the house, as I had years before her. She had a boyfriend, Mark Vitkauskas, who had already quit school and was working in a job that provided little security. When Margie was sixteen, she found out she was pregnant, and she and Mark got married. This marriage was as much a mistake for Margie as mine had been for me, when I stumbled down the same road eight years earlier. These marriages were doomed to similar outcomes because Margie and I were too young, too fearful, and too desperate for a way out. What looked like a better life in both cases was no more than the trap of turning our life choices over to the control of men. Our lives just became a continuation of the struggles we were familiar with from our family of origin. Unconsciously, we had chosen men with similar thought processes and similar disordered personalities. However, our bigger problem was our own skewed thought process, including our low level of confidence and the fear that we had no ability to take care of ourselves. Shame was the core issue; no one born into a family like ours could be expected to develop any degree of self-esteem.

Connie was now a Jehovah's Witness; she and her children attended Kingdom Hall and studied the Bible with a vengeance. Whenever Connie was enthusiastic about something, I was bombarded with her unrelenting insistence that I hop onto her bandwagon, which was supposedly the only one going in the right direction. I listened to her information and liked the idea of a Bible study, so she put me in touch with a Jehovah's Witness couple who lived in my area. The lady came a few times in the mornings to "study the Bible" with me, but I was never inspired by these Bible studies. I wanted to use my own Bible instead of hers, but she insisted that hers was the only true translation. My intuition told me that this was not for me; I had trouble believing as she did, and after two or three meetings, she stopped coming.

Chapter 14

Brief Reprieve before the Divorce

I was becoming more and more anxious about this move to New Jersey, which represented a change so bizarre and so extreme that it would change the whole landscape of our lives. Over the years, I had learned to love Atlanta, and I had made many friends there. Even though thoughts of moving did not really appeal to me, thoughts of freedom did. The move gave me hope for a life in which my children and I would be out from under the dominance of Jimmy Minor. In New Jersey, Jimmy would no longer have his mother to support him, hide the kids, and bail him out of jail. I hoped that it wouldn't be long before Jimmy would be on his way back to Georgia, alone. I just envisioned how it would all play out and hung onto that picture in my mind.

As summer approached, we made a quick sale of our house to an investor, who gave us a thousand dollars for our equity. Jimmy rented a truck, and Jack and Tommy came to help load the truck. The plan was for us to stay with Connie and Phil until Jimmy found a job, so we were going to put our belongings in storage in New Jersey until we could afford our own place. Of course, our little dog Cotton came with us.

Once we were in New Jersey, Jimmy had little trouble finding a job at a local body shop with a guy named Ed Matthews. Ed had the biggest ad in the yellow pages and had been in business for a long time. Everyone knew Ed Matthews. He was more than a little shady and was therefore the perfect boss for Jimmy. Like Jimmy, Ed didn't worry about taxes, which worried me a great deal. Nevertheless, I was grateful for the job and grateful to have an income again. I managed to hold onto the thousand dollars we got for the house, and I carefully deposited the money in a savings account at a local bank.

Mark Vitkauskas's sister offered to let Mark and Margie, whose baby was due in September, live in a small trailer that she owned. Even though this was a good opportunity for Mark and Margie to be on their own in free housing, the trailer was too small for a family of three, and it was parked in a sleazy trailer park.

With so many of us staying at Connie's, we were all under stress. The boys were beginning to fight among themselves, and we were all getting on each other's nerves. We had no luck renting an apartment because all the apartments in the area had two bedrooms, and landlords were not allowed to rent two-bedroom apartments to families with three children. However, Margie's in-laws happened to be selling their house on Cedar Swamp Road in a rural area of Jackson. It was a modest two-bedroom house that sat on 3.5 acres that was off the beaten path but close enough to everything. The house was covered with burgundy stucco and had a one-car garage. Even though all the rooms in the house were large, the floor plan was odd. The master bedroom and bathroom were in the front of the house, and everything else was in the back. The kitchen was long and narrow, which made the open living and dining area quite large. The pretty floor-to-ceiling woodburning stone fireplace gave the living area a feeling of warmth. A sunporch was separated from the living area by glass sliding doors. The house was built on a slab, and all the floors were tile. The best feature of this house was without a doubt the three and a half acres. The land was level with plenty of mature, well-spaced trees. Along one side of the property was a row of beautiful blue spruce. The in-laws said they didn't want to make a profit on the house and would be willing to sell it for a measly $16,000. We needed 20 percent down to qualify for a farm loan at an unheard-of (at that time) 5 percent interest. Daddy saw this as a deal we couldn't pass up, and he offered to loan us the $2,200 we needed to add to our $1,000 and buy the property. We applied for the loan and waited for approval.

During this time, Jimmy came home one evening and told me that he had seen Phil out at a local bar with a "girlfriend." Today, I would rethink my decision to give this information to Connie, at least until we had a place to move to. Back then, I felt that telling her was the right thing to do. I told her what I heard, but I also let her know that Jimmy was not the most reliable source and that she should check it out herself. Even though Connie promised me she would not let Phil know how she found out, she reneged on her promise, and Phil wasted no time telling us to pack up our things and move out. We packed our suitcases, loaded up the car, the kids, and Cotton and headed for a restaurant to decide where to go from there. We had no place to live while we waited to find out whether our loan would be approved. Had this house not been in the picture, we would have been on our way back to Atlanta, but we were not going to give up so quickly on our three-and-a-half-acre dream.

We scouted around for a motel that might allow us to rent by the week. The first one we called agreed to let us stay after we explained the predicament we were in. When we lived at the motel, Jimmy left for work each day, and the boys and I hung out at the pool, which we pretty much had to ourselves. After a couple of days at the pool, Jimmy and Scott learned to swim, and they loved playing on the twisted slide. This motel and its pool were a lifesaver for us. In ways I could never have imagined, Jimmy Minor and I became a unit for the first time in our marriage. We needed each other's cooperation and dedication to make this work, and we focused on what was best for our children and supported each other. Having no other choice, we had for the first time become a real family. At the end of each day, we all looked forward to Jimmy coming home, and then we would decide what we would have for dinner. I would call and place the order, and Jimmy would go and pick it up. Once the boys were asleep, Jimmy and I would watch TV together. We did really well for the first week or so, but the novelty of the pool soon wore off for the boys, and the motel arrangement wore thin on all of us. On the weekends, we tried to get away by spending time at Mark and Margie's. The boys complained that they wanted to go back to Atlanta; they missed their friends and wanted to move back into their house on Quillian Avenue. To be quite honest, so did I. At this point, we were all having regrets about this move; nevertheless, we all hung in there. The process of getting a loan approved seemed to take forever, and the day we got favorable news, we started jumping for joy. The next challenge concerned the moving date. Although Margie's in-laws were aware of our situation, they seemed unconcerned about it. It was a very long and difficult three weeks after the loan approval that the closing finally took place.

Soon after we moved in, it was time for school to start. Scott would be in first grade, and Jimmy in second. Mark was a constant ball of energy and missed having his brothers at home; even worse, since we were out in the country, there were no kids at all for him to play with. We had to leave Mark's swing set and sandbox in Georgia, so I bought him a new swing set, and Jimmy set it up in the backyard. These things did little to occupy Mark the way other children would have. I got a cat for Mark, and the cat became his companion for a while. Mark also made up an imaginary friend named Jackson, and Mark's stories about Jackson sounded so real that I sometimes caught myself believing that there was such a person. Mark was a delightfully beautiful child, just full of life, and I was constantly trying to think up ideas to challenge his curiosity. Jimmy and Scott adjusted well; they liked school and made friends easily. However, it didn't take long for me to realize how much more expensive the cost of living was in New Jersey compared to Atlanta. Property taxes were extremely high, even though the schools were crowded and the school day was limited to half sessions.

Ed Matthews introduced Jimmy to Dr. Bernake, an antique car enthusiast who, with his wife, owned a lab that did blood and fluid testing. Dr. Bernake approached Jimmy about working for him to restore his cars on a part-time basis that might eventually work into full-time. We were both invited to the Bernakes' house to talk about the new deal and sign an agreement to, as he put it, "protect them both." Dr. Bernake and his wife were affluent, and their house and land were impressive. I was excited about this opportunity, and I felt that the Bernakes were trustworthy people. But I worried about both the "agreement" and Jimmy's trustworthiness. Dr. Bernake presented this opportunity as huge and without limits, which sounded too good to be true, and Jimmy had a history of grandiose ideas that were no more than pipe dreams. However, I decided to just let it all play out on its own.

Mark and Margie's baby, Dawn Marie, was born in September. I seldom saw Connie, who was now working in a diner and in the process of divorcing Phil. Her affiliation with the Jehovah's Witnesses became no more than a fleeting wind that had blown out of her life, and now she was a devotee of astrology. Daddy still lived in Connie's house, but the arrangement was not working. Daddy spent more and more time at our house. Daddy's love was always farming, and he talked on and on about all the possibilities for our three and a half acres. He wanted badly to retire and get out of working the four-to-twelve shift that he hated; he only had a year to go before he would be sixty-two.

Winter soon arrived, and the boys and I enjoyed the snow. We made the biggest, best-looking snowman on Cedar Swamp Road. It was a fun winter for all of us. Jimmy took the boys out with him as he cut down one of the best-shaped blue spruce on our property for our Christmas tree. He also cut down a smaller tree for me to take to the school for the kids to decorate. We were blending into the New Jersey landscape, but I missed Atlanta and all my dear friends who had stood by me when I needed them. Occasionally, we would call and talk with one another on the phone, and I found myself wishing that I could visit them or they could visit me. I found Jackson, New Jersey, a difficult place to make friends. The people were distant and had their own agendas. Even in the spring when we signed the boys up for Little League, everyone seemed to have their own cliques, and I was an outsider.

I had now acquired the role of chief money handler in the family, and I had risen to the prominent place of number 1 woman in Jimmy's life. The house was no longer referred to as "Jimmy's"; it was ours. With Jimmy's mother out of the picture, I felt a new freedom, and I also felt that Jimmy and I were becoming more of a team. Even though I kept my distance to some extent and still had trouble trusting him, I no longer feared him. With my father around instead of Jimmy's mother, I felt safe. There was an unspoken respect between Jimmy and me, and our struggles seemed to bring us together as a family in ways I could never have imagined. Events were unfolding so different, and so much better, than I had ever expected.

As the weather warmed up, Daddy talked about retiring and having a garden. Another spring event was Jimmy buying a minibike for the boys to ride around the yard. I was afraid they would get hurt with it, but little Jimmy got the hang of it quickly. He and Scott had a ball with that bike. We also drove to the shore and let the boys enjoy the rides on the boardwalk.

Jimmy and Dr. Bernake had come up with an agreement for Jimmy to restore Dr. Bernake's cars, and they were now business partners. We were invited to parties at Dr. Bernake's house. Sometimes Daddy would stay with the boys while Jimmy and I joined Ed Matthews and his wife for a movie or for dinner at a restaurant. This was all so new to me. I was used to sitting home with the kids while Jimmy had his fun, and now I was included.

I soon gave up my expectation that Jimmy would be leaving us and moving back to Atlanta to be closer to his mother. Jimmy's attitude had greatly improved, and I was becoming acclimated to my new life. The abusive years no longer haunted me. I did not by any means forget the years of terror I had endured, but for now, I didn't allow bad memories to get in the way. I had found a place of contentment. It would take time for me to trust that the new reality would be a lasting one, but I was no longer dreaming of divorce. Frances kept in touch with Jimmy through his work number, which she used in order to avoid me. In late spring, Jimmy told me that his mother, Margaret, and Teresa would be flying up for a visit the following Saturday. They would arrive in the morning and leave that evening. I resigned myself to being as friendly as I could, and knowing that the visit was for only one day made it easier to tolerate. Once Jimmy's family arrived, they sat in our living room with Jimmy and rattled on making small talk for the entire day. I kept busy with the boys and tried not to intrude. I knew that I had now risen to the status of Jimmy's wife, with his mother taking second place. I figured that was what his changed attitude and sudden idea to move to New Jersey were really all about. I was now treated with as much respect as Jimmy Minor was capable of. A warm wind was blowing in my direction, giving me a freedom I had never before thought possible.

One day, Daddy discussed with us how much houses were selling for in our area of New Jersey. We had no idea how much our house was worth, but Daddy thought it was worth much more than we paid for it. The conversation drifted toward selling the house and moving back to Atlanta, with Daddy joining us the following year after he retired. I liked this idea because it sounded like a plan that would work for all of us. I felt it was unlikely that Jimmy would resort to his old behavior, and even if he did, I would have Daddy there to protect and help me. We called a local realtor, and we were shocked when he told us he could list our house for $25,000. Because of the difference in the cost of living between New Jersey and Atlanta, the move looked good, and we put the house up for sale.

Jimmy was on his best behavior. He was riding high and elated that we would soon be on our way back to Atlanta with enough money to buy a nice house with all the bells and whistles. Jimmy still found value in "things." His definition of success was tied to how he could impress others with what he had rather than who he was or how he treated others. Even though our values were still different, our relationship was at this point the best I could ever have hoped for.

That summer, the house sold for $25,000 to a cash buyer. We were in a state of disbelieving awe. Daddy was just as thrilled, and he looked forward to retiring and moving. I asked Jimmy about his contract with Dr. Bernake. "Don't worry about it," he snapped back. But I did worry about it because how Jimmy conducted his business dealings could have an effect on us as a family. Jimmy wanted to keep his business to himself because he knew I wouldn't agree with his underhanded, "screw you" type of thinking. As long as I had known Jimmy Minor, one thing was clear—he possessed minus-zero business sense. I worried that Dr. Bernake was never going to be informed about our move because Jimmy didn't care who he took from or lied to as long as he thought he could get away with it. Even when he gave me the impression that he was trying to do the right thing, I knew better than to trust him completely. My worry about the Bernake contract was a nagging, uneasy feeling, like walking on an ice-covered lake with weak spots that were vaguely visible. The possibility that this move would not happen the way we had planned, that Jimmy Minor would somehow ruin it for all of us, cast a dark shadow that I tried not to think about.

So far, everything was happening as planned. The morning of our closing, we loaded up the car and piled in our suitcases, the boys, and Cotton. It was a rainy, overcast day. There had been a hurricane in the Carolinas the night before, and we were getting the tail end of it. The closing was scheduled in a neighboring town on our way South. I took a last look at our house on Cedar Swamp Road as Jimmy turned the car around and drove forward down the long driveway. The closing went without a hitch. I remember the closing agent handing me the check for close to $10,000, and telling me not to consider this money a profit because it would be no more than a small down payment on another property. If we had planned to stay in New Jersey, that might have been the case, but we were on our way to Atlanta, and I knew that the possibilities there were quite different. We had arrived in New Jersey with $1000, and now a year later, we had $10,000. That was a windfall for us, and I was still amazed as I slipped that check into my purse and pulled the zipper tight. We were soon on the road, headed for Atlanta.

As we drove South, we witnessed the aftermath of the hurricane; in North Carolina, we saw an entire gas station underwater. Despite the storm damage outside the car, inside, it was the most pleasant trip I remember taking with Jimmy Minor. We were all together, without tension or fear. This was so different from the plan I had envisioned when we first went to New Jersey, and I expected Jimmy to return to Atlanta on his own. Now there was a new sense of harmony in our family. I was still tormented by a past that had never been resolved, but for now, I had a lot to look forward to, and I didn't want to look back. The dark spot in all this for me was Jimmy's deal with Dr.

Bernake; I knew Jimmy was hiding something, but I never could get any straight answers from him.

The day we arrived in Atlanta, we were invited to dinner with "the family." Their attitude toward me had also improved, so it was obvious to me that if Jimmy was happy with me, they were happy with me. Mike had now taken over the spot as the family hero. He played football and was Frances's pride and joy. Of course, of all his attributes, she was proudest of his size. The conversation always stressed how "big" he was rather than how smart, clever, or good he was. When we were invited to one of Mike's football games, I was reluctant to go because I never did acquire any interest in football, but I went anyway for the sake of family unity. The football game was a bigger deal than I ever expected. The family occupied one complete row of the bleachers. As we climbed up, there sat Margaret, decked out like a teenager with white knee-high boots and short shorts. She rattled on loud enough for everyone to notice her; Frances laughed at everything she said, which added to her obvious need for attention. The Minors were in their own grandiose world of fantasy.

The most exciting part of the return to Atlanta for me was reconnecting with my girlfriends, which was like coming home for me. We had so much catching up to do, and having friends added to my sense of security and freedom. Sandra and Danny invited us to stay with them until we found a house to rent, and within a few weeks, we were moving into a rental house in a neighborhood we were familiar with. I loved Atlanta, and I was glad to be back in the city that now felt like home. When I called a girlfriend I knew from Little League, she told me that she worked at Sears during school hours, and she encouraged me to apply for an opening there. The boys were enrolled in school that fall, and Jimmy landed a job at a dealership. One night, Jimmy came home from work with an almost new truck that he decided to buy without notifying me. I am sure he was impressed with himself as he wrote out the check in front his dealership buddies, paying for the truck without needing a loan. I felt pressured to find a house to buy before Jimmy could squander all our money showing off and making foolish purchases that we didn't need.

Sandra put us in touch with her friend Wendy, whose dad was a builder. We were invited over to take a tour of the house Wendy's dad had built her in a desirable section of Stone Mountain. This house was exactly what we wanted, so we made an appointment with Wendy's dad, Pete Bradford. We picked out a nice cul-de-sac lot in the Redan area of Stone Mountain, signed a contract, and we were on our way to having a new house built—a beautiful big house that we never in a million years would have dreamed possible. The house was an all-brick ranch with a full basement, and nothing, and I mean nothing, inspired Jimmy Minor more than that house. As I wrote out the check for $8,000 at the closing, we both felt a sense of unfathomable blessings. A few weeks later, Sears called me in for an interview, and a week after that, I started working part-time in the catalog department. Even though all was going in the right direction, I was still walking on eggshells, thinking something would come out of the woodwork to mess up our good fortune. I had all but forgotten about Dr. Bernake when a telegram arrived from him addressed to Jimmy. It read, "Imperative you contact me immediately." Jimmy cussed about the telegram and planned to ignore it, but I insisted that he contact Dr. Bernake and settle up with him. Jimmy finally agreed that he would, but I was worried that he owed Dr. Bernake more than we could pay him. Jimmy later told me that he had contacted Dr. Bernake, and everything was okay. I didn't believe him, but as far as I knew, Dr. Bernake never contacted us again.

It was late summer of 1972 when we moved into our new house at 1064 Jeannette Court. I kept my job at Sears. Not only did I love this job, but Sears allowed me to work every other Saturday through the summer and go back to the weekly schedule when school started. The arrangement was perfect for me and the boys. New houses were still being built, and the neighborhood was filling up with new families. The boys were happy and making new friends.

Our little dog Cotton hated the mailman, and he barked and growled like a maniac when he saw the mailman coming. One day, as Cotton did his "run the mailman off" routine, the mailman ran over him. The mailman did not have the courtesy to come to the door and let us know, and we were all devastated when we found Cotton lying dead in the street in front of our house. In tears and sadness, we dug a hole in the woods next to our lot and buried our little dog. The mailman was never popular with the boys after that. Sometimes, when they saw him coming, they would sit at the end of the driveway just so they could remind him about how he had killed their dog.

Daddy was now nearing retirement and excited about moving in with us; he could hardly wait to see our new house. I was enjoying decorating the house and putting it all in order. My life with Jimmy Minor was now as good as it was going to get, and divorce was no longer at the forefront of my mind. However, this better life did not in any way erase from my mind the previous ten years of terror. The effects of abuse do not just go away because the perpetrator for whatever reason decides to change his attitude. Even if I tried, I could not for one minute forget the night I was raped, the many nights of paralyzing terror, or the years of demeaning disrespect and captivity. Sometimes there were flashbacks, and sometimes those flashbacks were overbearing. I still had dreams that involved running, escaping, and trying to find a safe place to go.

One weekend, we bought a new bedroom suite, and it was the first time we ever owned matching bedroom furniture. When Jimmy came home from work the day the furniture was delivered, he walked into the bedroom to take a look. As he admired the furniture, he turned to me, looked me in the eye, and said, "I love that son of a bitch." It was a moment I will never forget. So far, in all the eleven years I had been married to him, I had never heard Jimmy use the word *love* in relation to me or the boys. I always knew that his real love was for "things," but it was at this particular moment that this fact suddenly became clear to me. However, as the days moved on, I could feel Jimmy inching closer to me, and he suggested doing things that he thought would please me. One Saturday, we planned a day at Six Flags, and it was a fun day for all of us.

One afternoon, as a thunderstorm approached, the sky became dark, and we knew that in a matter of minutes, it would be pouring down rain. Jimmy suggested that we move two lawn chairs into the carport and observe the storm. As we sat under cover and watched the sky open and the rain pour down, it occurred to me that Jimmy needed me. This new world was so different from the one I had known that sometimes I felt like Dorothy in *The Wizard of Oz*, imagining that the painful past was nothing more than a bad dream. I didn't see the hand of God in this miraculous change at the time as clearly as I do today. Today, I believe that my arrival on Jeannette Court was no more than the answer to years of pleading and praying for a way out. This was it. As I watched the lightning flash and the rain pour down in front of us, I felt an unspoken sense of gratitude for the moment. The rain danced in a rhythm that I believed was trying to send me a message that I couldn't interpret. I have gone back to that moment many times in my life and still find comfort in reliving it.

It was Christmas of 1972, and Jimmy was all excited because we had invited all his family to visit our new house for the first time. As they all gathered in the family room, I looked at them now from a different perspective. Jack and Diane were there with their three children and expecting the fourth. I felt sorry for Diane that nothing had changed for her; she was much more accepting of her situation than I had been. I wanted my life to count for something more than being someone's slave. I thought back to the day Diane and I spent together when we both lived in Wellswood Apartments. Even then, I knew that she wasn't as interested in fighting her way out as I was. I also knew that Jimmy and Jack were peas out of the same pod and that her life with Jack was not that much different from what I had endured. I felt sad that Diane and I didn't communicate with each other anymore. Our lives had moved in different directions.

New businesses and new subdivisions were popping up everywhere in our area, and a Chevrolet dealership had just opened on Covington Highway. I was delighted when Jimmy was hired there because the job included health insurance and retirement benefits, both of which we had been going without. However, after Jimmy had been a few months on his new job, I knew that something was not quite right. He never gave me a telephone number I could use to reach him while he was working. One day, when I needed to reach Jimmy, I looked up the main number of the dealership in the phone book, and when I called and asked for Jimmy Minor, I was told that he did not work there anymore. The man told me that Jimmy had worked there for about a month, then packed up his tools and left one morning. They never heard from him again.

Oh no, here we go again! was my first thought. That evening, I confronted Jimmy with this new information.

"Yeah," he admitted, "I found an opportunity to open my own shop in East Point. I am working for the owner right now, but he is leaving at the end of the month. Then I will rent the building, and it will be my shop." Of course, he built the situation up to sound as if we would be millionaires in the next six months. I didn't like this plan because Jimmy Minor was *not* a businessman. He was qualified to do the bodywork, but running a business, or running anything for that matter, he simply did not have the common sense to do. When I brought up the loss of health insurance he had not seen fit to tell me about, he claimed we would now have plenty of money to buy our own health insurance. I knew that prosperity and Jimmy Minor were never in harmony and that he and his warped ego were once more on the downward slide.

Our family unity, which had been so hard-won, was now dissipating. Obviously, Jimmy was keeping secrets again, and he was not treating me like a partner in the marriage. In addition, he was seldom home now that his shop took priority. Sometimes he would work all night and get home the next morning; occasionally, those morning arrivals included the smell of liquor on his breath. We never ate meals together or went anywhere together. The boys and I seldom saw Jimmy, except for a few minutes coming or going. Jimmy began to complain about my job at Sears and asked me to quit. He was annoyed when it was my Saturday to work and he had to stay with the boys because my job was standing in the way of his freedom to do as he pleased. I felt that the boys needed a father in their lives, but Jimmy had never been interested in being a participating parent. When fall arrived, the boys started school, and I started back to work during the week.

Daddy retired at the end of December of 1972, and in March of 1973, he packed up his things, drove to Atlanta, and moved in with us. Daddy loved our new house, and he was anxious to get the yard in shape. Daddy enjoyed yard work, and he and Jimmy went shopping for shrubs and had loads of topsoil delivered to fill in the low spots. Daddy had a perfect place picked out to plant a small garden. Daddy paid for a second driveway to be installed, which was part of a plan he and Jimmy made to buy and fix up wrecked cars. Daddy would buy the cars, Jimmy would fix them in our basement, and then they would sell the cars and split the profits. I was never privy to any of these plans, and Jimmy told Daddy not to tell me about any of it. Had I known, I would have warned Daddy against getting involved with Jimmy in any business venture. I could have clued him in as to who was going to benefit and who was going to get screwed in any deal. I often wonder why Daddy did not smell a rat. Didn't he think there was some good reason why Jimmy didn't want me to know? As I look back now, it becomes clear to me that in many ways, Daddy and Jimmy had the same distorted thought patterns, but that was something I did not want to admit at the time.

There was no kind of accounting being done by Jimmy or any hired help for his shop. When Daddy questioned Jimmy about his business income, Jimmy suggested that Daddy spend the day at the shop to see how it was run. Daddy could look over the paperwork and get an idea of what kind of income and expenses the shop was generating. Daddy went to the shop with Jimmy the following day. That evening, when they got home, Daddy had little to say, but the next day after Jimmy left, Daddy gave me the scoop. It was just as I thought; Jimmy had no idea how much money came in or how much went out. He did not know whether he had the income to support his family and the house, let alone buy health insurance. This "my own shop" deal was no more than a joke, an ego booster. I always suspected that, but now Daddy knew it too. Considering what he knew now, why would Daddy allow himself to be sucked into Jimmy Minor's rip-off schemes behind my back? Of course, at this point, I had no idea about the thousands of dollars Daddy was spending on Jimmy's schemes. Jimmy was soon sporting a motorcycle that he claimed someone gave him for payment of some bodywork he had done. I never believed that either. Jimmy was still gone most of the time, and when he did come home, he had been drinking.

Jimmy knew I was not happy with his shop dealings and his nights out. I remember one Saturday when I came home from work, and Jimmy had been gone since the previous Friday morning. I was in the bedroom changing my clothes when Jimmy suddenly appeared at the door. He said nothing, just looked at me. I noticed his extremely uncomfortable demeanor. I looked back at him as if to say, "What is it you want?" He finally blurted out the words I never thought I would hear come out of his mouth: "I'm sorry." Was I really hearing this right? His words caught me by surprise, and I wondered what he had done so different the night before that he felt the need to apologize. He knew at this point that tolerating his behavior was now a choice for me, and one of my choices was ending the marriage. The ball was now in my court, and he had much more to lose than I did. I felt Jimmy struggling through the rest of the day to get back into my good graces. I had planned to go to church the next day and take the boys, and Jimmy suggested coming with us. This was a bold step for him since he had always labeled himself Catholic, and going to a Protestant church was seen as a betrayal of his true religion. The next morning, we all attended a Baptist church. Jimmy knew he had given me little reason lately to stay with him, and his uneasiness with my self-sufficiency was evident. He knew I was sitting in a place of strength with all the resources I needed to move on without him. The tables had turned, and Jimmy Minor no longer held the power he once did when I was pregnant and had small children. Our eleventh anniversary came and went as usual, without any acknowledgment. As far as I was concerned, there was nothing to celebrate. If he felt the same way, why didn't he say so? I did know that even if he didn't love me, he wanted to stay with the family since we had now acquired all the trappings of the "things" he loved so much, which gave him the power to believe that he was in some way a success. Jimmy knew that he could lose his family, but the loss that he probably worried about the most had to do with the house and its furnishings.

Daddy loved working in the yard, planting new grass and shrubs. I ran the house and worked at Sears. Jimmy talked about making major improvements to the house, and he had a man come one Saturday to draw up a plan and give him an estimate. I was not included in whatever plans Jimmy had decided to make. While I kept busy, I listened as Jimmy and the builder talked about installing fancy columns on the front porch, building a larger deck, and finishing the basement. When the cost was added up, it was in the neighborhood of $10,000. As I listened to Jimmy's conversation, I realized that our new togetherness was not any more real than Jimmy was. If Jimmy thought it was acceptable to make plans to remodel this house without including me, then nothing had really changed. Nothing he owned would ever be enough to feed Jimmy's warped ego. I determined that I was not going to sign anything that put us in debt for $10,000, but I worried that this man was going to allow Jimmy to borrow the money without my consent.

This kind of worry had gone on far too long because I was married to a man I would never ever be able to trust. I would always be living on edge, never knowing what Jimmy might be doing behind my back. I was tired of this way of life; I had stuck it out way too long and spent too many years just hanging in there. Yes, life was better for me now that I was not being physically abused, but it was far from acceptable to be always worried about what my husband was doing behind my back. Thoughts of divorce once again danced in my head. For a brief time after our return to Atlanta, Jimmy Minor had a good job with benefits, which supported a newly contented wife, three thriving boys, and the house of his dreams. He got to live near his family and demonstrate to them that he had acquired everything that most men dream of. Unfortunately, this same family had indoctrinated Jimmy with values that made him unable to be satisfied with anything he might achieve; he was always compelled to go after more money, more needless luxuries, more overnight parties, more secret deals. He had to know what it would cost him, but he couldn't stop.

I opened a savings account in my name and started saving my money. When I talked to Daddy about my plan to leave Jimmy, I learned about the deals that had been made behind my back between my husband and my father. Daddy did his best to discourage me from divorce because he didn't want to lose all the money he had invested with Jimmy. As it was, Daddy was already discouraged about those dealings because he had paid for two wrecked cars that Jimmy was supposed to fix and sell, but Jimmy had yet to make any effort to fix them. Daddy worried that he would wind up losing thousands of dollars, including the $2,000 he had forked over for the extra driveway. I was shocked to hear all that had gone on behind my back, and I berated Daddy for getting sucked into Jimmy's deals. All this new information only fueled my determination to bow out of the Minor lifestyle. My time had come. I had news for Daddy. If he thought for one minute that Jimmy Minor was going to hold up his end of any of those deals, divorce or no divorce, he was mistaken. I knew this man and his manipulative ways better than anyone. For whatever reason, using other people and betraying their trust was built into Jimmy's psyche. As for Daddy, his decision to keep secrets from me meant that I was not able to warn him in time to preserve his savings. It was a revelation to me that he even needed such a warning; I had always thought Daddy was so much smarter than that. For the very first time, I was becoming aware of the many flaws in Daddy's judgment that I had so easily discounted in the past. Daddy always hid behind my mother as the source of his problems, but now that she was gone, his own flaws were exposed. I was seeing him now in a very different light than I ever had before. Nevertheless, I was grateful that he was living at my house because he was my safety net. I was not willing to live through any more years of regret, and I was in the perfect place to make my move. My children were in school, I had my friends and my father nearby, and I had a job.

I called an attorney and made an appointment to start the divorce process. I had no reason to believe that this time, the divorce was not going to happen; my promise to myself was finally going to be fulfilled. I remembered when the abuse was so intolerable that I was willing to die rather than allow it to continue. I remembered the despair, the urge to escape, and the fearful nights that I thought I might not live through. It was all over now; the end had finally come. I had no misgivings that hot summer day as I drove to the attorney's office. I gladly signed the papers and paid the attorney to start the process. Now that Jimmy was gone most of the time, coming and going as he pleased, we seldom spoke to each other. By the time he got home, I would be in bed, and I was up and gone before him in the morning. Jimmy must have sensed that something was up, and he finally mentioned something about coming home more often. This offer opened the door for me to speak to him. I responded, "It doesn't matter anymore where you go or what you do. I am not interested. I have filed for a divorce. So don't bother talking to me now. You are too late." He did not answer, but I could see his lips getting tight and the anger on his face rising. He followed me into the bedroom and stood there as he processed what I had just told him.

"So you're going to take away from me all that I have worked for?"

"I don't believe that anything we have is a result of your wanting to provide for us or your caring about anyone but yourself. So far, anything you have bought has been to benefit you, not us." I did not point out that his first concern about divorce was for his property, not his wife and sons.

He came closer, looked me in the eye, and said, "I know that for all the years we have been married you have never been with anyone else, but I can tell you that once you do, I will never want you again." I just smiled as I thought to myself how nothing about him had really changed; he still believed in his entitlement to stay out all night with other women while his wife remained pure. His threat only gave me a stronger reason to get off this bus to nowhere because Jimmy's belief in male superiority was ingrained in his thinking.

"So far, I have never been any more to you than a commodity. You have never given me one reason to stay. You always knew I wanted out, but my needs and wants have never mattered to you. Everything in our marriage has been designed and manipulated to benefit you, to feed your warped ego and make you look like someone other than who you really are. After all these years of tolerating your dominance and abuse, the door has finally swung open in my direction. I have choices that I've never had before. I would be a fool to stay with you any longer."

"If you go through with this divorce, I am going to tell little Jimmy that you were pregnant when we got married, and that was the only reason I married you." His threat seemed to imply that getting pregnant was something I did by myself. I was not going to change my mind because nothing could forgive Jimmy's lack of remorse for the years of extreme abuse. He believed that the abuse was justified because as a man, he had rights and privileges that I did not. For me, the end of worrying about Jimmy's next move was in sight. I had even more resolve now that I knew that his reaction to the divorce would be threats instead of sorrow. It would have taken nothing less than a supernatural intervention to stop this process for me, but I believed that the supernatural intervention in this case was God answering my pleas for help.

I was at my desk working the following Saturday when a supervisor signaled me to end the call and close my key. When I did, she told me that my husband had been involved in a motorcycle accident. The information she had received was that Jimmy was at a local hospital, being treated for scrapes to his arms. It would be another hour before our shift was over, and I didn't see the urgency to leave right away. I had ridden to work with Pat Wells that day, and she kept trying to convince me to go because "people were talking," and it would look better if we left. All the way home, Pat kept giving me advice that started with, "If that were my husband." I didn't argue with her or try to explain because she would never understand. She had been married as long as I had, but she had a real husband who loved her and helped her raise their children. When I arrived home, Jimmy was there. He had bad pavement scrapes on his arms but no broken bones. He had been wearing a helmet, which probably saved his life.

Through the next weeks, Jimmy was at home recovering. While I was at work and the boys were at school, Jimmy's goal was to make life as miserable as he could for Daddy, hoping he would decide to leave. If Jimmy could get Daddy out of the way, I would have less support and might not be able to go through with the divorce. Without Daddy's presence, Jimmy would have been abusing and threatening me, hoping I would give up as I had in the past. Jimmy's behavior only made me more determined not to back down, and I made it clear that it would be Jimmy who would leave, not Daddy.

We were sitting in the family room one afternoon when Jimmy nervously spoke up and addressed my father. "Well, Al, I'm going to have to ask you to leave."

"What? Leave? No, I like it here. I'm staying." Daddy continued to rock back and forth in his chair, and the anger grew on Jimmy's face. His lips tightened, and his face twisted. I remembered seeing that same face many times, when I had trembled in fear of what Jimmy's next move would be.

"This is my house, and I am telling you to leave." Jimmy's voice became louder, angrier, and more demanding. Daddy stood up and walked out to the front porch; I followed.

"You don't have to leave, Daddy. I have been through this before. If you leave, then I will be his target."

"Don't worry. I'm not going anywhere."

Just then, Jimmy appeared from the carport, and he walked up close to Daddy, shaking his finger in his face. "You bastard," yelled Jimmy, "I could kill you if I wanted to."

Daddy smacked Jimmy's finger away as if he were swatting a fly. "You're not a threat to me. I'm not afraid of you. Put your finger in my face again, and I'll smear you all over that driveway." I knew Daddy would not back away from Jimmy if in fact he started swinging, and I feared a fistfight might ensue.

"I'm going in to call the police before someone gets hurt," I said. I was shaking as I headed toward the kitchen. When I hung up the phone and Jimmy knew the police were on their way, he ran across the street to a neighbor's house to call his mother. When the police arrived, I explained to the officer what had happened. I could see Jimmy walking out of the neighbor's house as the police walked toward him. He told the officers that his mother was on the way to pick him up. The police waited outside with us and allowed Jimmy to go in the house and gather some of his belongings. The police stayed until his mother pulled up in her rescue mobile to save her boy once again. I watched as Jimmy angrily slung his things in the back seat and slid into the passenger seat. Frances's car pulled away from the curb, and I watched as it turned off Jeannette Court. I knew this had been the final showdown, and Jimmy would never be back.

Daddy had been there this time to witness Jimmy Minor in action. It was just a small taste of what had been going on for years, but this time, I had someone in my corner to support me. I was pretty sure Jimmy was not going to be calling in the middle of the night, threatening to kill me or pounding on the door, demanding that I let him in. He wasn't man enough to stand up to another man who wasn't going to back down when threatened. Jimmy had played the part of the good husband in front of my father all those years, but it only took one evening for the truth to come out.

The court date was set for late August. In the meantime, Jimmy had collected a nice settlement from the insurance company for his motorcycle accident, and he hired a hotshot lawyer to contest the divorce. On the day of the hearing, I felt confident when I took the stand next to the judge's podium. Jimmy's lawyer aggressively questioned me, trying to portray Daddy as the problem. He tried to make the case that this divorce was happening only because Daddy lived with us and refused to leave when Jimmy asked him to. The attorney argued that it was Daddy who should pay child support, not Jimmy. He kept insisting that I tell the judge how much income Daddy had, and I kept insisting that I did not know, which was the truth. When all the questioning was over, the judge wrote some figures down and told the attorneys that Jimmy was to pay $25 per week per child and that he was allowed visitation with the boys. This was all temporary until an agreeable solution could be reached between us. Jimmy was allowed to come to the house one time to take whatever tools and personal belongings were his. The judge ruled that due to Jimmy's past record of violence, he was only allowed this one opportunity and was never to come into the house again for any reason.

When the hearing was over, I was on my way to freedom, or so I thought. I had to pinch myself to believe that this was actually happening. This was the moment that I had many times thought would never come, when I was severely oppressed and in desperation. I was not only rid of Jimmy Minor but his family as well. This course of events serves to confirm that bad behavior, hidden by dishonesty, will eventually find its way out of hiding. I was astonished that the truth had surfaced without any action on my part. I could have never in a million years planned, dreamed, or imagined that events would unfold as they did. I am always amazed at how things changed, not when I most needed them to but when I had begun to heal. It had been six years since the trauma of 1967, and pain no longer dominated my thoughts and my life.

I was well aware that getting Jimmy to pay the court-ordered child support was always going to be a struggle. I quickly applied for a full-time job at Sears, and my request was accepted within a month. After six weeks, I would be eligible for benefits, and my children and I would finally be covered with life and health insurance.

As Pat Wells and I rode back and forth to work together, I finally shared with her some details about my marriage. She and her husband were both Christians and were active in their small Baptist church. She encouraged me to come to her church, and the boys and I started attending on Sunday mornings. I struggled to grasp any sense of comfort at that church, and I felt that I just did not fit in. I tried to explain my feelings to Pat, but she didn't seem to understand the problem. She kept insisting that the problem was with me, and she suggested that I get involved in a Wednesday night Bible study led by the pastor. I agreed to try it, but the class only made me more uneasy. The class consisted of six women led by the fiftyish, married pastor. As we all sat in a circle, I could feel the pastor eyeing me up and down. His eyes always focused on me when he should have been addressing his teaching to the whole class. I became so uncomfortable in that class that I stopped attending the Bible study, but I did continue to attend the Sunday service. Pat was very critical of my decision and kept pressuring me to get more involved. I tried to explain my feelings of discomfort around the pastor, but she insisted that I was reading him wrong. When the pastor was gone for a few weeks, I was told that he was in the hospital suffering from depression. When he came back, he began calling me. Every Sunday morning, the phone would ring so early that it woke us all up. The pastor's voice sounded nervous as he would kind of sing his words, something to the effect of, "The service starts at a certain time. Get out of bed, get dressed. I will be looking for you!" I stopped going to that church altogether, and after such a negative experience, I was reluctant to try another church. I did not understand church life; I got no benefit from it and found it to be more of an annoyance than a help. I was resolved that I was simply not a church person.

One afternoon, Jimmy called. "Are you ready to apologize?" he asked.

"Apologize for what?"

He changed the subject. "Why don't you go out and have some fun? Why don't you go out on a date?" he asked with an air of arrogance in his voice.

"I don't think that is any of your business," I answered before hanging up.

He never contacted me again. The boys had told me he already had a new girlfriend named Barbara. Whenever the boys went to see him, Barbara was part of the visit. I was glad he had found someone because that would take his focus off me. I did not envy her in the least.

I had now graduated to a full-time position in what Sears referred to as the front office where all the incoming orders were processed. I caught on fast, but I found the work to be too simple and boring. After I complained, they trained me on the teletype machine, which was a welcome break from tearing apart orders for eight hours. Sears was good about promoting from within. I kept watching the board for other full-time jobs that were posted. When another position that I felt qualified for became available, I applied for it and was accepted. This new position was at a higher level; it paid more and consisted of a variety of new tasks they would train me to do.

Daddy oversaw the boys as they left for school and when they got home. It wasn't long before Jimmy's child support checks started to bounce. Jimmy was still working at his shop. I contacted my attorney, who sent letters to Jimmy warning him of the consequences if he didn't catch up on the child support payments. Jimmy ignored them all. Making ends meet out of a small amount of money was familiar to me. I knew how to handle money well; I made do with my salary, and Daddy occasionally pitched in. My attorney finally served Jimmy with an abandonment notice. A police car pulled up at his shop, handcuffed him, put him in the back seat, and took him to the county jail. By now, Jimmy was behind in his child support more than $700. My attorney called to tell me that Jimmy had been in jail for four days and that Jimmy's mother could come up with $400. I could feel the attorney's sympathetic tone toward Jimmy's situation, which annoyed me. The lawyer advised me to settle for the $400 so that Jimmy could be released, arguing that Jimmy couldn't earn any money while he was in jail. I always found it odd that Jimmy's family, which always bragged about how much money they had, all of a sudden didn't have any. I felt victimized, but when the lawyer implied I had no other choice, I reluctantly agreed. When I received the check from the attorney a few days later, it was for only $300 since the attorney took his part off the top. I was getting educated as to how the system worked and what to expect in the future. It just validated what I already knew. Depending on Jimmy Minor for child support or any other kind of support was fruitless. I was going to have to earn my own way and take care of my children, and any child support I was lucky enough to receive I would consider as a little extra.

Chapter 15

Effects from Years of Abuse Surface

My marriage had been a long twelve years of abuse, dominance, captivity, and extreme fear. I welcomed my new freedom, but I did not understand how the past twelve years had taken its toll on my mental well-being. I now know that I was suffering from post-traumatic stress syndrome and in need of counseling. Time would tell me that I was anything but mentally stable enough to handle my new freedom. However, at the time, I was in denial, and I was sure I would be fine now that the abuser was gone. The denial left me blind to my feelings, my needs, and my identity. There had been so much denial in my past that had I suddenly been forced to see the truth, I would have died from the sudden shock of exposure.

I later learned that post-traumatic stress had changed my whole personality. I had been chronically traumatized, first by my mother and then by my husband, and I no longer had any baseline state of calm or comfort. My life had been so full of anxiety that I had no ability to reason. By the time Jimmy Minor was gone from my life, I had lost all touch with reality, and I had no ability to determine right from wrong or to differentiate between acceptable and unacceptable behavior. I was fighting a build-up of fear, hurt, frustration, deprivation, and loneliness, and I was not aware of my need to seek help. I looked fine, my life was moving in a new direction, and my goal had been accomplished. I had no doubt that my children and I were on the road to live happily ever after. The problem was that I no longer knew what I believed in. While it is clear that ordinary, healthy people may become entrapped in prolonged abusive situations, it is equally clear that after their escape, they are neither ordinary nor healthy. The traumatic memories stay in suppression, waiting to be acknowledged either by acting out or talking it out. As long as I continued to believe that my freedom rested on some outward condition, i.e., Jimmy leaving, I was no more than a slave to circumstance. The real problem was inside me. True freedom is an inner state of awareness, not a change in circumstance. I was still in bondage and on a journey of spiritual and mental decline. What I didn't know was that it would take years before I would find my true spirit, be free, and start climbing toward the light.

I started out in this marriage as many do with the right intentions to take the vows seriously and stick it out through good times and bad. Unfortunately, the disrespect and abuse in my marriage made commitment the wrong path for me. I stayed way too long; the safety and well-being of my children and me should have been a higher priority. I realized later that I had recreated my childhood environment in my own marriage. Jimmy Minor and my mother were both highly disordered people. Throughout my childhood, as I watched my mother act out her insanity, I listened to my dad tell me how wonderful she was and that what I was seeing was not really happening. In this house of denial, I did not develop a healthy belief system of my own. Later, I mirrored my father's coping mechanism and kept looking for something wonderful about Jimmy Minor long past the time when I should have known it was hopeless to expect him to change his ways.

My life had turned a significant corner, and as I looked forward to a new beginning and a better life for myself and my children, I was not prepared for the downhill spiral I would experience in the months and years ahead. My fall from grace started when a neighbor's friend asked me out to celebrate New Year's Eve. It didn't matter to me that Tim was five years younger than I was because I had no plans to pursue a relationship with anyone. After all, my divorce wasn't final yet. Tim made reservations for dinner and dancing at a nice restaurant. This was the first time I had been out on a real date with someone who treated me so well. Even though it was an enjoyable evening, I had no intention of going out with Tim again. I was too busy with three children and a full-time job. Unfortunately, Tim did not feel the same way. He would "stop by" on weekday evenings to hang out, have a few beers with Daddy, and play with the boys. At first, I didn't feel that he was intruding because he was affectionate and showered me with attention. I had been deprived of affection for so many years, and Tim fed my suppressed emotions. He lifted me up on a pedestal with a clear message that I had value and that my life was important. On the weekends, he would take me out to dinner at nice restaurants. He catered to me, paid attention to my needs, and wanted to be with me all the time. I allowed Tim to dominate my life for a time, but after a few months, I began to feel smothered and wanted to break it off. Daddy was happy having Tim around since he had gained a drinking buddy. I, on the other hand, was not happy with Tim's drinking. More than that, I found myself overwhelmed with trying to keep up with all my responsibilities. I became worn-out, going to bed late, getting up early, and spending less and less time with my children. Tim and Daddy were now dominating my world as they sat on the deck discussing over their drinks about how great things were. In the spring of 1974, my divorce from Jimmy became final.

As I tried to pull away from the relationship, Tim became more domineering and more demanding. He criticized the boys and how they were being raised, insisting that parenting should be done exactly as it was in his perfect upbringing. I realized that he brought up his reservations about my parenting style in order to convince me that I needed his "help." I began to feel more and more violated and overpowered. I knew that Tim was invading my time, my space, and my life, but I did not know how to go about ending the relationship. This time, I had no one on my side because of Daddy's friendship with Tim. I again felt trapped and wanted out, and I started sliding backward emotionally. I was having trouble sleeping at night and having trouble making decisions for myself. I became so worn down by both Tim and Daddy that after some time, I stopped trying to get rid of Tim. After that, the feeling of entrapment was as real as it had been when I was with Jimmy. My life had spiraled out of my control. Tim and Daddy were now in charge; they were running the show. I worked at my job at Sears all day, and at night, I ran the boys around to their Little League practices, washed clothes, cooked an evening meal, and cleaned up. After dinner, Daddy and Tim would retire to the deck to drink a few six-packs and share complaints about how I handled everything. In their opinion, I should be taking Jimmy back to court to get more child support. Neither of them suggested helping me with anything, and my attempts to dole out some of the responsibilities were never taken seriously. I wanted to get rid of Tim, get my thoughts together, calm down, and find some sanity in my life so that I could go back to being a mother. I knew that getting Tim out of my life was going to take a strong stand on my part and that the stress of accomplishing the break against Daddy's wishes would prove way too traumatic for me. I already had more stress than I could handle.

Sporadically, Jimmy would take the boys for a weekend, using Barbara as his gofer. Barbara was Jimmy's puppet and chauffeur. She never worked anywhere long enough to support herself and was totally dependent on Jimmy. When he came along, Barbara was willing to do whatever he needed her to do and to live any way he provided for her, which was a poor living to say the least. Her standards were like his, and I believe that she was the perfect match for Jimmy Minor.

One weekend when the boys were visiting their dad, they were out in the yard building a tree house without any adult supervision. Scott and Mark got into a squabble about who was to use the sledgehammer, and Scott slung it to Mark. The hammer hit Mark in the head, and he collapsed and was rushed to the hospital. The impact of the hammer on Mark's head had put pressure on his brain, and he was scheduled for surgery the next day. The doctor had to make a cut in Mark's scalp in the shape of a horseshoe in order to repair the bone. Mark was only seven years old, and the doctor said that it was because of his young age that the surgery was so successful. After a week in the hospital, Mark came home. He had to wear a special helmet to protect the stitches, and I had to watch him carefully. Mark's class sent him get-well cards and gave him a special sand art project that he loved. I felt blessed that my insurance with Sears paid all the medical bills, with the exception of a co-pay of $150. When I asked Jimmy if he would help with the $150, he flatly refused.

Tim continued to "drop in" whenever he wanted to. By now, I felt helpless and did not know how to stand up for myself against the dynamic drinking team of Daddy and Tim. I feared conflict at all cost. I tried to talk to Daddy about the situation when Tim wasn't around, but of course, Daddy loved the status quo and was not going to encourage me to do anything to change it. I was no longer devoting the time and attention to my children that I knew they needed. Because I felt so bad about myself, I began to dissociate from my children. Dissociation, which lies at the heart of traumatic stress disorders, provides a mental escape, a method of coping with an unacceptable situation. I became insensitive to both my pain and my children's pain because I was now functioning on a robotic level. I knew that any changes I tried to make would upset Daddy's and Tim's applecart, and I would be downgraded to "ungrateful for all they did for me" after the divorce. I was still fear-driven, and I wondered why Daddy's and Tim's needs mattered so much more than mine. Who was I anyhow? I was acting a part just to accommodate everyone else. I needed serious counseling but was too beaten down to think clearly. I knew this situation was not good for me or my children, but for now, it was all I could do to keep going, working all day and caring for a family all evening in my depressed and sleep-deprived state.

Tim's parents seemed to be nice people. They were well respected in their community, and if they had any problem, it was their unwillingness to see any faults in their children. Tim's mother shared with me many times that Tim's drinking worried her, but she blamed his excessive drinking on the service. His parents owned a boat on Lake Erie, and each summer, we were all invited up to go out fishing on Lake Erie. The boat was impressive, and it was a fun time for us. Despite Tim's mother's worries, there was never any shortage of beer supplied during our trips there. Of course, Tim didn't allow his mother to witness any of his anger and hostility. When we were alone, Tim constantly rambled on about how his parents could not really afford to take us out on these boat trips, and he made sure I knew how much it cost to fill up the boat with gas. A couple of times, we took trips to Florida, but these vacations were never pleasant for me or the boys because Tim constantly found fault with everything we did. Neither I nor the boys ever did anything right according to Tim. Some days I just wanted to plan a trip to anywhere that included just my children and me. I wanted to take us away from our home situation, even if just for a few days. I longed for my family to be free to be ourselves and do what we wanted. However, a trip like that would have taken some planning, and I feared what would happen if Tim found out about our going somewhere without him. His angry outbursts were becoming terrifying to me, so I cowered away from standing up for what I knew was right. I had not learned how to communicate my needs because I did not feel as if I had any rights. I had gone from being terrified of Jimmy to being terrified of Tim, but in this case, Daddy always sided with Tim, which made my father a major problem in the chaos.

Despite my difficult homelife, I excelled in my job at Sears and had the opportunity to apply for better positions. My salary was also moving up. Although Jimmy seldom paid his child support on time, I managed my money well and was able to make ends meet. Daddy's best contribution was that he was there to see the boys off to school since I had to leave before anyone was up, and he was there when the boys came home in the afternoon. In the winter, Daddy would sometimes go to Mexico for a month to visit his brother Ferd or to Canada to visit other relatives. Daddy came and went as he pleased, and during the seven years that he lived with me, we never discussed money. His money was his own; he never gave me any money, nor did I ever ask him for any. I managed with what I had.

Although I had a good job and a nice home, I was extremely insecure. I had allowed Tim to stay in my life way too long, just as I had with Jimmy Minor. My raises at Sears always annoyed Tim because my financial stability was a threat to him. My job was the most important tool I had in my quest to find a way out of this relationship. However, I knew I needed other kinds of help in order to fight for my rights and the rights of my children. Without a healthy support system, my ability to make rational choices continued to slip further away. I feared stepping out of that box and turning my life upside down. But oh, how I wanted to. I dreaded coming home from work each day, and I remember planning how I would handle whatever crisis might greet me. If this happened or that happened, I would just do this or that and put an end to Tim's presence once and for all. These escape fantasies consumed my drive home each day, but every day as I arrived home, I lost my courage. My stress was so extreme that I finally asked my doctor for sleeping pills, and the pills did give me some needed rest in the short term.

Daddy and Tim were the only ones who found any joy in our living arrangement. Trying to talk to Daddy about it was like talking to a brick wall because he was so happy with his drinking buddy. When Daddy went on one of his trips, he would be sure to tell Tim, "Take care of things for me while I am gone." I would cringe at his words. In our daily lives, their idea of "taking care of things" was no more than sitting out on the deck drinking beer and talking for hours about how I was not handling things as I should. Daddy was rapidly losing his "hero" status with me.

Tim would sometimes talk about getting married, but that was something I knew without reservation would never happen. Tim believed that marriage was what I wanted, and he would dictate to me how things were going to be "when we were married." One thing he emphasized was that we would never get divorced. It was difficult for me to express to him my true feelings because if I said the wrong thing, his anger would surface. In order to avoid confrontation, I said nothing, which he interpreted as agreement on my part that we would be married. However, nothing could have been further from the truth.

As time went on, I realized more and more how my relationship with Tim was not very different from my relationship with Jimmy Minor. Our life was never about me, about how I felt or what I wanted; it was all about Tim and what he wanted. Tim thought that we should all agree with his beliefs and act according to his rules. Anytime I attempted to break off the relationship, Tim would find a way to get back into my good graces. When Tim stayed away for a week, I would gather up my children and go to church. I had found a Church of God not too far away, and we started attending, irregularly, but attending. Somehow, I thought of seeking God as a way to find some peace and some semblance of sanity in my unstable life. I was always seeking a solution but never understanding how to make change happen for me. Even though I went looking for a new beginning, I really had no clue as to what I was really looking for. Somewhere inside me, I felt that real change was somehow connected to finding God.

The more I tried to pull away from Tim, the more he became obsessed with me and spoke about marriage. One of his schemes to bond us forever was the purchase of a dog. Tim was always talking about his perfect childhood, and part of that perfection was his springer spaniel dog. Tim decided to purchase the same-breed dog for the boys. Although Skipper was supposedly my boys' dog, everything had to be done according to Tim's rules, and fights were ongoing about "the dog." Nothing we did was ever good enough for Skipper, according to Tim. He would blow up about Skipper's care, and his anger fueled more and more fear in me. Now breaking up with Tim would be complicated by our sharing both my boys' dog and my father.

I began to question myself as to why I kept finding myself in relationships in which I felt trapped and without choices. I know now that these dead-end, anger-fueled relationships had everything to do with my childhood. I kept unconsciously recreating my childhood trauma, and this time, I even had Daddy's words validating that nothing could or should be done to change the situation. Whether Daddy was excusing my mother or Tim, he always asserted that there were no solutions, which implied that I was stuck and that I had no right to change. I had to separate my thinking from Daddy's thinking. I didn't believe what he believed, but I felt powerless to break away from Tim without the help of the only solace of my childhood and the "hero" of my divorce.

Through these years, I was slowly but surely losing the respect of my children and the closeness I once had with them. The situation gnawed at me because as much as I knew that my children's home environment was toxic, I could not pull myself together to do anything about it. I had lost my ability to nurture and to be a close part of my children's lives. I broke it off with Tim more and more often now, but I was never strong enough to keep my resolve.

In the spring of 1976, Mark, who had always been a tough, energetic kid, began showing signs that something was wrong. Scott was the first to notice. He came to me one day and said, "Mom, something is wrong with Mark."

"What do you mean?" I asked.

"He can't keep up with us when we are out playing. He has to sit down on the curb."

This was so unlike Mark that it worried Scott and then me. I asked Mark what was wrong, and he said he didn't know but that he was losing strength in his legs and hands. I immediately made an appointment with Mark's pediatrician to have him checked out. I noticed that Mark had trouble rolling down the car window and that his gait did not look normal. I was terrified. Mark's doctor was mature, had a great way with kids, and gave me a feeling of confidence that he would get to the bottom of the problem. When he examined Mark that day, he said that he suspected something was wrong but could not pinpoint exactly what the problem was. He told me to take Mark home and have him stay off his feet for two days. At the end of two days, I was to bring Mark back in, and the doctor would again examine him to see if he could figure it out. We did as he instructed. At the next appointment after the same examination, the doctor strongly suspected that Mark had some condition, but he could not identify what it was. He referred me to a pediatric neurologist. Not knowing was the worst part. I was now observing Mark struggle to lift almost anything. I thought about his head injury just two years earlier. Could that have something to do with it? I asked the doctor and was told that there was no possible connection.

I called the church we had attended a few times, explained the problem, and asked for prayer. I was assured that the pastor would be notified, and Mark would be on their priority prayer list. Again, it was in these trying times that I found comfort in knowing that

I believed in God, and I trusted that he was going to help me. In hindsight, throughout my life, God was continually drawing me in, trying to get my attention, but I only responded in times of crisis when I had nowhere else to turn. I found comfort knowing that this body of Christian believers knew the problem and were praying for a positive outcome.

The next week, when it was time for our appointment with the pediatric neurologist, his appearance made me wonder about his common sense. He wore a loud plaid shirt with a nonmatching dotted bow tie, all of which gave him a clownish appearance. However, once he started asking questions and talking to me, I realized that this specialist's appearance held little importance. I was extremely impressed with his knowledge and expertise, which were obvious the moment he asked the first question. He lifted Mark from the examining table, stood him on the floor, and asked him to walk. As he observed Mark's gait, he looked me in the eye and said, "He has polyneuritis. I can tell from the way he walks. The walk is always the same." He put his hand on my shoulder and continued, "He will get better from this. It is a form of the polio virus, but unlike polio, it runs its course and gets better. I would like him to go into the hospital for tests, to rule out any other possibilities. Its cause is not known. This condition is also known as Guillain-Barré syndrome, named after the doctor who discovered it over seventy years ago. More severe cases can be life-threatening, but Mark appears to be only mildly affected and should recover completely." His words were extremely comforting to me. I was relieved that the doctor had put a name to Mark's illness, followed by the magical words that he should recover completely. The prayers I had requested came to mind. How I loved the Lord at that particular moment! Even though I knew Mark's condition would get worse before it got better, I trusted this doctor that Mark would return to health.

Mark's hospital tests ruled out any other possibilities. He came home, and his condition deteriorated through the next month or so. When I brought Mark back for his next appointment with the neurologist, he was in a wheelchair. The doctor lifted Mark onto a table to examine him, and as he asked me questions about how we were coping with Mark's illness, tears rolled down Mark's face. The doctor looked him in the eye and said, "You will get better. Do you understand what I am telling you?"

"Yes," Mark answered reluctantly. I realized that I needed to spend more time with Mark, finding things that he could do and assuring him that he would get better. This was a terrible, debilitating disease, but the condition came with not only the hope but the assurance that he would get better. For a nine-year-old boy who wanted to get back to running and playing with his friends, the wait was not easy.

The weeks of Mark's convalescence were trying at best for all of us, but we persevered. Although I was not happy with my father's drinking and his friendship with Tim, we could not have made it through Mark's illness without Daddy. Because he looked after Mark during the day, I could continue to work, and without my salary, we could have been in big financial trouble. When Daddy spent time outdoors working in his garden, Mark had trouble getting his attention, so I bought a whistle for Mark that he could blow when he needed something. Since school was still in session and Mark could not attend, he was eligible for a tutor to come to the house once a week to teach him privately. This program was a godsend. Mark looked forward to these sessions; he thrived on the individual attention, and he passed the fourth grade with his class in June of 1976. Scott graduated that June from seventh grade, and I attended the graduation ceremony with Mark in his wheelchair. I was very proud of Scott, who looked too grown-up as he walked up to receive his diploma. I realized how quickly the years were slipping away.

Throughout the summer, Mark began to make progress, ever so slowly. One afternoon when I came in from work, he showed me how he could stand up without any help, using the back of the sofa for support. Mark was gaining strength as well as confidence, just as the doctor told me would happen. Another day when I came in from work, Mark was gone, having found a way to scoot his butt along the floor to get where he was going. A week later, he was walking, holding onto a piece of furniture or balancing with one hand on the wall for support. Mark had a bunny that he kept in a cage in the basement. He figured out how to inch down the basement stairs and open the cage to let the bunny out so they could play on the walkway. When school started in September of 1976, Mark had recovered well enough to attend every class but physical education. By the end of the school year, he had made a full recovery, and to this day, there are no signs that he ever had polyneuritis.

Also in 1976, Bruce Springsteen's name was beginning to surface in the newspaper and occasionally on TV. Daddy and I knew that this musician was none other than Bart's friend who played with him in the band the Castiles in Freehold, New Jersey. Springsteen had signed with a recording company, and his music was gaining recognition. Whenever I heard Springsteen's name, it brought back memories of Bart and how deeply his death had impacted my life. A few years later, in 1979, the book *Born to Run* was published. This was the story of Bruce Springsteen's humble beginnings and his miraculous rise to fame and fortune. The book talks about his life growing up in Freehold, about our neighbors Tex and Marion, and about how Tex became their first manager. On page 25, there is a picture of the Castiles, with Bart in the middle holding the drumsticks. Bruce Springsteen wrote all his own music, and Daddy and I believed that his song "Born in the USA" was a tribute to Bart.

In the summer of 1976, as Mark was recuperating, Tim suggested that we take a vacation to Florida to visit Busch Gardens. We went on the trip with only Scott and Mark; Jimmy stayed home with Daddy. I knew this was wrong because Jimmy should never have been left out of anything we did together as a family. Tim was the outsider, not Jimmy. This trip gave me the fuel to charge ahead with putting a final end to a relationship that was now over three years old. I felt great shame for the fact that Tim was still dominating my family. I had to be brave enough to step out and pay whatever consequences were necessary to make the breakup stick.

By spring of 1977, I had figured out how to end to my relationship with Tim, and I was not as fearful of the consequences as I had been in the past. Fear is a powerful force, but I knew that if I didn't act now, this fiasco would only continue. Tim drank too much, and he was a poor influence on my children. Although Tim never lived at our house, he was there most of time that we were home. I knew the boys wanted him out of our lives and were depending on me to make that happen. I was feeling stronger and more determined to do whatever it took. I carefully made my plans each day on my way home from work, when I was alone and able to think things through without distraction. Now that Mark was better, Daddy was planning to travel to Mexico with his brother in March of 1977. I knew that the month that my father was out of our house would be the best time to move forward with the breakup. Daddy had never wanted to lose his drinking buddy, but the party for Daddy and Tim was about to come to an abrupt halt. I didn't care who liked it and who didn't; I was willing to do whatever it took to end Tim's hold on my family.

I made an appointment with a counselor for the Saturday after Daddy left for Mexico. I explained to the counselor that I was there for help in ending a long-term relationship. I know now in hindsight that I just needed some support, even from a stranger, to give me the courage to go through with the breakup. After that one session, I felt a new sense of freedom. On my way home, I stopped at the mall and bought a new outfit because I had plans to go out that evening to a singles dance for the first time since I had been divorced. It would have taken more than one counseling session to get a lifetime of warped priorities straightened out, and I was not interested in further counseling at the time. I believed that Tim was the problem and that breaking up with him was all I needed to do to get my life back on track.

Jimmy had taken the boys that weekend. As I walked in the door, the phone was ringing, and it was Tim. He knew I had gone to see a counselor and asked how it went. I gave him few details and ended the conversation. I assumed that he must have known it was over, and I felt a tremendous sense of relief. It was a beautiful spring day, and I was happy and excited, thinking about my plans for that evening. I took my bags into the bedroom and began trying on my new clothes. I was standing at the bathroom mirror looking at my new outfit, tags dangling everywhere, when I heard a sudden banging at the kitchen door. I knew it had to be Tim, and I quickly changed clothes and ran to the kitchen. I was afraid he would knock down the door before I got there to open it. "What took you so long to get to the door?" he grumbled.

"I had the bathroom door closed and didn't hear you right away," I answered.

"Okay, this is the plan," he explained. "My parents are coming for a visit, and you and I are going out to eat with them, and we are going to talk."

"I won't be going," I said confidently.

He grabbed me in a rage and pulled me down on the floor. He held me there with his finger pointing at my face, demanding that I go with him and his parents. The fire in his eyes terrified me, and I became paralyzed with fear as I realized we were alone in the house. I tried to scream, but nothing came out; I fought to get up, but he was not going to let me. I finally gave up fighting, and once I was able to speak, I said, "Okay, if you just let me get up, we can sit down and talk about it." I knew this was what he wanted to hear as a first step to my agreeing to go along with his plan. He backed away, and I slowly stood up.

"That's more like it," he said.

I felt that going along with him was safest because he would calm down when he thought that he was again in control. I leaned on years of experience with a violent mother and a violent husband. When I was up and firmly on my feet, I slowly walked toward the kitchen, saying that I needed something to drink. Tim stayed in the family room and waited for me to return. As I walked past the carport door, I slid my hand onto the doorknob, quickly opened it, and ran for my life across the street to a neighbor's house.

My house was on a cul-de-sac, and my neighbor's house sat across the street up on a hill. As I stood at her front door, desperately ringing the doorbell, it soon became apparent that she wasn't home. I kept looking back to see if Tim was coming after me. I could clearly see my house below, and I walked behind some shrubs and hid, watching to see whether Tim would come after me or just get in his truck and leave. Eventually, he walked out through the carport door and got into his truck. As I watched Tim back out of my driveway, I felt relieved. He glanced up at the neighbors' house as he drove by, but he did not stop. My eyes continued to follow his truck as he turned off Jeannette Court. I was still terrified that Tim might come back, so I stayed put for at least half an hour. When I felt it was safe, I walked back down the hill to my house, locked the door behind me, and checked all the other locks. I sat down on the sofa, shaken but unscathed. Tim was gone, finally gone. I felt relieved that the ordeal was over and that I had done what I intended. The violence that I had feared for so many months did occur, but I got away. My backup plan in case Tim did return was to call the police. However, there was comfort in knowing that his parents were coming to visit him, which would keep him from making any stupid moves. That evening, I dressed up in my new outfit and went to the singles dance. I felt free, energized, and ready to move on with my life.

Throughout the following year, Tim stalked me. He followed me to work and back every day, no matter how many times I changed my route. He would drive behind me so closely that if I had stopped short, he would have rear-ended me. He would call my workplace and inquire if I was there. I received cards and letters from him every day, sometimes two a day. Back then, there were no stalking laws in place as there are today. Tim started to hang out at my neighbor's house across the street because he liked being able to watch my house. I ignored all his attempts to contact me. When Daddy returned from Mexico, I told him that Tim and I were no longer together. I made it plain to him that Tim was not allowed in my house under any circumstances. When I found out that Daddy let Tim visit when I wasn't home, I was infuriated. Daddy's disrespectful attitude made me hope that he would eventually make plans to move out. I could not handle my father continuing to be best buddies with my stalker.

Even though my dysfunctional childhood did not lead me to alcohol or drug addiction, it did lead me to many other life-sabotaging behaviors. As I look back today, I wish I had continued my counseling sessions. The idea that "once the abuser was gone, the problem is solved" was as silly with Tim as it had been with Jimmy. The real problem was with me. I did not know how to make rational choices or how to put my priorities in the right order. I had few role models to help me to know how to live a sane life, how to create a loving home environment, or how to become an effective parent to my children. I can see now how Tim and Daddy fed my neediness and validated my fear that I needed to be "taken care of." They made me question my ability to make my own choices, to parent my children, and to live my life as I chose.

As I started dating others, the same pattern of neediness continued, and whenever a relationship ended, I overreacted, and my life spun out of control. I kept recreating the chaos I had grown up with. In the years following, I slipped in and out of periods of depression; I was neurotic and losing my grip on reality. My life had turned into a wild ride. I wanted to reconnect with my children, to the closeness that we once had, but I couldn't slow down long enough to work on that goal. The boys were busy with their friends, and I had lost touch with their needs. Since Daddy had lost his drinking partner, he spent less time around the house and was now hanging out at the neighborhood bar. I became a regular at the singles dances and was befriended by other single women. We banded together at the local Atlanta singles bars, searching for some misguided fun. It was my first step off the high road that made the next step even easier, and I began slowly sliding down a slippery slope of desperation and regret, unaware of the consequences I would later pay. I was searching but not finding, looking in all the wrong places with my wrong motives, which only created wrong results. I knew this lifestyle was not who I really was, but I didn't know how to stop it. I was trapped in a life of focusing on externals, which creates a drive for esteem, power, and security. I always sensed the wrongness of my life but had no resources to free myself. The false self was no more than living a lie about who I really was, an image dedicated to the world's approval of me. It was how I diverted my attention from the importance of internal issues and true reality. These insatiable drives within me emerged out of my childhood where the environment I grew up in never provided these things. By living in my false self, I was compensating for my wounded childhood.

Daddy's brother Ferd was having some health problems, and Ferd's longtime neighbor Gerry offered to come in and nurse him through his illness. When Daddy went to visit, he and Gerry became friends, and I was thrilled when Daddy told me he and Gerry planned to get married. He was seventy-five, and she was eighty. Gerry was Catholic and insisted that they get married in her local parish. Daddy still believed that religion was ridiculous, and anyone with half a brain should be able to figure that out. He laughed at Catholic rituals, especially how they paraded around the sanctuary blowing incense. Although Daddy claimed that religion was an insult to his intelligence, he and Gerry were married by a priest in her church. Daddy did enjoy sharing wine with the priest after the ceremony. Daddy moved to MacTier, Ontario, Canada, to begin his married life with Gerry. I was happy that Daddy was moving on with his life, and his leaving Atlanta was a blessing for both of us. I felt that he deserved a good woman, a companion, someone who would have a drink or two with him, since this was the one thing he was unwilling to give up under any circumstances. Daddy's marriage also gave me the freedom to move on with my life without any interference from him.

Now that both Tim and Daddy were gone, I had gained my freedom but did not know how to use it wisely. I slid more comfortably into the drinking, dancing, and dating scene. I was moving in the wrong direction, racing downhill so fast that I could barely stop myself. This lifestyle disconnected me even further from my children, and I regret these years more than any I have lived through. I was in deep denial, still affected by the memories of the abuse I had suffered and the hateful lies that I had been told for so many years. I worked at trying to appear as if I was in control when my life was clearly out of control. I rented out a spare room in my house for extra income. I knew how to rent rooms; in many ways, I had regressed back into my childhood. I was blindly stumbling through the fog and darkness, trying to find a flicker of light somewhere. I felt extremely needy, wishing there were someone I could trust, someone who would love me and treat me with the respect I felt that I deserved. I thought Daddy would be proud of me for hanging out in bars; the bars were full of men like Daddy, and I was now no better than they were. My warped thinking was being fueled by alcohol, and any healthy thought patterns I might have once had were being destroyed. I was living in a world of risky behavior, and the drinking gave me false courage that allowed me to behave in ways that were not really me.

In order to draw more attention to myself, I began to focus on my appearance, and I worked hard to look perfect in every way. I often shopped for new clothes. I was a perfect size 10 and dressed like a model, with flawless makeup and every hair in place. I smiled a lot, trying to look happy, together, and carefree. I thought that if I just looked better, smiled more, and pretended to be happy, then my life would improve, and I would draw better people into my life. I was setting a poor example for my children. I did come home from work each evening, cooked dinner, and kept my house clean in order to make my life look much saner than it really was.

Back then, I didn't understand what was wrong with me, but today, I understand the progression of post-traumatic stress disorder and how that disorder erodes the personality. After being chronically traumatized throughout my childhood and young adulthood, I was living a life of hiding and pretending, which was a direct result of my faulty belief system, which altered an unbearable reality. My memories of severe trauma were still in suppression waiting to be acknowledged, and the only way I knew to express myself was by acting out. Needless to say, I now understand the unquestionable advantages of talking it out over acting it out, but I was so traumatized that I could not bring myself to verbally express the trauma of my past to anyone. It would take a radical encounter with the truth to lift the fog I was in.

Barbara was becoming more and more of an annoyance and a troublemaker. When Jimmy gave her the orders, she jumped, and she was good at doing his dirty work. She was always calling, trying to stir up trouble, and as time went on, she began to take on the looks and personality of Jimmy's mother. She loved gossip, and Jimmy expressed his hostility toward me through her. The boys had their own opinion of her; they thought she was ignorant, and they called her family a bunch of hillbillies. She claimed to have had fifteen or more brothers and sisters, some of whom she had never met. I held no hostility toward her because I was glad that she was stuck with Jimmy Minor instead of me. Jimmy had trouble supporting both

Barbara and his sons. When he fell behind on his support payments, I filed abandonment charges against him. This action required him to pay through the court, which was a much better deal for me. There was now a probation officer assigned to Jimmy who checked up on his payments, and I no longer had to call Jimmy for any reason. I received support checks from the State of Georgia instead of waiting for Jimmy Minor's personal checks that were never any good.

    Today, as I look back, I realize that Sears had become a vital part of my existence. I had moved up the ladder to a position that afforded me a comfortable living. I still have many wonderful long-time friends I met while working at Sears. I never got involved in any of the cliques; there was a gossip grapevine that could be quite vicious. Sears in Atlanta was a large organization with close to three thousand employees in the building on Ponce de Leon Avenue. Keeping my social life separate from my work life was a wise decision because I managed to gather friends without making enemies.

    I was part of a group of girlfriends who hung out on the weekends at the Sheraton. One Friday night, I walked into the ladies' room, and on the counter next to the sink, someone had left some religious tracts. I picked one up and read it, but it had no effect on me. From time to time, I would think of those tracts left on the counter, but I dismissed them, thinking of them as "for someone else, not for me." I did not allow myself to remember the many times throughout my life that my prayers had been answered. I was in a different time and place now. I had elevated myself to the status of glamour girl, but in reality, I had done nothing but lower my standards and headed down the road to disaster.

Chapter 16

Healing Takes Place

The years came and went so fast. My memory has lost some years completely, and others I can remember only in bits and pieces. The boys were growing up right before my eyes, and one day, I woke up and realized I was the mother of a group of unruly teenagers who were skipping school, drinking, smoking, stealing from me, and lying about everything. Their behavior was a wake-up call for me. My sons were acting out the family system of irresponsibility that I had grown up with, and I was the one of the key players in that dysfunction being passed on to them. Their teenage years, like mine, were spent without access to healthy role models. I should have been the one to model responsible adult behavior for them, but I was acting like an irresponsible adolescent, consumed with getting back the youthful fun I had missed in the past. I had no clue how to parent these teenagers when I had never been parented myself. I had missed out on some of the best years of my sons' lives, and now they were running wild. I asked Jimmy if he would be willing to take Scott because I was afraid Scott would get into some kind of serious trouble if he didn't have the kind of firm male discipline that I was unable to give him. Jimmy agreed, but only if I relieved him of the twenty-five-dollar-per-week child support he paid for Scott. Scott went to live with his dad, but the same day I signed off on lowering Jimmy's child support payments, he sent Scott home, saying that he couldn't afford for Scott to stay with him. However, my agreement to stop the child support payment for Scott was irreversible. That incident left me wringing my hands in frustration as to why my life never worked out for me. However, this time, when I felt that I was a victim looking through the fog for answers, I began to take a good look at myself. Surely there had to be a better purpose to my life. Maybe the change had to start with me.

The hot new place to socialize for my group was now the discotheque T-Birds, which was just a few miles from where I lived. I had made plans to meet one of my girlfriends there for a drink one Friday night, and while I waited for her, I sat at the bar and ordered a Coke. It was early, not yet very crowded, and as I sipped my Coke, I became aware of my surroundings. There was a woman on the dance floor who had obviously had too much to drink. She had one arm missing, and she was sloppily trying to follow the beat of the music. I could feel her pain because, like her, I was missing something important in my life, perpetually off the beat, and wandering around in circles, looking for fun. This sudden awareness of what I was seeing and where I was made me want to run somewhere and hide. I couldn't stay any longer; I got up and left. As I drove home I began to cry, praying and asking God to help me. I had prayed this same prayer many times before, but this time, it was different. I was finally connecting with God through tears of remorse for the years I had wasted. I was seeking forgiveness, and I knew at that very moment my life was changing. I knew that this profound change that had taken place within me was real, and I would never be able to explain it.

That same week, I received an invitation in the mail to a Bible presentation on prophecy being hosted by a local church. The following Friday night, I went to my first Bible class. As I stepped through the door of the church, I was directed to a table to receive a loose-leaf notebook and a name tag. The people were warm and friendly, and for some strange reason, I felt extremely happy to be there, as if I were in the right place. I was then directed into the sanctuary, where I viewed a movie about the end-of-life prophecy according to the Bible. The class was divided into four parts for four consecutive Friday nights, and I came back for each one. When the last presentation ended, a young girl from the audience came up onstage and told how she had started these classes at the insistence of her mother, kicking and resisting, but now she was glad she had come. The girl said she wished to sing a song to the audience, and she proceeded to sing "You Light Up My Life."

In the weeks ahead, I lost all desire to go out with my girlfriends to bars. They called often, inviting me and asking what was wrong with me, but I told them I was simply no longer interested in going out with them. They were puzzled as to what had changed with me, and at this point, I was not sure what it was. I just knew that something larger and stronger than myself was moving me in another direction. The mask had been removed, and the real me was coming back! This profound change in me happened so suddenly that my children were the first to notice. I had instead an insatiable hunger driving me forward on my search for truth.

I went to a Christian music store and bought a series of tapes by Amy Grant. I began to work on redecorating my house that had been neglected for too long, and as I worked, I played these tapes over and over. I sanded and shellacked doors, painted closets, took up old carpets, and replaced old window treatments. Each Sunday morning, I set out to find a church. I visited many different ones in my neighborhood, not knowing exactly where to go or even what I was seeking. I had an unrelenting motivation to move forward, to seek, to find answers, to rise above and understand where I had been and where I was going. When I think back to those days now, I realize that the power that so strongly urged me on was not my own power but a power greater than me. Each day, I became more and more aware of a fact or truth that I had not seen before in quite the same way. I was looking at everything in my life from a different angle, putting my priorities in order. I was elated with my newly found happiness and contentment. I began to relax as all fear and anxiety disappeared. The terror that held me captive for so long was gone, and I was free. I felt clean and elevated: lifted and so very grateful for this miracle connection with God. How all this happened was without logic but was a true miracle. When I stopped resisting and allowed Jesus to enter my belief system was the moment when real change took place, giving me the freedom to move forward toward a healthier quality of life. I had received a free gift that I could not have bought at any price.

I watched a new church being built on Hairston Road as I traveled each day to and from work. One day, I noticed a large sign out front that read Hairston Road Church of God. I knew I wanted to visit that church as soon as services started. Eventually, I learned that the congregation was holding services in the gym. The first Sunday morning I attended, I was welcomed by a redheaded gentleman at the door. He had a humble demeanor and a welcoming smile as he said good morning and handed me a bulletin. The gym was a large room that was informally set up with three sections of folding metal chairs, with a wide aisle in between each section. I quietly slid into a seat on the back row. The music started, and the choir filed onto the stage, taking their places in rows of seats set up in the back of the piano. Each person carried a songbook. The choir began to sing a series of melodies, and their music was easy to follow, uplifting, heavenly, and joyful. I could feel the words of the songs feeding me like no other words ever had. Many of the people lifted their hands in praise to God, and the atmosphere overflowed with love and joy. As the music continued and the spirit became stronger, people stood up, clapping and raising their hands as they sang. I felt safe and at peace for the first time in my life. I knew I belonged there.

The following Sunday, I was back, and I returned for the evening service as well. The atmosphere and the music were feeding me and filling me with a joy that I had never before known. I began attending every service Sunday and Wednesday evenings, and I noticed many of the same people at each service. They all spoke to me but did not ask any questions; I was becoming a familiar face to them. I could literally feel my life being rewritten through the words in the music. After the Wednesday night service one evening, I slid into the front seat of my car and began to cry. That night, many of us had gone down to the altar, knelt, and prayed. I surrendered my life to God, thanking him for the change within that I could have only acquired through repentance.

Repentance is defined as a change of mind that results in a change of behavior. Repentance must include facing up to prior decisions and actions that were wrong. Repentance frees you to change direction and to connect to what you truly believe and who you really are.

In the days and weeks ahead, my life was changing before my eyes. Light flooded my consciousness, and I saw the world from a different perspective. I felt secure, free of anxiety, and finally able to let go of the past. After being a-pack-and-a-half cigarette smoker for twenty-five years, I quit and never picked up a cigarette again. I had been born-again with a new strength that surpassed all understanding. I was no longer afraid to think for myself or express my feelings. This inward transformation was the result of a surrendered life. I had finally come in from the cold to a place of warmth, love, and truth. This change marked the end of my life as I had known it. For most of my life, I had been staggering down a crooked trail that led only to destruction. Whether I was accepting the dominance of inappropriate men or acting out as a manic party girl, it had all been the same crooked trail. After my surrender, I was on a path of accountability, contentment, and joy. It was as if I had been plucked out of my own life and allowed to look through a new window and see the world through new eyes. Pleasing the world had lost its influence on me. Jesus began to serve as the parent I never had, and as I studied his Word, I learned the value of truth, love, and forgiveness. When I believed what was true, this higher thinking pushed me to grow in directions I had never before thought possible.

In December of 1986, Daddy's wife, Gerry, suffered a stroke and passed away. I flew up for the funeral so Daddy would have at least one family member with him. Daddy was now eighty years old. I knew he would want to move in with me, now that Gerry was gone, because he had made many friends in my neighborhood. I also knew that I was no longer willing to tolerate alcohol in my house. I remember my conversation with Daddy when he called a month later asking if he could come back. "Daddy, that's fine. You are welcome to come back, but there are changes. I am now a Christian. There will be no alcohol allowed here."

"Oh, that isn't a problem for me."

"Okay, well then, come on."

Despite what he said, I knew that not drinking in the house would be a problem for him, but I also knew he wasn't going to admit it. Daddy came as planned, and as I expected, I could sense his discontent with not being able to drink. A few times, I found a bottle hidden behind the living room sofa. Daddy finally told me that he was taking a trip to New Jersey to visit Connie. He insisted he was just going for a visit, and he would be back. Daddy must have complained to Connie about the alcohol ban, and it wasn't long before I received a letter from Connie filled with criticism. She berated me for not letting Daddy drink at my house, arguing that he didn't have a problem with alcohol. I wrote her back suggesting that he live at her house where the drinking flowed freely since he would be much happier in that environment. With three teenage boys now experimenting with alcohol themselves, I could not afford to condone any drinking in my home.

As I looked back on my life, I was now aware that alcohol had been the enemy in many ways. Alcohol is a mind-altering drug with extreme powers to destroy, and I had been powerless against it as a daughter, as a wife, as a mother, and in my own behavior. I now knew that I had choices, and I was not going to let destruction continue to infiltrate my family. My life was on the mend, and I needed to protect myself and my children by making better choices and stepping up as a role model. Daddy never came back, nor did he ever tell me that he wasn't coming back. I knew why; he didn't have to say anything. I also knew that in order for me to live a healthy life, I had to disconnect from the influence of my family of origin. The strong hooks and warped thinking that had once so strongly influenced me were gone, and they had to stay gone. Daddy's decision to live at Connie's was right for him and a relief for me.

I began to bow out gracefully from contact with my family, slowly detaching from them. I would no longer fit into the role they had programmed for me, and I was not willing to compromise with any of their self-defeating beliefs. I had a new strength born out of a connection to God that I had been seeking for most of my life. It pleased Daddy to believe that religion was nonsense, but I could no longer worry about his needs and beliefs at the expense of mine. In a moment of truth, it became clear to me that it was Daddy's advice and influence over me that had kept me blinded and bound for so many years. Connie had also had a strong influence on me, and I realized that her domineering personality had made it easy for me to follow her down some paths that were wrong for me. Connie and I had both struggled for Daddy's approval, starting when he was all that we had to depend on. I could see how I had tiptoed around them, trying to go along with their beliefs, but I no longer needed their approval. When the blindfold of my childhood was removed, I finally understood why I had so many problems as an adult. I clearly saw why I was drawn to men who would never really be there for me, why I had difficulty getting close to people, and why I had such a hard time asking for help. I had been repeating all my childhood patterns, but now I felt free to stop.

As time went on, I continued to attend the Hairston Road Church of God. I joined the church, was baptized, and sang in the choir. I made new friends, some of whom I am still in contact with. These people loved me as if I had been there my entire life; they knew little about me, but my past didn't matter to them. They welcomed me into their world and treated me as part of their family. Since I had grown up without much of a family, this was the very first time in my life that I felt loved, secure, and a part of something I believed in. My church family modeled for me what it was like to be full of joy and contentment and happy to be alive. I worked at reconnecting with my children, whose lives were now going in separate directions. So much time had passed, and there was no way to go back and redo the years I had missed out on. Nevertheless, my sons knew there had been a drastic change in me, and they had a new respect for me, just as I had a new respect for myself. I began to focus on my sons and did what I could to make amends.

After almost a year of Christian counseling, I joined the Al-Anon groups that were designed to help codependents of substance abusers. It was time to face reality. Facing the truth about how I had been acting was extremely painful, but the process was necessary in order for me to heal. However, I was still not strong enough to tell the story of my mother or the abuse in my marriage in the counseling sessions. Although, I would recommend to anyone that talking it out is a better alternative than acting it out as I did. Sometimes the trauma is just too extreme, and talking it out is not possible until a certain amount of healing has taken place. I was now ready to leave the past behind and move on with my life. After my surrender, the continual pain, intense fear, and darkness that I had lived with for so long, either in real time or as repressed memories, no longer dominated my life. I was free from post-traumatic stress, empowered, happy, truly alive, and moving forward. I looked at the world from a different angle now that my conscious and unconscious selves were in harmony. Throughout my adult life, I had believed that I would achieve freedom when I separated from this husband or that boyfriend, but I finally learned that there would be no freedom until I surrendered to God.

As an adult, my main problem had been that once I was finally free from the terror of my marriage, I regressed back to childhood and adolescence. My childhood and marriage had left me hungry for love and approval, and I sought those things from the men in my life. When I first met Tim, he catered to me as if I was a treasured child, and I became addicted to that kind of attention. After Tim became controlling and I broke up with him, I simply transferred my craving for attention to the men at the bars. In the bar scene, I could be sure to get attention for my looks, and I had no idea how shallow and unfulfilling that kind of attention really was. Through immoral behavior and decisions, I had screamed out to the world, acting out my story without telling it. One of my problems was that I was looking for men who could parent me rather than partner with me. Since I had never had a real childhood, I did not mature as most people do. I lived with the constant confusion of wanting to be a child while being expected to be an adult, of needing parenting yet being expected to be a parent. My adolescence did not foster the usual process of self-discovery, nor did my early adulthood help me to know who I really was. As the child of alcoholics and as the wife of an abuser, I only knew how to act out whatever role I had to in order to survive another day. Finally, with the help of God, I broke through the shell of the roles I had taken on as a means of survival, and I found my own inner center of value and direction. At last, I was able to meet my true self and grow up.

Once I was no longer striving to get my own needs met, I was able to look around me and see the needs of my children, who had been tossed by the wayside. This inner healing was the moment I had been waiting for all my life. The future was a blank slate to be filled as I wished, but I was not without guidance. This is a story of survival. It is about my stunted growth and finally my emergence into authenticity, like the caterpillar that turns into a butterfly and is forever free.

As I finish this memoir, I am sixty-five years old. When I look back on my messy life with all the wrong turns, failures, and days I wish I could rewrite, I am in awe of God's grace, how he picked me up, dusted me off, and allowed me to close the door to the past. How grateful I am for today and for the life that I now enjoy.

About the Author

Charlotte Lauver was a child of alcoholic parents who created an environment that was detrimental to the nurturing and well-being of their children. Out of desperation, she married to escape, only to find herself in an extremely abusive marriage. Finally, the pain and fear led her to escape again, finding healing through God's amazing grace and a life of peace and joy.

Today, her life is filled with gratitude as she spends her days doing the things she loves: writing, gardening, cooking, and spending time with her husband and grandchildren.